ЖУПЕЛЪ
И.Б.'15.

Spirit Beings in European Folklore 3
*Compendium3: 255 descriptions – Russia, Belarus, Ukraine, Poland, Romania, Hungary, Bulgaria, Czechia, Slovenia, Serbia, Croatia, Albania, Georgia, Turkish regions, Roma-culture*
Author: © Benjamin Adamah
2022


Lay-out: Sylvia Carrilho
Editor: Orenda Bol


ISBN 978-94-92355-57-7


Publisher:

VAMzzz Publishing
P.O. Box 3340
1001 AC Amsterdam
The Netherlands
www.vamzzz.com
vamzzz@protonmail.com

– 255 DESCRIPTIONS –
Russia, Belarus, Ukraine, Poland,
Romania, Hungary, Bulgaria, Czechia,
Slovenia, Serbia, Croatia, Albania,
Georgia, Turkish regions, Roma-culture

# SPIRIT BEINGS
## IN EUROPEAN FOLKLORE 3

COMPILED & EDITED BY
# BENJAMIN ADAMAH

# Contents

# INTRODUCTION

*Compendium 3* of this 4 volume-series *Spirit Beings of European Folklore* focuses on the Slavic countries, the Balkans, the Carpathians, Albania, Georgia, and the Turkish and Roma peoples. Initially written as a single encyclopedia of about a thousand pages, we decided to divide this manuscript into four separate compendia and use a cultural-geographical format, describing alphabetically the spirit beings of a more or less coherent segment of Europe. Each compendium is a stand-alone work, but when purchased together with the other volumes can also be enjoyed as part of the whole series – see also *From the same series* at the end of this book.

The classification into cultural-geographical formats is not solid because many creatures overlap with creatures from other areas or are (basically) the same creature under a different name, which, however, almost always has elements integrated from the region and culture where it is locally known. This is especially true of *Alp* or *Mare*-like creatures, *Goblins* and *dwarf*-like spirits, spring- or fountain-spirits – which often have roots in the Greek *Nymphs* – as well as a spirit like *Lady Midday*, *Mittagsfrau* in German, of which there are also Eastern European variants such as the *Poludnitsa* described in this *Compendium 3*. The creatures of Eastern Europe, especially in the cultural border regions, regularly overlap with creatures from the German-speaking areas and Baltic states, while Greece is seen by many folklorists as the cradle for the various seductive female water-spirits such as the *Rusalka, Samodive* etc. These ethereal femmes fatales contrast sharply with the conspicuous amount of *Vampires* and *vampiric Revenants* that abound in Slavic, and to some extent, Turkish culture. Compared to the areas described in Compendia 1, 2 and 4, this volume stands out for its content of sinister creatures and recurring dead.

The four-volume series *Spirit Beings of European Folklore* is the result of much translation work. In addition to the books added in the literature list, and apart from other online sources, I collected a substantial amount of useful wikicommons-licensed data fragments, which I edited into new, often more complete texts, after translating the texts from German, Spanish, Portuguese, Basque, Polish, Russian, French, Czech, Lithuanian, Latvian, Estonian, Finnish, Swedish, Norwegian, Romanian, Hungarian and other sources. In particular, my knowledge of German and Lower

Saxon (the language I grew up with and spoke as a child) proved very useful, and made it possible to make accessible much unique folklore that has never before been presented in English. Of great value in creating *Compendium 3* were two works of W.R.S. Ralston, M.A. (1828-1889). Some years ago this nineteenth century folklorist initiated in me a deeper investigation into Slavic folklore, which took shape in this particular book. I want to mention Ralston's *Russian Fairy Tales – A choice collection of Muscovite folk-lore* (1872) and *The songs of the Russian people, as illustrative of Slavonic mythology and Russian social life* (1872).

**– Benjamin Adamah, Amsterdam, August 6, 2022**

# A

## Äbädä

*Äbädä* (Tatar: Әбәдә; Azerbaijani: Әbәdә; Turkish: *Ebede*) is a *forest-spirit* in Tatar mythology and also a figure in the folklore of Siberian peoples. The spirit resembles an old woman or a *Wild Man*-figure. The spirit is generally believed to be harmless, though legend also tells how to protect oneself from the creature. Äbädä is a being that is similar in nature to the Turkish *İyes*. The Äbädä protects the birds, trees and animals of the forest; he appears in the shape of a man with blue skin, two great horns, green hair, and a long green beard covering his face, carrying a club or whip indicating his rulership over the forest. He can shape-shift into many different forms. As a human, he looks like a peasant with glowing eyes, wearing his shoes backwards. Should one ever encounter an Äbädä, one must thwart him immediately by turning all one's clothes inside out, and putting one's right shoe on the left foot and the left shoe on the right.

## Al, Ali or Hal

The *Al* or *Ali* is first documented in European literature in the middle of the 19th century. The *Ali*, *Al* or *Hal* (Persian: آل; Armenian: Ալ or Ալք; Mongolian: Гал; (Qal); Oirat: һал; Russian: Алы) is a class of demons in the folklore of the Caucasus, Iran, Central Asia and Armenia. In Georgian lore the *Ali* (ალი) is a type of Lilith-like demon that afflicts pregnant women, the elderly, and infants who happen to stumble into remote woods, caves, and ruins. In general the Als or Alis are demons of childbirth, interfering with human reproduction. The Al is known by various other names, including *Alk* (meaning gorge, or world interior) in Armenian and Kurdish, *Ol*, *Hāl* and *Xāl* in Tajikistan and Afghanistan, *Almasti* or *Albasti* in Central Asian Turkic-speaking countries, and *Halmasti* among the Dards. *Alis* can be male or female (the females being known as *Alkali*); male Alis generally appear monstrous, while female Alis can shift between tempting beauty and hag-like ugliness. Their name may be related to the word for "flame" (ალი). It is suggested that conceptions of its appearance may derive from folk memories of relict hominins like the cryptozoological *Almas*.

In Armenian tradition, the Als steal the lungs, liver and heart of women in childbirth, pregnant women, and women who have just given birth. They also destroy embryos in the womb, causing miscarriages, and can steal babies forty days after childbirth, replacing them with *Imps*. They are male and female. They have clay noses and fiery eyes, and appear with sharp fangs, disheveled hair, copper claws, iron teeth, the tusks of a wild boar and sagging breasts, resembling a crone. After stealing the organs of a woman, the Al attempts to escape and cross the first available source of water, after which the woman cannot be saved. Apotropaic wards against Als include methods also used against other demons (such as charms, prayers, iron objects, onions and garlic), and preventing the Al from reaching water. In Iran, the Al is a bony, thin old woman, with a clay nose, red face, and a straw or wicker basket hanging from her shoulder, in which the liver or lungs of the young mother are placed. In Central Asia, the Al is customarily a fat, ugly and hairy crone with sagging breasts, one of them hanging over one shoulder, while hanging over her other shoulder is a woolen bag in which she has placed the heart and liver of her victim.

According to many Near Eastern traditions, Al was the first mate designed for Adam by God. But since she was made of fire and Adam of earth, they were incompatible. The arrival of Eve made Al very angry, which is why she attacks pregnant women (as does *Lilith*, Adam's first wife and second mate, who is not supposed to have had any children). Sometimes Al carries a pair of scissors. When the creature wears its hat, covered with small bells, it becomes invisible. It prefers dark and damp places, like stables or dark corners of houses.

## Ala

An *Ala* or *Hala* (pl.: *Ale* or *Hali*), in the folklore of the Balkan Slavs of Bulgaria, Macedonia and Serbia, is a female demonic spirit of the air. Ale are considered to be demons of bad weather, whose main purpose is to lead hail-producing thunderclouds into the direction of fields, vineyards or orchards, in order to loot the crops. When they fought among themselves for territory, they would throw ice at each other, causing a hailstorm. Being extremely voracious, Ale particularly like to eat children, though their gluttony is not limited to Earth. It is believed they sometimes try devouring the Sun or the Moon, causing eclipses, and that it would mean the end of the world, should they succeed. When people encounter an Ala, their mental and physical health, or even life, are in peril; however, her favor can be gained by approaching her with respect and trust. Being in a good relationship with an Ala is very beneficial, because she makes her favorites rich and saves their lives in times of trouble. The appearance of an Ala is diverse and often vaguely described in folklore. She may look like a black wind, a gigantic creature of indistinct form, a huge-mouthed human-like or snakelike monster, a female dragon, or a raven. They were often imagined as winged snakes, living in dark storm clouds. They could also take the form of birds or animals, and only a man with six fingers was able to recognize them.



## Alkonost

*Alkonost* (pl.: *Alkonosty*; Russian: алконст *Alkonst*, алконос, *Alkonos*) is the name of a legendary figure of Russian folklore. They are birds that have the face of a beautiful woman. Alkonost comes as a name from Greek mythology, derived from *Alkyone*. Alkyone was transformed into a kingfisher by the gods. The creatures reproduce by laying eggs. They lay them on the seashore and then roll them into the water. Thereupon the sea calms down for six or seven days and is stirred up by a storm as soon as the young hatch. The Alkonosty are the magical birds of happiness and hope. In contrast are the *Sirin*, the birds of sorrow and grief. The Alkonosty are well-disposed towards humans, while the Sirin are less so. For the Russian Orthodox Church, the Alkonost is the personification of the divine will. She lives in paradise and leaves it only to deliver messages in our world. Her voice makes everyone who hears her forget everything around them. The earliest image of the Alkonost is found in a book miniature from the 12th century. In modern neo-paganism Alkonost appears as an incarnation of *Khors*, a Slavic god of uncertain functions, mentioned since the 12th century, and mostly interpreted as a moon god.

## Almas

*Almas*, evil forest-spirits in the folklore of the Vainakh people of the North Caucasus (Chechens and Ingush). There are male and female *Almas*. Almas-men are fierce creatures, covered with hair and looking terrifying. On their chest is some protuberance that looks like a sharp axe. In some tales the female Almases have an extraordinary beauty, but are also evil, insidious and dangerous. In other stories they are huge terrifying creatures with enormous breasts, thrown over their shoulders. The favorite occupation of the Almas is dancing in the moonlight. Almas live in the woods on the highlands. Sometimes Almas get into a love affair with a hunter. Luck in hunting, according to legends, depends on the benevolence of the Almas. The Vainakh people of the North Caucasus were Islamized comparatively late, during the early modern period, and a trend has arrived to reconstruct some of the elements of their pre-Islamic religion and mythology, including traces of ancestor worship and funerary cults. The Nakh peoples, like many other peoples of the North Caucasus, such as Circassians and Ossetians, had been practicing tree worship, and believed that trees were the abodes of spirits. Vainakh peoples developed many rituals to serve particular kinds of trees. The pear tree held a special place in the faith of Vainakhs.

In Mongolian folklore, an *Almas*, *Alma* or *Almasty*, among other variants (Mongolian: Алмас, Chechen: Алмазы, Turkish: *Albıs/Albız* or Albastı), is a cryptid, folk creature or deity, said to inhabit the Caucasus and Pamir Mountains of Central Asia and the Altai Mountains of western Mongolia. The term "almas" and numerous variants thereof appear in Mongolian, Turkic languages and Iranian languages. The name is connected to a variety of place names (toponyms) in southwestern Mongolia, including Almasyn Dobo (the Hills of Almases), Almasyn Ulan Oula (the Red Mountains of Almases) and (the Red Rocks of Almases). Folk belief in the Almas in Oburkhangai and Bayankhongor has resulted in a name-avoidance taboo there, wherein the entities may be referred to as *Akhai*, meaning 'uncle-brother'. The folk traditions of Darkhad include the deity *Almas khara Tenguer*, meaning "Almas the Black God" and associated with highland prairies and mountain forests. According to Rinčen, the god may be offered edible wild roots and wild animal meat.

**Spirit or humanoid?**
Nikolay Przhevalsky in his *Mongolia, the Tangut Country and the Solitudes of Northern Tibet* (1876) describes the Almas, as related to him under the name *Kung-guressu* (man-beast), as follows:

*"We were told that it had a flat face like that of a human being, and that it often walked on two legs, that its body was covered with a thick black fur, and its feet armed with enormous claws; that its strength was terrible, and*

*that not only were hunters afraid of attacking it, but that the inhabitants removed their habitations from those parts of the country which it visited."*

Heaney suggests that the Almas should be identified with the *Arimaspi*, a group of legendary humanoid creatures said to inhabit the Riphean Mountains. In 1992, a group of scientists went on an expedition to search for the Almas in the Caucasus Mountains.

## Archura

The *Archura* or *Arzuri* (Chuvash: *Апçури* Arçuri "half man", Tatar: *Apcypu, Arsuri*; Turkish: *Arçura*; Russian: *Арзюр, Arzjur*) is a shapeshifting woodland spirit, who protects the wild animals and forests in Chuvash and Turkic mythology. The Archura is represented as a tall, naked woman with long (to the ground) hair, with a body covered with wool, only her genitals are exposed. Her eyes are *"as large as oatmeal sacks"*, her breasts hanging down; she puts them on her shoulders while walking. In some myths, the Archura has a black face, long hair, three arms, three legs, and four eyes: two in front and two behind. In some other myths the Archura were endowed with such features as a very large head and eyes the size of a millet seed. The Archura was also represented in other guises: human, usually as a peasant with glowing eyes, or as a gray-bearded old man or with a beard made of living grass, a giant, a *Satyr*-like figure with a tail, hooves, and horns, or an animal. The Archura has for example a close bond with the gray wolf (Turkish: *Bozkurt*). Legend describes him as wearing a red scarf and wearing his shoes on the wrong foot. He also had no shadow. Archuras protect the animals and birds in the forests and tell them when to migrate. They are mischievous beings; they utter horrible cries and can imitate voices of people familiar to wanderers and lure them to their caves, where the Archuras will tickle them to death. Archuras can scream wildly in different voices, bark like a dog, squeal like a pig, roar like a horse. They often sit in trees or run ahead of men, laughing impudently and showing their genitals. Archuras usually chase a man in the woods, taking all sorts of images: a sheep, a hare, a flaring fire, a pile of bread, etc. In such cases it is impossible to address them, as they immediately disappear, and when this happens the forest begins to whistle, hoot, crackle and all kinds of horrible inhuman voices are heard. Archuras are very afraid of iron, whips, fire, water, dogs, and the crackling of bird cherries on a fire. If a traveler in the woods has bird cherry branches burning in the fire, she will not approach him. The creature loves to ride horses, so it can be caught by smearing tar on the horse's back.

Despite their rough way of pulling pranks, they aren't intrinsically evil; although they enjoy misguiding humans and kidnapping young women, they are also known to keep grazing cattle from wandering too far into the forests and getting lost. Sometimes more than one Archura inhabits a forest, and then they will fight for their territory, knocking down trees and scaring animals. According to a number of myths, Archuras are born from murdered people or suicides. The Archura enters the body of a suicide or murder victim and carries it through the forest, frightening passersby. In some regions, it is thought that the soul of a roadkill or suicide cannot find peace and becomes an Archura. There are also versions where the souls of illegitimate babies, abandoned in the forest, sick people, or the dead whose remains are not buried, or who did not get their proper funeral rituals, can turn into Archuras. In contrast to the myths it is however more likely the Archura or Arzuri belongs to the nature-spirits. The term "Arzuri" may go back to the ancient name of the deity, close to the Slavic *Shchur*. Another name of Arzuri – *Varman tura*, means "forest god" – and is similar to one of the names of the wood spirit *Urman iyase* (Lord of the forest) of the Kazan and West Siberian Tatars. The Southern Chuvash consider Arzuri to be the wife of *Übede*, therefore they also call her *Varman amashe* (Forest mother).

## Avet

*The Avet* (pl. *Avetes*), *Avetinja* (Serbian: Аветиња), *Havetinja* (Serbian: Хаветиња), lit. "ghost" is a character in the folklore of the Serbs and some other South Slavic peoples, a night-spook or nocturnal *Bogeyman*, a restless spirit. It is assumed that the name came from Arabic, Turkish or Proto-Slavic. In the beliefs of the South Slavic peoples, the *Avetes* are equated with the unruly souls of dead young people, suicides and deceased sinners. It is also believed that the Avetes are the spirits of people who have not lived their own lives but had their lives managed by others. Avetes have a lot in common with "earthbound spirits", or better: *"spirits trapped in an obsession"*, as that is what so called earthbound spirits are, but their appearances and *Goblin*-like behaviors suggest they are something else; they may even appear in the shape of a bat, for example. Beliefs about Avetes exist in Serbia, Croatia, Montenegro, Macedonia and Bosnia Herzegovina. According to legend Avetes appear, as a rule, at night. They break into homes, steal women's clothes, wear them, and then return them. Usually the Avetes do this, so that no one notices the loss. People sometimes hide their clothes and store them in hard-to-reach places. Garlic is used for protection against Avetes.

# B



## Bába

*Bába* in Hungarian folklore means "old woman". Bába was originally a good Fairy who later degraded and became evil. Although she had magical abilities, she was not a *Boszorkány* (witch). She was thought to live in fountains, and if young children went too close to her lair, she lured them in.

## Baba Hârca

*Baba Hârca* is a witch in traditional Romanian folktales, who steals stars from the sky, hides in the waters of a cave or lives high in a tree, and sometimes gives helpful advice to heroes engaged in some struggle. *Baba Hârca* (Baba the Old Witch) is also the title of the first Romanian operetta, composed in 1848 by Alexandru Flechtenmacher, born in Iași in 1823, with a libretto by Matei Millo. The premiere took place on December 26, 1848 in the Teatrul Național din Copou in Iași.

## Baba Yaga

*Baba Yaga* – Russian: *Yaga, Yaga-baba, Egi-baba, Yagaya, Yagishna, Yagabova, Egiboba*; Belarusian: *Baba-Yaga, Baba-Yuga, Yaginya*; Bulgarian: *Baba Yaga*; Ukrainian: *Baba-Yazya, Yazya, Yazi-baba, Gadra*; Polish: *Jędza, Babojędza*; Czech: *Jezinka, Ježibaba* (witch, forest woman); Serbian: *Baba Jaga*; in Slovak: *Jaga Baba, Ježi Baba* – is a generally well-known character in Slavic mythology and folklore (especially fairy tales). She is depicted as an ugly, large, hunchbacked old woman with a long hooked nose, bony legs and hanging lips, possessing magic objects and endowed with magical powers. In a number of fairy tales she is likened to a witch or sorceress. Most often she is a negative character, but sometimes Baba Yaga acts as a helper. In addition to Russian fairy tales, she also appears in Slovak and Czech fairy tales. It is also a ritual Christmas character in the former Slavic lands of Carinthia in Austria, a Shrovetide character in Montenegro, and a night spirit in Serbia, Croatia and Bulgaria.

In Slavic folklore, Baba-Yaga has several enduring attributes: she is able to bewitch, fly in a stupor, dwells at the edge of a forest in a hut standing on chicken legs (or propped up with pancakes), surrounded by a fence of human bones and skulls. She lures good folk and small children to her, supposedly to eat them. She pursues her victims in a mortar, driving it with a pestle and covering her tracks with a broom. According to folklorist V.Y. Propp, there are three kinds of Baba-Yaga:
1. *the giver* (she gives the hero a fairy tale horse or a magic object);
2. *the child-snatcher*;
3. *the warrior*, fighting with the hero of the tale after which he/she passes
   to another level of maturity.

Baba-Yaga's dual nature in folklore is connected firstly with the image of the mistress of the forest, who needs to be placated, and secondly with the image of the malicious creature, who spits up children to roast them. This image of Baba-Yaga is associated with the function of priestess, who guides teenagers through a rite of initiation. So, in many fairy tales Baba-Yaga initially wants to eat the hero, but after fattening them up she lets him/her go, after giving them a ball, or some innermost knowledge, or the hero-figure runs away on its own. The image of Baba-Yaga is linked to worshiping an ancient totem, which was among the patrons of the tribe and was worshiped together with the cult of worshiping nature. She also has traits of a tribe's patron spirit, as she is a prophet, and in fairy tales it is Baba-Yaga who guides the hero to the right path, as she knows everything. As a family patron spirit, associated with the cult of the home, she has such attributes as a stove, a pestle and a pomelo.

In Serbia, Montenegro and Croatia the creature is called *Baba Roga* (Horned Baba) and scares little children when they are capricious and do not want to go to bed. In Montenegro (in Risan) in the Shrovetide dressing ceremony, one of the participants dresses up as Baba Ruga

(Grandfather's Baba) and carries a "child" (a doll) on his arms. The image symbolizes the ancestors and is believed to provide fertility for the coming year.

## Babay or Babai

*Babay* or *Babai* (Russian: Бабáй) is a night spirit in Slavic folklore. According to beliefs, he abducts children who do not sleep at night or behave badly. He is also called *Babayka* (Russian: Бабáйка), although this term may also be applied to his female equivalent. "Babay" is translated as *grandfather* or *old man* in Tatar language. The term, alongside its synonym, *Baba*, is most likely of Turkic origin. Because Babay is useful for parents as a *Bogey*-character, his appearance is rarely described. This is to encourage children to imagine him in his most terrifying guise. However, in some legends Babay is described as a pitch-black and crooked old man. He has some physical defects, such as muteness, no arms, and lameness. Babay has a bag and a cane. It is believed that he lives in forests, swamps or gardens. At night, he wanders through the streets and puts the children that he encounters on the way into his bag. Walking along people's homes, Babay peers through the windows and watches the children. If they are not sleeping, he starts to make scary noises. Like the *Bogeyman*, the Babay hides under children's beds, and may grab the children when they get up.

## Bagienniki

*Bagienniki* are lesser known water-spirits in Slavic folklore. They were akin to the bathhouse spirit *Bannik.* and ruled by *Wąda*, lady of the lakes and the shallow streams, also known as the *Queen of the Underwater Lawns*. The influence of Bagienniki on humans was regarded as mostly positive. They usually stayed at the bottom of shallow swamps and ponds and only occasionally emerged from the surface of the mud to take a breath. They were capable of emitting an oily substance from the nostrils, which were located between the eyes or on the forehead. This substance was so hot that it burned the victims it hit, but it was also provided with notable healing abilities for rheumas, deep wounds, indigestion, heart illness and even infertility. The creatures were unlikely to attack humans. The presence of Bagienniki could be detected by the bubbles on the water's surface, or by its darker and muddy color.

*Bannik* (1934) by Ivan Yakovlevich Bilibin (1876-1942)

# Bannik

The *Bannik* (Russian: *Bainnik, Bynushko, Banniy, Bainik*; Belarusian: *Lazennik, Laznik*) – is a demonic character in the beliefs of the Eastern Slavs. The Bannik belongs to the *house spirits* and lives in the bathhouse. Sometimes he is not regarded as a unique entity but simply as a *Domovoy* who prefers to live in the bathhouse. Usually invisible, he sometimes takes the form of a naked old man covered with mud and leaves, or twigs from a broom. He can also appear as a man with long hair, and can turn himself into a boar, dog, cat, frog or a white hare. The Bannik lives behind a sauna heater or under a shelf. He likes to sweat after several shifts of people in the bathhouse, and washes himself exclusively with dirty (unclean) water that ran off human bodies. The Bannik is believed to take a bath after midnight and people are not allowed to be in the bathhouse during that time. The third firing (or fourth, depending on tradition) was reserved for the Bannik, and, given his inclination to invite demons and forest-spirits to share his bath, no Christian images were allowed, lest they offend the occupants. In the Smolensk district it was usual for peasants who quit a bath to leave a bucket of water and a whisk behind for the Bannik who took their place. A special feature of the Bannik is that he participates in sacred fortune telling sessions. At midnight girls approach the open doors of the bath with their skirts up. If the Bannik touches a girl with his airy hand she will have a rich bridegroom – if naked, a poor one, and if wet, a drunkard.

The Bannik is blamed for all bathing mishaps. His favorite activities include scalding people with boiling water, throwing stones at the sauna heater and banging on the wall to scare the steamers. The Bannik only hurts (skinning and scalding to death) those who break the prohibitions badly. To placate the Bannik, they leave a piece of rye bread with plenty of coarse salt, and also make sure to leave some water and a piece of soap in the cauldron. To avoid the Bannik from doing harm people took a black chicken, without plucking its feathers, strangled it and buried it under the threshold of the bath. According to legend, a Bannik's red invisible hat, which he leaves to dry on the stove, can be stolen at midnight sharp. After stealing it, one must run straight to church, but if one fails to make it, the Bannik will catch up with the thief and kill him/her. Yet any evil creature is very afraid of iron, and the Bannik is no exception to that.

The female *Bannikha* is called *Banniha, Baynitsa, Banya matushka, Obderiha*. One can see a shaggy, ugly old woman. She may also appear naked, or as a cat. She lives under the doormat. Another version of the female Bannik is *Shishiga*. She is a demonic creature who pretends to be a friend, and after she lures her so-called friends into the bathhouse, she can scald them to death. The Shishiga is shown to those who go to the bathhouse with bad intentions and who do not pray.



## Bełt

*Bełt* (also: *Błąd, Błęd, Błądzeń, Błądzón, Bbłędnik, Błud, Bludón, Obłęd*; from Old Polish: *Bełtać* – to muddle or to err) is a malicious and invisible *field* or *forest-demon*, appearing in the tradition of eastern Little Poland. He confused travelers and led them on the wrong path. He would sit under a stone at crossroads and guide people walking in the fields at night, especially drunkards, causing them spatial disorientation. Shrines were erected in such places for protection against his harmful activity. The Bełt is also mentioned as a kind of Alp who harasses horses at night.

## Berehynia

A *Berehynia* or *Bereginia* (ru. Берегиня) is a female spirit (Vila) in Slavic mythology, which notably came to be regarded as a "Slavic goddess" with a function of "hearth mother, protectoress of the home" in late 20th century Ukrainian romantic nationalism, centered on matriarchal myth. The word originates from pre-Christian Slavic mythology, but in the modern usage it has two meanings. The confusion in the name's etymology owes to the fact that a Slavic word *bereg* (берег) may mean either a "river bank" or "to protect". Originally, obscure shadowy ghost-like Fairies similar to *Rusalkas*, Berehynias lived along the rivers, lakes and ponds and were considered ill-tempered and dangerous. A water-bank where they thought to be found were to be avoided by young men and women, especially in the dark.

## Bezkost

In Slavic, especially Polish lore, *Bezkost* is a term used for evil inclined specters, also called *Upiorami*. They are restless dead, emanations of the souls of people who do not deserve to be laid to rest, or who have been bound to this world by a curse or spell. These beings are often unaware of what they are doing, and happen to be aggressive towards the living.

The Unquiet dead-phenomena in general was comprehensively
documented by the Swedish-American psychiatrist and physician Dr.
Carl Wickland in his *Thirty Years Among the Dead* and the phenomena is
widespread and not bound to any specific region on Earth.

## Bibi

One day a year the Romani tribes of the Balkans pay honor to a *Vampire*-
like being they call *Bibi* (aunt). She is described as a tall, thin, and
barefoot woman wearing a red dress, who is accompanied by two small
girls. Some sources also include two white lambs to its entourage. Bibi
visits homes at random. If invited inside, she blesses the home with good
fortune; however, if she is turned away, the inhabitants of the house will
fall ill with cholera. If there are children in the home, Bibi will choke
them to death, but their bodies will show no signs of the attack.

## Bichura

*Bichura* (Tatar: *Бичура*; Turkish: *Biçura* or *Bıçura*) is a typical
multitasking, pranks pulling household-spirit in Tatar/Turkic folklore,
that lives behind the stove or in the cellar. It has a lot in common
with most Slavic and Middle and West-European household-spirits.
Traditionally, every house is said to have one, though it was also believed
that Bichuras did not live in all houses. Sometimes, a special room was
set aside for them. A plate of food and a few spoons were left in that room
for the night. With the Tatars, the *Bichura* was represented in the form of
a woman of small stature with an ancient headdress. It was believed that
she could live in houses under the floor, or in bathhouses. The Bichura
will pull the hair of a woman to warn her about an abusive man and
moan and howl to warn of other kinds of coming trouble. It lookes after
the chickens and does other kinds of housework. The spirit sometimes
comes out at night to spin and often looks like a man in a red shirt,
although it may also take on the appearance of a cat or dog. If the spirit
shows itself, it forewarns death, and if he weeps, a death in the family
has to be expected. According to Tatar folklore a Bichura could harass
horses in the stable overnight, as well as steal the grain of a neighbor in
order to feed the horses of the owner of the house he lives in. When the
Bichura is unhappy, it plays nasty *poltergeist*-like tricks on the members
of the household. The Bichura does not cause any essential harm but can

act very disturbing and in different ways at night; it shouts, plays, laughs, jokes, drags a sleeping person from place to place; puts things out of place or hides them. It can also disturb the peace by moving and rattling small objects, breaking dishes, leaving muddy little footprints, causing the walls of a house to creak, bangs on pots and produces moaning sounds. The Tartars have a saying about this spirit: *"Where did this thing go; didn't the Bichura steal it?"* If people closed their chimney at night, she will open it, and she is generally naughty in many other ways. When the family members can determine the cause of their Bichura's discontent, they can rectify the situation and return things to normal. However, most families live in harmony with the creature. If not, this means one has to banish the spirit from the house, either by dismantling the entire building or by bringing a bear into the house as Bichuras are afraid of this animal.

In some ethnic groups of the Trans-Kama region the term Bichura referred to spirits, which were represented as a small-sized woman wearing an ancient headdress, an analogue of the *Bannitsa* or *Kikimora*. The Bashkirs have a *Bisura*. Bashkirs represented the *Bisura* in the form of small humanoid creatures, of which both sexes wear red shirts. It was believed that they lived in remote forests on the glades. People who wandered into their domain were persuaded to copulate with them, and were then patronized by them. The Bichurs of the Mishar Tatars were a type of evil spirits of feasts. In some groups of West Siberian Tatars, Bichura corresponds to the spirit *Sary tsats* (the yellow-haired).

## Bieda

In Slavic folklore *Bieda* (Poverty) is an immortal demon bringing misery, bitterness and hardship to people. She was depicted as a skinny woman who sucked the vitality out of people. She was able to incarnate in some object, such as a log. The best way to get rid of her misery was to direct it towards your enemy.

## Bieluch

*Bieluch* or *Duch Bieluch* (Spirit Bieluch) is a legendary ghostly being of the Chełm Chalk Tunnels, the guardian of the treasures hidden there. The Chełm Chalk Tunnels (in Polish *Chełmskie podziemia kredowe*) are a system of tunnels dug into the chalk under the city of Chełm in eastern

Poland. The tunneling began in the Middle Ages for chalk mining and was discontinued in the 19th century. The tunnels also served Chełm's inhabitants as shelters during raids, wars and pillage. The system is now open solely for tourists. In total, the network of tunnels stretches for around 15 kilometres (9 miles). Bieluch is believed to be the spirit of the white bear on the coat of arms of Chelm. According to folklore you can meet Bieluch during sightseeing in one of the underground chambers. He emerges from the darkness and tells you how he used to scare thieves and treasure hunters. At the end of his tales, he promises to grant one wish made in the dark with his hand placed on the chalk wall in the Wishing Chamber. While still a living bear, Bieluch lived in a chalk cave on Chełmska Mountain under three oaks. One day, after returning from hunting, the bear found a hiding place lit with an eternal candle. Blinded by the glow of the fire he fell into the chalky tunnels. Only when the land of Chełm was in danger, the bear would emerge from those tunnels again.

## Bies or Bes

*Bies* or *Bes* (Russian: бес) is an evil spirit or demon in Slavic mythology. The word is synonymous with *Chort*. After the acceptance of Christianity the Bies became identified with the Devil, corresponding to the being referred to in Ancient Greek, as either *Daimon* (δαίμων), *Daimónion* or *Pneuma* (πνεῦμα). *Bes* is a kind of demon from Serbian folklore. When a Bes possesses a human or animal, the demon causes extreme rage. Bes is evoked when on Sunday somebody spits in a fire or throws something in it. Some folklorists claim that *Besomar* (from *bes*: anger, rage) and *mora* (torture, death) is king of all Bes spirits, a demon that is connected to disgust and hatred that had similarities with a *Werewolf* or a *Vampire*. According to others Besomar is another name for *Chernobog*. Chernobog (Latin: *Zcerneboch*, lit. Black God, reconstructed as Proto-Slavic Čьrnobogъ, from čьrnъ = black + bogъ = god) is the god of bad fate worshiped by the Polabian Slavs. He is first mentioned by the Saxon monk and chronicler Helmold (ca. 1120-1177) in the *Chronica Slavorum* (Chronicle of the Slavs), a medieval chronicle which recounts the pre-Christian culture and religion of the Polabian Slavs. It describes events related to northwest Slavic tribes known as the Wends up to 1171. About the cult of Chernobog he writes:

In later Polish folklore *Biesy* were evil, annoying spirits, which were often depicted as having a limp on one leg. They usually inhabited forests and swampy areas, but over time popular culture secondarily associated them with the Bieszczady Mountains. The research of linguists denies that the name Bieszczady originates from *bies*, but it does not stop the locals from spreading the legend of *Bies* and *Czadi* – two types of devils, who through their conflict contributed to the formation of the mountains.

## Błędnica

*Błędnica* is a Slavic, female *forest demon*, which is said to have led people astray, leaving its victims alone in the depths of the forest to die of starvation or be eaten by wild animals. The evil entity is most often described as a young and pretty girl. It is believed that the only way to chase the demon away was to use some strong spells, or to sacrifice something, either at one's home or during the hunt.

## Blud

The *Blud* (Блуд) is a character of Ukrainian, as well as Russian and Polish mythology, an unclean force that leads one astray. Other names of the character: Ukrainian: *Oblud, Obluda, Man, Mana, Obiinik*; Russian: *Vodylo, Vodka, Uvodydna, Manilo*; Polish: *Bełt, Błąd, Błęd, Błądzeń, Błądzón, Błędnik, Błud, Błudón, Obłęd, Zwodziciel*. The word *blud* itself is pan-Slavonic and in most Slavic languages means "mistake, delusion, wandering." Often the Blud was represented as something invisible and non-personified, but at the same time real, and sometimes could appear in the form of an animal or human. According to some *bylichkas* (stories about supernatural encounters), a person under the influence of Blud is not able to orientate himself on the terrain on which he found himself, and may wander for a long time, walking in circles, sometimes even in a small space. It is as if insurmountable obstacles arise before him, or he simply becomes unwell and loses all bearings. The Blud leads the person until he or she finds himself or herself in some difficult place. In some cases, the lost person may die. It was believed that one could get lost both at night and during the day. There are also locations or places which are more than average infested with by unclean forces. In a number of cases people explained the effect of a Blud by conscious or unconscious violation of prohibitions, rules of behavior in natural space.

Normally the Blud is a formless demonic spirit. At the same time, in a number of stories the Blud appears in the form of a goat, dog, cat, bird, a human of any gender, class or age, sometimes as a dwarf, an object (like for example a haystack) or a light, usually a *Will-o'-the-wisp*, which like the Blud, in the shape of a bird tries to lead a person astray. When two people are walking together but with some distance between them, the Blud may imitate the voice of one of them and thus lead the other of track; the one whose voice is imitated is usually as if petrified and deprived of his or her strength when this happens. As a rule, however, the Blud has no audible manifestations. It was generally believed that the Blud also had no attachment to any particular place, although it was also told that there were locations where the chance of getting lost was greater, for example, in the Ukrainian Carpathians there was a forest that was called "Blud". It was also believed that the Blud "clings" to places where someone committed suicide, where a murder was committed, or where an infant strangled by its mother was buried.

There was a number of rituals that were performed in order to not get lost or to find the right way if already lost. There were several precautions that could be taken to prevent a Blud attack, or getting possessed by one. Often Christian prayers were recited, or a metal object was carried along. One could also carry a piece of bread, especially the so-called *zabutni bread*, that is, one that was forgotten in the oven after baking. Some horse-dung, or a four-leaf clover put into the shoe (for Serbs) was also used. It was believed that the Blud could not affect first-borns and those who ate unpeeled garlic. If one had to pass by the grave of someone who had committed suicide, one had to throw a branch, stone or lump of clay on it. Similarly, in the Chernivtsi region, in order to propitiate the Blud, they tossed tree-branches in certain glades in the forest.

# Błudnik

*Błudnik* is a regional *Blud*, that was said to haunt the region of Łużyce (Poland). Like all *Blud* it was said to be a mischievous *Gnome* who used to lead people astray and decoy them into swamps.

# Bobak

There are several ways of portraying *Bobak* in Slavic culture. Some people believed that it was a *Bogeyman* of some unspecified features, sometimes taking the form of a white dog or a cat. In the south-eastern region of Łódź, Bobak was said to be the name of so-called *Odmieniec* (a child changed by demons) and it was considered to have been replaced specifically by a female demon called *Boginka-mamuna*. What differentiated the demon from a normal child were its taciturnity, non-motility and its lack of appetite, at least when home-dwellers were present. Left alone at home, Bobaks were voracious and fond of alcoholic beverages. When such a demonic child grew up, it used to be handicapped and mistrustful of people, but this happened rarely as they used to die in their infancy. According to some sources from Wieluń, in turn, Bobaks were mischievous *dwarves*, while in the region of Kutno they were believed to be small devils or diabolic children.

# Bobo

A *Bobo* is a supernatural creature from Polish folklore, probably a demon from Slavic beliefs. This small, ugly and malicious creature, was later used as a *Bogey* to scare children in order to discipline them. Bobo is also known as: *Bobok* (Wielkopolska, Małopolska), *Babok* (Kujawy), *Bebok* (Silesia). The creature is mentioned in the *Peregrynacja dziadowska* (Grandparents' Peregrination) written in the early17th century, according to which the Bobo was supposed to beat children and do various kinds of harm to the family. He could be propitiated by offering food.

# Boginka

*Boginka* (goddess; pl.: *Boginki*) in pre-Christian Slavic beliefs was a female demon, a personification of natural forces, hostile to humans. Later she is often equated with *Dzvozhona*, *Mamuna* and *Rusalka*. The name is derived from the word *bóg*/*bogini* (god/goddess). With time, in popular belief, the term goddess was replaced by the borrowed term Rusalka, and people began to identify the Boginka also with other demonic spirits, such as *Strzygami, Dziwożonami, Topielicami, Mamunami.*

The Boginki lived in swamps, lakes, rivers, forests and mountains. They could be found near the water while washing scarves with wooden tadpoles. Near Cracow, there was a well-known story about a miller whose pillar by the bridge kept breaking down. A mysterious stranger advised him at a fair to move the post because Boginki lived under the bridge and they disturbed the post. When the miller followed the advice, the bridge stopped breaking. When someone approached their habitat, the Boginki could kill the daring person (usually a young mother) with blows from the tadpoles or kidnap her. Women who died in childbirth, suicides and child murderers were to become Boginki. They were represented as ugly women with sagging breasts, large heads and crooked legs, or as just beautiful young women, usually naked. According to the highlanders of Pieniny, the goddesses had black hair, black eyes and a light complexion. They lived in streams and ravines near villages. Because they loved green peas, they snuck into fields where peas were sown and destroyed the harvest. They also exchanged newborn babies and kidnapped women after giving birth. Boginki would attack women after childbirth and exchange children for them. There were several variations on this belief, including:

* The Boginki come to swap the child in the house at noon (when the mother goes out into the field to bring food to the elderly housemates) or at midnight when everyone is asleep.
* The Boginki appear in pairs, accompanied by a man with a horned hat: the group enters and slaps the mother in the face or hits her, then takes her healthy (unbaptized) child and leaves a skinny, screaming child behind.

A swapped baby became a changeling. This was indicated by certain external features of the child, such as a large head, bulging eyes, intellectual disability, and certain behaviors, such as crying, speech impediments, bad coordination of movements, etc. The Boginki also abducted women to become mothers of their children and "exchanged" them, or tormented them with postnatal depression. Women in this condition became unnaturally withdrawn or demanding, and annoyed their surroundings. This was explained by the earlier abduction of a young mother by Boginki to swamps or wet meadows: there the creatures would roll the woman in the mud, twist her arms and legs, beat her on the back with tadpoles. Among the Pieninic highlanders, Boginki would tickle a young mother to death. These various descriptions of the appearance and behavior of the Boginki have many indications of the folkloric accounts of both the *Wild Women* and the *Ruselkas.*

**Protection against the Boginki**
Highlanders from the Tatra and Beskidge mountains and residents of ancient western Galicia knew the protective effects of St. John's wort *(Hyperium perforatum).* When Boginki (in the Tatra mountains – *Dzwożony)* carried a kidnapped young mother, she could cling to this flower and the Boginki, fearing its power, then angrily dropped the woman. According to the Krakowiaków and Hucułów, a confused child had to be taken to the border (of a village/field/road etc.), then beaten to make it cry loudly and sent away. It was believed that the Boginki, feeling sorry for the fate of their child, would take it away and leave the previously stolen human child on the spot. It had to be beaten with a rod on a dirty road and was also given water from an eggshell to invoke the Boginka. The windows and doors of the house where the woman with the newborn child lay were covered with consecrated Easter palms and/ or bell flowers to deter the goddesses, and garlands were hung in front of the windows. Herbs and flowers were also placed in the baby's crib. In the regions of Tarnów and Rzeszów, people were advised to make incense from the herb "podróżnik" (Chicory – *Cichorium intybus L.*) to perfume the house and the woman during childbirth. After childbirth, women were not allowed to go outside for a while to prevent abduction.

---

# Bohynia

In the Ukranian Hutsul folklore the *Bohynia* (goddess) or *Diva-Baba* (virgin midwife) or *Bisytsia* (She Devil) can be a beautiful woman or an ugly old Hag, who gains great magical powers, including flying ability, by throwing her abnormally long breasts over her shoulders. She has the nasty habit of stealing babies, though she can have a baby by herself. No matter whether this child was conceived by a demon or human father, it is usually born as a demon, with an abnormally big head, long ears, thin legs and a protruding belly. The child is weak, sickly and ugly and only learns to walk at seven years of age. It plays stupid, but possesses secret magical knowledge. As a changeling it sucks the blood out of the nipples of its human mother.

## Bolotnik

In Slavic folklore the *Bolotnik* is a male swamp-spirit. There are many descriptions of Bolotnik. Usually he was portrayed as a man or an old man who has big, frog-like eyes, a green beard and long hair. His body is covered with dirt, algae and fish scales. Other legends say, that Bolotnik is a dirty, fat, eyeless creature that motionlessly sits at the bottom of the swamp. In some legends Bolotnik is also said to have long arms and a tail. Like the *Vodyanoy* or *Rusalka*, he lures and drags people into the water or swamp if they get close to the edge. To lure people to the marsh, Bolotnik quacked like a duck, mooed like a cow, gurgled like a black cockerel or squawked terribly. He also cultivated intoxicating herbs near the marsh, mostly rosemary, and created *will-o'-the-wisp* cradles on the surface of the water. When someone was already in the swamp, the Bolotnik grabbed him by the feet and slowly, but inevitably, dragged him down to the depths. In some legends he is married to *Bolotnitsa* (or *Bolotnica*), a female swamp-spirit, similar to a *Rusalka*. In other legends he has neither wife nor children. In Poland, *Błotnik* is often associated with *Boruta*, the most well-known Polish demon from the Polish town Łęczyca.

Bolotnik has a lot of names: *Bolotny* (Russian: болотный; literally swampy), *Bolotny dedko* (Russian: болотный дедко; old man of the swamp), *Shut bolotny* (Russian: шут болотный; swamp jester), *Bolotny chert* (Russian: болотный чёрт; swamp devil), *Bolotny leshy* (Russian: болотный леший), *Tsar bolotny* (Russian: царь болотный), *Boloto* (Russian: болото; *swamp*), *Antsibal* (Russian: анцибал), *Ancibul* (Russian: анцибул), *Antsibalka* (Russian: анцибалка), *Antsibalit* (Russian: анцибалит), *Anchibal* (Russian: анчибал), *Anchibol* (Russian: анчибол), Belarusian: *Balotnik* (Belarusian: балотнік), Ukrainian: *Bolotyanik* (Ukrainian: болотяник), *Ocheretyanik* (Russian: очеретяник), Old Polish: *Błotnik*.

## Bolotnitsa

In the Russian North it is believed, that *Bolotnitsa* or *Bolotnica* is the mistress of the swamp and tundra. Like the Bolotnik, there are many different descriptions of her. In some legends she is a *Rusalka* (or Rusalka's sister). It was believed, for example, that a girl, who had died in a swamp or was carried away by an unclean spirit, could turn into the Bolotnitsa. In some places the Bolotnitsa was considered to be more like a

nature-spirit that had no connections with the human race. A Bolotnitsa
was usually portrayed as a beautiful young girl with pale-white skin and
goose legs instead of normal legs. To hide them, the Bolotnitsa would sit
on a giant water lily, putting her legs under her. She would lure people
into the swamp with a weep for help, pretending that she is drowning.
If they were charmed by her beauty, people would get close to her. She
would then pounce on them and slowly pull them to the bottom of the
swamp. It was believed that the Bolotnitsa liked singing. *Bolotnitsi* (pl.)
were also able to cause storms, rain and hail and in some legends the
Bolotnitsa is not described as a beautiful girl but as an old swamp hag.



## Bòrowô Cotka

*Bòrowô Cotka* or *Borowa Ciotka* is a Kashubian good-natured spirit of the
forest and protector of forest animals. She gives toys, sweets and nuts to
lost children and protects them from witches and *Maniewid*. She was able
to turn people who destroyed trees and scared off the forest animals, into
junipers.

## Bosorka

*Bosorka* (pl.: *Bosorkani*; Rus.: Босóрка; Hung.: *Boszorka, Boszorkány*;
H. Slavic: *Bosorka*; Ukr.: босорка, босоркáня – *Bosorka, Bosorkanya*;
Rum.: *Bosorcoi*) is a folkloric character of the Carpathian peoples, a
witch or wizard with *Vampire* features. The word is of Hungarian origin.
It may in turn have come into Hungarian from Turkic languages, of the
Turkish *Basyrkan* (Nightmare). In Hungarian folklore the Boszorkány
or Boszorka can mean as much as: *witch, sorceress, spirit of the dead,
Bogeyman, night ghost*. In Romanian folklore the Bosorcoi is mentioned
mainly in Transylvania. Other variant names are *Bosorcan, Bosorcaie,
Bosorcă, Bosorcaië, Borsocaîe, Borsocaie, Borsocane, Bortsokană, Bosărcăi,
Bursucăii*. It was said that a child born with a caul, a living adult and
a dead person could all become *Borsocaîe*. To prevent a dead person
from becoming a Bosorcoi, it was advised to put garlic in his/her mouth
and lay the dead person face down in their coffin. A Bosorcoi could be
recognized by a tail on the torso, on the head, or behind the ear. The
Borsocaîe could turn into a hare, a dog, a wolf, a fish or a bird. It was
up to the midwife to determine what kind of animal the Bosorcoi-child
would turn into. In addition, it was believed that there were Bosorcoi not

only for animals, but also for wind, for dance, for anything. To turn itself into an animal, a Bosorko would simply whistle.

**Bosorcoi-vampirism**
Bosorcoi were believed to steal milk from cows, suck blood from humans and cattle, and try to pierce them with an arrow. The midwives admonished the Bosorcoi-infants not to do the latter, otherwise they would *"slit their throats with an axe"*. There were the following incantations against taking away milk: *"Let milk come back to the cow, as the stars come back to the sky and as the dew comes at night, let not the Bosorkoi interfere with it"*; *"St. Peter met her, St. Peter, mooing and roaring. St. Peter asked: "You cow, why do you moo, why do you roar?" – "How can I not moo, how can I not roar; he has hurt my leg, he has jinxed my calf, he has taken away my milk."* The wounded leg when the milk is taken away is very characteristic of a Bosorcoi.

Slavic mythonyms with the root *bosor-* are present in Polish, Moravian, Slovak and Ukrainian folklore. Thus, the term *bosorka* is known in 21 Ukrainian-Carpathian colloquialisms; the word ведьма (witch) was used in the Ukrainian Carpathians, except in Verkhovina and in places where the beliefs in the creature have been practically erased. The word is known in most of Slovakia, especially in its western and eastern parts. The root *bosor-* is present in the following words denoting its feminine character: Polish – *Bosiorka, Bosorka*; Slovak and Moravian – *Bosorka, Vozorka*; Ukrainian – *Bosórka* (Hutsul), *Bisurka, Bosirka, Bosorkanya* (Rusian), *Bosurkanya* (Boyki), *Bosurganya, Poshurkanya*. The male characters are named as follows: Slovak – *Bosorák, Bosoroš, Bosorkáň*; Ukrainian – *Bosorkun*; *Bosurkun* and *Bosurkach* (boyki); *Bosorka* (lemki). In Transcarpathia, the term "bosorkans" is also used for certain insects like the silver-headed and dead-headed butterfly and flat-headed dragonfly.

**General appearance**
The Slavs combine in the image of Bosorka the images of the East Slavic witch, the West Slavic goddess and the South Slavic demons. It was believed that the more souls a Bosorka has (from one to three), the stronger and more harmful she is. In different parts of the Ukrainian Carpathians different concepts of the image dominated: in Transcarpathia the Bosorkani mostly meant "witches" and "healers", while in Boik and Hutsul the witch who takes milk from cows dominates. People who

could become Bosorkani: one who is possessed by a dead persons' spirit
or the seventh girl in the family. In Transcarpathia the number of local
Bosorkani was estimated as large: a pair, and even 10-15 in every village.
There were places where it was enough to whistle on ones fingers for
any number of Bosorkani to appear (Transcarpathia). In Transcarpathia
the Bosorkans either were brought close to *Ghouls* (Ukr. *Opiritsya*)
or they were believed to become Ghouls after death. In the Ukrainian
Carpathians, the male image of the Bosorkun was usually more positive.
Often Bosorkuns were opposed to Bosorkani, and their power increased
rather than disappeared or decreased after death.

Bosorkani were believed to look beautiful during the day, while at night
they took on an ugly appearance: shriveled face, red eyes, crooked mouth,
hairy legs. Bosorkani could also be depicted as flat-chested women
dressed in white, with long skinny arms and thin legs, with chicken
feet and a tail. In one of the Transcarpathian festivals, a boy imitating
a Bosorkan used to wear a white dress or sheet, smeared his face with
flour, inserted prosthetic fangs of white fodder beets into his mouth,
and attached a birch broom or pomelo for a tail. Then he would spit the
water he had collected in his mouth, gallop, beat his tail, squeal and howl,
trying to catch other children, lick them and kiss them, smearing flour
on their faces. Although it is noted that Bosorkani can be any age, in
mythological stories they are often elderly. Bosorkani have the ability to
appear as a *Werewolf* or other were-animal: they can turn into toads, cats,
dogs, chickens, pigs, owls, a chamois, snakes, bats, but also into a wheel,
a poker or a laundry roll. They could also make themselves invisible.
Bosorkani were believed to know about herbs and gather them for their
own purposes.

According to some folk beliefs, Bosorkani visit a coven every new moon
or at the end of the month. They then fly on a broom, a poker, a shovel, a
crusher or a barrel. In doing so, they fly out through the chimney. They
could also travel in a cart harnessed with black cats, or ride on a horse-
turned-husband or another person. The Bosorkani were believed to be
accompanied by a strong wind. These gatherings could take place in
empty houses, in deep ravines on mountain-tops (for example, Mount
Bujora is mentioned), or in caves. There the Bosorkani, together with
Ghouls and others, indulged in orgies. Generally, they like to dance in the
moonlight.

**Effects on people**

Bosorkani were mainly attributed to the following activities:

- taking milk from cows (taking straw, grass, dung from someone else's yard
- collecting dew on the pasture on canvas, which then became milk or stealing milk from a cow in labor); doing other harm to the household and livestock
- taking revenge on those who recognized her; casting spells
- sending spoilage, disease, death, the evil eye
- intimidation and leading people astray (Transcarpathia)
- luring and ruining lads
- strangling victims at night
- substituting a human child for her own – ugly, whiny and living for only seven years
- taking milk away from women in labor (touching her bed; drinking from her mug – Ukrainians of eastern Slovakia)

Bosorkani were believed to affect the weather, in both harmful and useful ways: causing hail, rain, thunderstorms, wind, storm, drought or fire. According to folk-belief, during the funeral of a Bosorka it rains heavily. Bosorkani caused drought by charming snakes, which began to fight with each other, or by tying two feathers under the left wing of a rooster. Bosorkani were believed to be more active on St. Lucia's Day, Christmas Eve, the Day of the Three Kings, St. George's Day, Thursday and Friday of Holy Week, the first day of May and St. John's Night.

**Protection**

The ability to see them was given by wearing quills of garlic sprouted through a snake's head. A woman who came before the *Polaznik* into the house on Christmas Day could be counted as a Bosorka. (Polaznik is called the first guest in Slavic traditions, a ceremonial guest, sometimes called the "divine guest", who comes to the house at Christmas or on some holiday between St. Demetrius day and Epiphany to bring luck, prosperity, health and wealth for the coming year.) Garlic, parsley, holy water, salt, a passion candle, a wreath of ears of corn, thorny plants, brooms, or a harrow were considered as amulets for cattle against Bosorka; cows were given bread baked with dried herbs or fruits of rose-hip, or hawthorn and the barn was fumed with nutshells of the nuts that were eaten on Christmas Eve. To prevent the spoiling of milk, it was ritually salted and a piece of bread was pierced three times; watery milk or milk with blood was beaten with a branch of thorns or filtered through it, or through a fork with a knife, lying crosswise. To protect children, they hung a small sack with salt or garlic, or a wolf's tooth, around their necks; they turned their shirts inside out and put iron objects in their cradles. Elderberry, elm, gooseberry, and thorn branches were also used to protect the house.

## Boszorkány

Outside Hungary *Boszorkány* is usually translated as "evil witch". This is incorrect. The word is derived from the Turkic word *baszargan, baszirgan,* which has the same meaning in Turkish, and is a derivative of the Old Turkic verb *basz* (to press) – the origin of the Hungarian word *baszni* – and it appears that the Boszorkány has more in common with the *Alp*-type and the etheric or vampiric version of the *Revenant.* Gábor Lükő (in his *Ethnographic symbol library of soul forms*) attributes the belief in the Boszorkány to the spiritual beliefs of the Stone Age or Bronze Age peoples and the theory of transmigration of souls. According to these beliefs, the soul of a dying person leaves the body at the moment of death and then, for a certain period of time (usually a short or long month, which is 20 to 40 days) it remains in an intermediate state of wandering between the earthly world and the afterlife. During this time, it can pose a threat to the living and return to relatives and, by entering through their noses and mouths, cause illness in their stomachs (which can be averted by various practices). According to Lükő, this belief may be a distorted remnant of an even more primitive but logical belief, namely that this wandering soul, in its original form, was a threat only to women, because it wanted to return to the womb instead of the stomach, with the obvious intention of being reborn. In any case, the returning spirit, bringing evil, sickness and pain, may be closely related to the Boszorkány, who was originally a creature who, according to superstitious belief, would settle on the sleeping person's breast and, as the name suggests, would press it, squeeze it, and thus cause tormenting dreams or even illness and death. The word Boszorkány is a playful, affectionate form of the word witch.

One of the names given to witches in the Hungarian-speaking regions was *Bűvös-bájos, Bű-bájos,* and their activity was bewitching-beguiling. The meaning of these words was connected with evil and the depraved.

The interesting thing in this case is the meaning, origin and connection of the root words *bű* (witch) and *báj* (charm) with witchcraft. They are derived from the Old Turkish word *báj*, which means "bond" or "shackle". The Hungarian words *báj* and *bájos* have lost their pejorative connotation over time, and only the figurative meaning of "fascinating" and "immobilizing" has been preserved, hidden deep in the meaning. The original meaning of the word is best preserved by the meaning of "witch as enchantress" (i.e. bewitching, captivating). The word *bű* means "sinful", "horrible" but also has a link to "enchanting".



## Božalość

*Božalość*, also transliterated as *Božaloshtsh* or *Bozaloshtsh*, is a messenger of death in the folklore of the Wends and Lusatian Sorbs. The name was translated in German ethnographic sources as *Gottesklage* i.e., "God's Lament". An 1886 article *Das Spreewaldhaus* by W. v. Schulenburg associates the Božalość with the elder bush and describes it as a woman dressed in white with long braided hair and red eyes from crying under the window of those about to die:

> *"Sambucus nigra; weil einst die Božalość kam, die Gottesklage*
> *(die im Fliederstrauch sitzt), ein Weibchen, weiss gekleidet,*
> *mit langem verwilderten Haar und rothen Augen, als*
> *man H. brannte. Nach Hartknoch glaubten die Litthauer,*
> *unter Hollunderbäumen hätten Götter ihren Sitz,…"*

(Sambucus nigra; because once came the Božalość, the gods lament (who sits in the elder bush), a female, dressed in white, with long feral hair and red eyes, when one burned H.. According to Hartknoch, the Lithuanians believed that under elder trees the gods had their seat,...)

The white hair makes her reminiscent of the Rusalka, however the braid does not. In Russia the braid of the Rusalka was a symbol of their freedom and their wildness. That the Božalość has a braid indicates that it isn't free or entirely a nature-spirit (unless we presume that its braid was a later edition). The fact that she cries for those about to die would make it similar to the *Domovoi* and the *Banshee* (of Celtic mythology) which are ancestor spirits. It seems quite possible then that the Božalość is the spirit of a dead girl which is still bound, or in some way connected, to her family. A parallel creature is *Bože sedleško*, described as a crying child in white clothes. The name is of unclear etymology (the apparent association with the word translated as "seat" is unclear). While there is an agreement that *Božalość* means "God's Lament", the opinions about the etymology differ. In some opinions it is the contraction of *Boža žaloć*, i.e., "God's Pity". Another opinion is that the word *glosc* in the meaning of "lament" can be found in manuscripts from as early as the 17th century, and the attribute *Boža* i.e. "God's", was added in folklore later on, as were the poetic usages: "God's wind", "God's Sun", etc.

## Brodarica



The *Brodarica* or *Brodavica* is a female Slavic demon of Serbo-Croatian and Bulgarian folklore. She was believed to be a genus of Vila. She inhabited bodies of water – mainly fords and shallows, which she guarded and protected from men.

## Brzeginia

In Slavic folklore *Brzeginia* or *Brzeginka* was originally a female demon inhabiting the shores of water-bodies and mountains and guarding treasures hidden underground. Later on this role was taken over by the *Rusalka*.

## Bubus or Mumus

In Hungarian folklore, the *Bubus* or *Mumus* is an invisible, malevolent creature of the Bogeyman-type that scares children. It is known by other names, such as *Zsákos ember* (the man with the bag), *Bákász* or *Bakurász* or *Böbös*, which is more commonly used in Transylvania. The Bubus is mostly associated with darkness, but there is no description of the figure itself. It has been suggested that the reason why there is no description of him is that he is the embodiment of everyone's own fears. In the vernacular, Bubus or Mumus is still used to discipline children, for example *"Ne sírj, mert elvisz a Mumus"* (Don't cry, the Mumus will take you away) or *"Hallgass, mert jön a Mumus"* (Be quiet, the Mumus is coming).

## Buka

The *Buka* or Russian Bogeyman is a folklore character who used to scare
naughty children. In the past, the Buka was often used to scare children
(*don't go, the Buka will eat you*), to keep them out of trouble, for example,
so they wouldn't go out at night. In folklore, the Buka is depicted as a
scary creature with a huge open mouth and a long tongue, with which the
Buka grabs children and, after throwing them down its throat, devours
them. The Buka also goes out only at night, wanders about in yards and
houses, and carries away children who are still outside. In everyday life
the word "buka" often refers to an unsociable, uncommunicative, sullen
person.

Before being turned into an NLP-method to scare off children, the Buka
seems to have been some sort of nasty *Goblin* – a small evil creature that
lived in the closet or under the bed. He was seen only by children, and
children suffered from him, because Buka was very fond of attacking
them at night – grabbing their feet and pulling them under the bed or
into the closet (his lair). He was afraid of the light, which could kill him,
and of the faith of adults. He was very afraid that the parents of his child
victim would believe in him. There was a counting rhyme to take away
the fear for the Buka:

| | |
|---|---|
| Раз, два, три, четыре, пять | *One, two, three, four, five* |
| Букой вздумали пугать. | *The Buka is scaring the living daylights* |
| | *out of you.* |
| Три, четыре, пять и шесть, | *Three, four, five and six,* |
| Вы не верьте, что он есть. | *You can't believe he's there.* |
| Пять и шесть, а дальше семь, | *Five and six and then seven,* |
| Буки, братцы, нет совсем. | *There's no Buka at all, brothers.* |

## Bukavac

*Bukavac* or *Vodeni bik, Vodenbika* (Serbo-Croatian: *Bukavac, Bukavac
noisy*) is a demonic creature of folklore, resembling a *Werewolf* or *Vampire*.
Beliefs in him are recorded in Srem (Serbia, Croatia). Bukavac is sometimes
described as a six-legged monster with deer antlers. According to folk
beliefs, it lives in large bodies of water (lakes, marshes), comes out of the
water at night, makes a lot of noise (hence the name; in Serbian the word
*buka* means "noise"), jumps on people and animals, and strangles them.

*Baba-Yaga Dancing with Old Man,* mid-18th century

## Bzionek

The *Bzionek* is a forest-demon from Silesia, named after the elderberry. It is described as a caring *dwarf*-like spirit who protected the homestead from evil spells and lived under an elder bush. For this reason, people held this plant growing near their homes in pious reverence. It was forbidden to cut down, dig up, or burn the elderberry in a stove. Water was poured under it after washing the deceased, to ward off misfortune. Sometimes a child with a high fever was brought under the lilac bush, in the hope that the Bzionek would take away the illness.



# C

## Căpcăun

A *Căpcăun* is a creature in Romanian folklore, depicted as an *Ogre* who kidnaps children or young ladies (mostly princesses). It represents evil, as do its counterparts *Zmeu* and the *Balaur*. The Romanian word *căpcăun* appears to have meant "dog-head" (*căp* being a form of *cap*, meaning "head", and *căun* a derivative of *câine*, "dog"). According to Romanian folk-beliefs, the Căpcăun sometimes appears with two heads, sometimes with the head of a dog and the body of a man. It is said that these beings can transform into several animals (from bear to deer and so on). Its main characteristic is anthropophagy (eating human flesh). In the legends, the Căpcăun has his own land, a land without flowers or any kind of life and very gloomy and dark, full of ghoulish creatures that do not hesitate to attack any passers-by. The term Căpcăun also means "Tatar chieftain" or "Turk chieftain", as well as "pagan". Some linguists consider Căpcăun to be an echo of a title or administrative rank, such as *kapkan* (also *kavhan, kaphan, kapgan*) used by various Central Asian tribes who invaded Eastern Europe during late antiquity and the medieval era, such as the Pannonian Avars, Bulgars and Pechenegs.

## Chesme

In Turkish folklore *Chesme* is a cat-shaped well (or fountain) spirit or *Nymph*. She was said to lure youths to death. She also has a strange shape-shifting ability to appear as a corpse surrounded by mice. The word

Chesme translates to mean "fountain cat". Sitting on a rock near a source of water, the creature sings a siren-like song to lure men to it, attacks them and tries to drown them by draining her victims of their life-force.

## Chichiga

The *Chichiga* (Russian: шишйга, also named *Lechenka*, лёшенка) is a female *Goblin*-like creature in Russian folklore and Slavic mythology. She is described as a small hunchbacked being, living in reeds, with a preference for small streams and ponds. According to tradition, she walks around naked and with her hair down, harassing passers-by, especially drunks. She sleeps all afternoon and appears only at dusk. Chichiga plays an important role in the mythology of the Komis – a Finno-Ugric people of Russia, living mainly in the Komi Republic – according to whom she lives in the river Kama, which she sometimes leaves to sit on the riverbank and comb her long black hair. Seeing a Chichiga is fatal. Anyone who spots the creature will soon die of drowning or some other cause. Chichiga is also the nickname of a Russian off-road truck, the GAZ-66.

## Chobold

In Polish lore the *Chobold, Chobard, Chochold* is a Warmian-Masurian demon, guardian of the homestead and hearth, borrowed from the German *Kobold,* however instead of a *dwarf* in a red robe he could also appear as a bird, usually an owl or hen. Chobold was most likely to spend time near human habitation. He sought the company of man and desired to have a protector in him. Appearing in the form of a hen, when taken into a household he could bestow wealth on the host, demanding comforts and good treatment for the time he served, and when neglected he would take away all his possessions, bestowing them on someone else who took better care of him. Only the sign of the cross kept him from stealing. A Chobold was by nature vindictive, dishonest, but loved peace and quiet, so he was assigned a place in the attic of the house, hiding his existence from others. His preferred food was noodles. During the day, while being nurtured, he did not leave his abode, at which time he shrank to almost invisible proportions. At night he developed his strength and activity. A relationship with a Chobold led to the loss of one's peace of mind and salvation, while quarreling with him led to the loss of worldly possessions.

# Chochlik

In Polish and Lithuanian folk tales the *Chochlik* (from Old Polish:
*chochoł* – meaning something like "on top of the head") is a mischievous
or naughty spirit. According to folklorists Bronisław Trentowski and
Joachim Szyc it was a Slavic household deity who took the form of a cat
that guarded the pantry. When angered, he could smash and overturn
furnishings and wreak havoc with supplies.

# Chowaniec

The *Chowaniec* (also: *Hodowany, Chowany, Utrzymywany, Wychowywany*;
Czech: *Skřítek, Kristek*; Slovak: *Škriatok*; Ukr.: хованец, годованец) is
a Slavic *household-spirit*. He is depicted as a little man or a *Gnome* with
a gray beard, who hides during the day but comes out at night to look
after the household. He is cuddly and kind, but people were afraid to
offend him. The creature lived behind the stove or in the chimney, where
it was left unsalted food. Like other spirits of this type one could create
a Chowaniec by an "egg-armpit variable"; one should carry the first egg
(znosek) laid by a black hen for nine consecutive days. During that time,
one had to refrain from bathing and pious prayer. On the ninth day, the
creature was supposed to hatch, though there were no guarantees.

# Chuhaister

The *Chuhaister* or *Chugaister* (Ukrainian: Чугáйстер) is a Ukrainian
spirit of the forests, related to the *Leshie* and *Woodwose/Wilder Mann*. He
is specific to the Ukrainian Carpathians, unknown to other Slavs, except
in some parts of Bulgaria. He is also called лісовий чоловік – *Lesovyi
cholovik* (forest man), лісовий дід – *Lesovyi did* (forest grandfather), гай
– *Hai* (Grove), очугайстер – *Ochugaister*, чугай – *Chugai*, лісовий дід –
*Lesovyi did* (forest grandfather), and simply дід – *Did* (grandfather), and
ночник – *Nochnik* ("night light" in Transcarpathia). The origin of the name
Chuhaister is unclear, but it may be related to the Proto-Slavic root *čuga*,
meaning "to guard". The origin of the second part of the word is unknown,
although it has been linked to the word for "stork", (Ukrainian: лелека).
The word may be of foreign origin. The use of descriptive names like "forest
man" etc. is probably related to the taboo of the pronunciation of names of
demons among the Slavs. A number of authors however spelled the name
of the character with a capital letter, thus treating it as an individual.

Chuhaistras are masculine and humanoid in shape. According to legend, the Chuhaister was once an ordinary man who did something bad to his neighbor, who in reaction cursed him to live in the woods until the end of time, unable to die. Since then he has wandered alone through the dark dense forests and wild mountain tops, both in summer and winter, and no one can harm him, neither man nor beast. Over the years his clothes have worn out, and the Chuhaister now walks naked. He has long hair and a white beard, and his body is covered with white or black wool, so that it is very difficult to recognize a man in him. Usually the Chuhaister appeared as a giant: big, tall as a fir tree – from two to seven meters in height. There are indications that he has blue eyes, or eyes like a toad, that he is toothless and lisping, that he has claws on his feet, or even hooves. Sometimes the Chuhaister was described as dressed in white clothing, or being one-legged. There are legends that there is only one forest man, or that there are seven brothers, or that there are altogether only three or four Chuhaistras. Sometimes the Chuhaister was imagined as a whirlwind falling down on a forest and bringing down the trees. He was believed to have a cheerful disposition and loved to dance and sing. It was also believed that Chuhaister hunted down and devoured dangerous female forest-spirits or maidens known as *Mavkas, Nyavoks, Mavoks, Mayeks, Lesovitsa(uk), Povetrul(uk),* or *Forest witches.* Knowing the paths they walk, he hides in the foliage and waits for his prey to appear. When it passes by, he jumps out, grabs it, tears it in half (by stepping on one leg and pulling at the other) and then eats it. According to some Hutsul representations, when the forest man chases his victims, he is accompanied by a strong wind. The Chugaister gets angry if his victim tries to run away and hide, his loud voice rolling with the howl of a storm in the treetops. In order to get close to the *Forest-Maidens,* the Chuhaister could turn himself into a wolf, since they were not afraid of wolves. By his hunting of the Forest-Maidens the Chuhaister prevents the harm they can do to people, especially to the men working in the forest. There was a belief that if it were not for the Chuhaistras, there would be so many of these spirit-creatures that they would destroy the whole population.

It is usually pointed out that the Chuhaister is not dangerous to people and even treats them with sympathy, greeting them when they meet and urging them not to be afraid of him. He likes to warm himself, chat and smoke by the people's fire in the forest, or roast a captured Mawka on it. Sometimes, however, the Chuhaister takes people into a furious dance, which can be very exhausting or even fatal to them. Carpathian woodcutters used to leave a bowl of soup as a sacrifice for the toothless creature. According to other views, the Chuhaister does not like and even despises villagers, except for those who spend a lot of time in the woods and *"knows the forest customs"*. In the lives of other people he usually does not interfere, but if someone interferes with him, he can retaliate severely.

## Cicha

In Polish folklore the *Cicha* (proceeding quietly, silently, without noise, without tumult, secretly, stealthily, suddenly) is a malevolent demon in the form of a little girl that kills people, especially children, without warning and abruptly. She traveled the world in the form of a small, young girl with raven-black hair, a swarthy complexion, with large, bulging eyes and wearing a white robe. She wore a garland of poppies in her hair and wrapped her braid with a bloody scarf. Wherever she passed, plants withered, birds and insects fell silent, and a deadly smell was in the air. In cemeteries, she would dig up old graves, take out the bones, and bury them again. She held a black steel rod in her hand, with which she touched children, causing their immediate death.

## Cikavac

In Serbian folklore the *Cikavac* is a strange *Tulpa* or thoughtform-like creature, imagined as a winged bird-like animal with long beak and a pelican-like sack, which was created by some sort of witchcraft ritual. A Cikavac could be obtained by taking an egg from a black hen, which would then be carried by a woman under her armpit for 40 days, during which time she would not confess, cut her nails, wash her face or pray. The Cikavac would then suck honey from others' beehives and milk of others' cattle, and bring it to the owner; it would fulfill any of the owner's wishes, and also enable its mistress to understand the language of animals.

## Cmentarna baba

The *Cmentarna baba, Cmentarna kobieta* (Cemetery woman) is a demonic female character in folk tales from the Polish Radom-region. She was dressed in a long, black gown, had shiny white teeth, and was

armed with long claws. Wandering around cemeteries, she brought
misfortune upon people she encountered. It was believed she also dug up
graves to scatter the bones of the dead, most often of those who died a
sudden death. People she encountered, she tried to drag to the graves.

## Ćmuch

A *Ćmuch* is a Slavic Water-Sprite or Marsh-demon, found in legends
of the Laskowiak people from the Tarnobrzeg area, in Subcarpathian
Poland. This slothful creature lives in water reservoirs and marches or
in their vicinity. It looked like a huge frog with small round ears and
it had a short, slightly curled, pointed tail. According to lore he always
sat in a crouch. His presence was betrayed by strange noises such as *"a
sudden splash of water of something invisible"* or strong swirls of air over
the surface of the water, relative booms and humming of the water in
some place. The Ćmuch was reluctant to approach people. It frightened
especially those who were lazy and unwilling to work.

## Cmuk

*Cmuk, Ćmok or Ćmuk* is the name of a home-demon from the folk beliefs
in the Polish Wielkopolska region, which maintained that in the corner
of every house lived a demon in the form of a snake. The snake had to
be worshipped in order not to punish the family by death, and could not
be killed. The name of the demon is derived from *smykania*, meaning
"slithering".

## Csordásfarkasa

The *Csordásfarkasa* (shepherd-wolf) of the Hungarian folk beliefs in
Göcsejben and in the eastern part of the language area can be a man
who turns into a wolf after he has killed a lot of people and animals. Also
shepherds, who have been insulted and oppressed by their masters in
life, were believed to avenge themselves as raging wolfs on their masters'
flocks after death. After their revenge is satisfied, they lose their wolf form
and find rest in the grave. The Csordásfarkasa has different local names.
It is called *Farkaskoldus* in Hontban, *Szakállas farkas* (bearded wolf) in
the Tiszántúl and in the north-east, and *Küldött farkas* (sent wolf) in
Transdanubia.

Apart from a frustrated shepherd, any outsider opposed to the community could become a Csordásfarkasa: a quack who was more or less excluded from the village community, a person caught in an attempted theft, an unsympathetic village landlord, or a foreigner of another nationality. The Csordásfarkasa is depicted as both a more classic *Werewolf* (a living person able to change into a wolf) or a revengeful phantom creature in wolf-shape. Particularly ferocious wolves were often mistaken for people in the shape of wolves. The most typical beliefs, some widespread and some local, are:

- The ability to metamorphose can be acquired in infancy, for example through the carelessness or malice of a midwife.
- If a midwife puts a newborn through the remains of a birch tree three times, it will become a Csordásfarkasa at the age of seven, taking the form of a wolf or a human at will.

Others acquire the ability as adults. Becoming a wolf and reverting back into a human being is usually done in a similar way, e.g. by moving through the same remains of a birch tree three or seven times. In some beliefs this Werewolf was half animal, half human in appearance. A wolf thought to be a wolf of the pack with certain characteristics that distinguish it from a "real wolf", like a better sense of smell, or *"having its belly where its back should be and its back where its belly should be"*, was also thought to be a Csordásfarkasa. The transformation into a wolf can be prevented; for example, in human form, a cross could be made three times with a red-hot piece of iron on its back. There are also historical records of the Csordásfarkasa dating back several centuries. According to a 1653 trial, a herdsman, who kept watch at Szombathely, was accused of *"attacking cattle with the wolves, with the help of the Eördegh"*. A trial in Nyíregyháza in 1734 mentions three witches in the form of wolfs attacking animals. The belief in Werewolves faded out in Hungary in modern times, but survived into the 20th century mainly in western Transdanubia and Transylvania.

## Čuma

A *Čuma* or *Kuga* (Serbian: чума, куга) personifies the plague in Serbian mythology. The Čuma was usually imagined as an old (rarely as young) woman dressed in white. Saying "Čuma" out loud was taboo, so euphemisms as *Kuma* (godmother) or *Teta* (aunty) (Serbian: кума, тета) were used. Čumas were believed to live in a faraway land, from where they set out to infect people with diseases. They hate dirtiness and are especially eager to infect a dirty house, hence if plague would appear in the vicinity, it was believed that every house and its occupants must be thoroughly cleaned; which was of course a useful belief that actually really helps preventing diseases. Offerings of food, clean water, basil and a comb could also be made to her.

## Czart or Czort

*Czart*, also known as *Czort*, *Chort* or *Bies* (Czech *Czert*, Russian *Czort*, Russian чёрт) is in the beliefs of the Slavs the demon of evil, known mainly in the Ruthenian tribes, where the Czart replaced the old Slavic *Bies*. In the folk dialect it is called *Kusy*, and in Christian beliefs – *Devil*. After the acceptance of Christianity the Bies became identified with the Devil. For example, *biesy* (Russian pl. of *bies*) is used in the standard Russian translation of Mark 5:12, where we have the devils entering a swine. In Ukrainian *bisy* or *bisytysia* means "to go mad". The Slovenian *bes*, Croatian *bijes* and Serbian *bes* mean "rage" or "fury". Most likely the Czart has gradually developed itself from an original nature daemon into the Christian Devil, although it never completely solidified into the latter due to its many folkloric connotations.

In folk beliefs Czart is depicted as a lame man. He inhabits swamps, forests and bodies of water, and also manifests himself in whirlwinds, which gave rise to the theory that the Devil was the personification of the destructive power of the wind. The Devil sent bad weather and disease down on people and encouraged them to commit suicide. He could take the form of a snake, dog, pig or black cat. In Slavic mythology, Czart once led a fight with one of the gods, during which he was wounded in the leg, or was thrown from the sky and broke his leg. Another version of the myth tells of the tail being bitten off by a dog sent by a god. After Christianization the term Czart became synonymous with the word Devil, while the original meaning and function of Czart has been lost and is now reconstructed on the basis of folklore.

The etymology of the word has been derived from the term *czarny* or *czary* (black or sorcery), and similarity to the Lithuanian *kyréti* (to anger), as has also been pointed out. Another possibility is the connection with the words *krótki, skrócony* (short, shortened) (cf. English: *short*, German: *kurz*, Latin: *curtis*), which is also indicated by the term *Kusy*, that is sometimes used for the Devil. The name in this case would come from the fact that the Devil had one leg shorter than the other leg.

In Czech folk tales, *Čert* is not an evil character per se. It is often trying to tease people into selling their souls in exchange for something (money, power, completion of a task). This often ends badly for evil or greedy types of people, who are tricked into getting useless gifts and then are carried into Hell. At other times, Čert changes roles from trickster to tricked as he loses a bet against a hero, who outsmarts him, winning his soul back. This way, Čert is often tricked to build castle walls in a day, dig fish ponds or even whole river banks, move large stones, or create hills and mountains. Čert is often a smallish hairy man with a tail, horns and one or two hoofs. But he is a shapeshifter and he tries to trick people in his nicer forms, before they even realize what he is. In these forms, he is often represented as a handsome young man, count or huntsman. Often, this transformation is not complete, so one can recognize Čert by small horns hidden in black curly hair, or a single hoofed leg hidden in a high boot.

In Turkic its name is *Çor* (Chor) and people in Anatolia know him as *Çorabaş* (Chorabash). *Çors* are spiritual creatures – mentioned in pre-Islamic texts and oral tradition – who inhabit an unseen world in dimensions beyond the visible universe of humans. Folk narratives mention that the Çors are made of fire, but that they can also interact physically with people and objects and likewise be acted upon. Like a human being, the Çor can also be good; *Ak-çor* (White Chor), evil; *Kara-çor* (Black Chor), or neutral. An exorcist is called a *Çoraman* in Anatolia.



*Boruta* (1876), woodcut by Jan Holewiński (1871-1927) after a drawing by M. E. Andriolli

# D

## Damk

In the Kashubian folklore of Pomerania (North Poland) the *Damk* is
a spirit who takes care of hermits, outcasts, and quiet introvert people
without a sense of humor.

## Dev



In Armenian mythology and many various Armenian folk tales, the *Dev*
(in Armenian: դև) appears both in a kind and in a malicious role, and
has a semi-divine origin. A Dev is a very large being (in Turkish dev
means giant) with an immense head on his shoulders, and with eyes as
large as earthen bowls. Some of them may have only one eye. Usually,
there are *Black* and *White Devs*. However, both of them can either be
malicious or kind. The White Dev is present in Hovhannes Tumanyan's
tale *Yedemakan Tzaghike* (Arm.: Եդեմական Ծաղիկը), translated as
"The Flower of Paradise". In the tale, the Dev is the flower's guardian.
*Jushkaparik, Vushkaparik,* or *Ass-Pairika* is another chimerical being
whose name indicates a half-demoniac and half-animal being, or a
*Pairika* – a female Dev with amorous propensities – that appeared in the
form of an ass and lived in ruins. In one medieval Armenian lexicon, the
Dev are explained as rebellious angels.

## Devi

*Devi* are many-headed *Ogre*-like giants whose heads can regenerate if
any of them are cut off, like the *Lernaean Hydra* in the myth of Hercules.
These malevolent giants live in the underworld or in remote mountains,
where they hoard treasure troves and keep their captives. In Georgian
folklore, they live in family units, usually consisting of nine brothers.
*Bakbak-Devi* was the strongest and most powerful of the Devis. To defeat
them, heroes would outwit them by means of various tricks and games.
Their name is related to that of the *Daevas* of Zoroastrian and Persian
mythology, derived in turn from Proto-Indo-European *deiu̯ó* (god).

# Dhampir

A *Dhampir* (also *Dhamphir* or *Dhampyr*) is in south-eastern European folklore the child of a *Vampire* father and a human mother. In the Balkans, it was believed that male Vampires have a great desire for women, so a Vampire would return to have sexual intercourse with his wife or a woman he was attracted to while alive. In one case, a Serbian widow tried to blame her pregnancy on her dead husband, who was said to have turned into a Vampire, and there were cases of Serbian men pretending to be Vampires in order to reach the women they desired. In Bulgarian folklore it was said that Vampires sometimes deflower virgins. The sexual activity of the Vampire seems to be a peculiarity of the South Slavic Vampire belief, in contrast to other Slavs, although a similar motif also occurs in Belarusian legends.

The word Dhampir (definite form *Dhampiri*) possibly derived from the Albanian *dham* (tooth) plus *pir* (drinker/drank) (standard Albanian forms: *dhëmb* and *pirë*). So Dhampir means in fact "toothdrinker" in Albanian. In the rest of the region, terms such as Serbian *Vampirović*, *Vampijerović*, *Vampirić* (and Bosnian *Lampijerović*, etc.) literally meaning *Vampire's son*, are used. In other regions the child is named *Vampir* if a boy and *Vampirica* if a girl, or *Dhampir* if a boy and *Dhampirica* if a girl. In Bulgarian folklore numerous terms, such as *Glog* (hawthorn), *Vampirdzhiya*, *Vampirar*, *Dzhadadzhiya* and *Svetocher* are used to refer to Vampire children and descendants. Dhampiraj is also an Albanian surname. Some traditions specify signs by which the children of a Vampire can be recognized. Albanian legends state they have untamed dark or black hair and lack a shadow. In Bulgarian folklore, possible indications include being "very dirty", having a soft body, no nails and bones (this last physical peculiarity is also ascribed to the Vampire itself), and *"a deep mark on the back, like a tail"*. In contrast, a pronounced nose was often a sign, as were larger than normal ears, teeth or eyes.

# Diabeł Boruta

*Diabeł Boruta (Boruta the Devil)* or simply *Boruta*, also known as *Mudman* is a devil living in the basement of the castle in Leczyca. Diabeł Boruta has long been known in the Leczyca region. It is derived from the Slavic demon *Boruta*, also known as *Lesze* or *Borowy*, who was believed to live in the forested and swampy surroundings of present-day Leczyca.

*Borowy* was the guardian of forests and the patron saint of hunters. It is also believed that the name *Borut* comes from a pine forest – in Old Polish, pine is simply *boruta*. Boruta is represented in various ways. According to legends he can take various forms. The typical and favorite, hence the most common character, is Boruta the nobleman, also called *Boruta tumski* or *Black*. He was a tall nobleman with a long black moustache, black eyes, dressed in a rich cape covering his tail and a cap covering his horns. However, Boruta also appeared in other forms and was found in various places:

- as a bird with huge wings (*Boruta błotny – Błotnik = Boruta mudskipper*) he was found on meadows and moors near Leczyca,
- as a big fish with horns *(Boruta topielec = Boruta the drowning man)*, he was seen in the waters of the Bzura River,
- as a fast black horse *(Boruta koń – Boruta the horse)* galloping at night on the fields around Leczyca, he was also seen in Panoszow, the sound of hooves was heard and the silhouette of a speeding, beautiful horse was seen,
- in the form of an owl he was *Boruta sowa* (Boruta owl),
- as a wolf he was found in the forests,
- as a sitting, hooded monk, holding a shiny kettle in his hands, he was seen near the sunken robber's castle in Panoszów,
- in the guise of *Boruty młynarza (Boruta the miller)*, he haunted the local mills at night. He would later distribute the flour he had ground to the poor inhabitants of the town. The presence of this devil could also be confirmed by a fire that would suddenly start and quickly go out.

In all the legends devoted to the devil Boruta, he shows great cunning, cleverness and superhuman strength. He usually outsmarts people with his "devilish tricks". However, in many legends, he also appears as a benefactor, helping the poor.

## Legends

According to legend, Boruta was originally a nobleman living in the 14th century. His landed estate and wooden castle were located on the western side of the Liswarta bend in the meadows between the villages of that time: Ługy and Niwki (the contemporary names of these villages are Ługi-Radły and Panoszów), as indicated by numerous archaeological excavations. Around 1360, while building the castle in Leczyca, King Kazimierz Wielki (Casimir the Great) was driving nearby and got stuck

in his carriage on the wide marshes. A strong young man called Boruta
helped him and in return received the castle. There are legends that
Boruta, when settling in the castle, took a pot of gold with him, but it
was so heavy that he could not carry it, he dragged it and in this way he
carved the bed of the Liswarta river.

There are many versions explaining how Boruta later became a devil.
Supposedly, at the end of the 14th century, the Duke of Masovia entrusted
Boruta with a treasure, which, however, he did not manage to get back.
Therefore, to this day Boruta sits in the dungeons of the castle and guards
the deposited chests of gold. Another legend tells that Boruta and *Rokita*
went to an inn in Lodz to drink the local beer. Their thirst was really
great and they drank many beers. The innkeeper was worried about this
and wondered if the guests had enough money to pay. He told them that
he would not bring another beer until they had first paid for the beers
they had consumed already. Rokita only laughed, threw a few gold coins
on the table and demanded that the innkeeper bring them more beer.
When he returned with another portion of the drink and tried to pick up
the gold coins thrown by the devil, it turned out that they were burning
his skin like fire. The innkeeper screamed in pain and heard the devil's
laughter coming from the clouds of smoke in the place where his guests
had been sitting a moment ago. The beer he had brought a moment
before had already been drunk, and there was no trace left of the coins.

## Djall

*Djall* or *Dreq* became the personification of evil in Albanian mythology
and folklore. The name is also used for a demon of fire. In modern
Albania Djall is the name of the Devil. The name Djall derives from
the Latin *diabolus* (devil). Alternative forms are *Dreq* or *Dreqi* from the
Latin *draco* (dragon), *Satan* and *Shejtan* and the Albanian god of youth,
known as *Dyalos* in antiquity, parallel to *Dionysius*. He was demonized
by Christianity to represent the Satan. (cf. Romanian *Dracul*). There is a
parallel with *Lucifer*, once the Roman god of Dawn and sometimes called
*Morning Star* (Venus), but later demonized by the church into the Devil
or one of the major demon princes.

# Dobilni

In Georgian folklore the *Dobilni* (the ones who became sisters) are
disease-spreading spirits, usually appearing in the form of women,
children or animals. Dobilni towers *(dobilt k'oshk'i)* were built in
Khevsurian shrines to keep them at bay. Some Dobilni are benevolent,
such as *Princess Samdzimar* of the Khevsureti legend, who is invoked for
an easy childbirth, the birth of healthy children, and women's health in
general. Benevolent Dobilni were also invoked at certain shrines in order
to bless cattle, and also for the protection of travelers.



# Dobrochoczy

*Dobrochoczy* is a Polish forest-spirit. It was a rather kind creature towards
people, and is generally believed to have been a good spirit. He helped
travelers reach their destinations and took care of the injured. However,
he severely punished dishonest or wicked people who polluted the forest
thicket with their presence. The angered spirit could send illnesses and
other unpleasant ailments. The favor of this demon could be obtained
through an offering of bread and salt. Dobrochoczy looked like a tree, so
that he could camouflage his presence from strangers entering the forest.

# Dola

In Slavic mythology and folk-belief, *Dola* is both the personification
of fate and destiny, and a guardian spirit that takes care of the home,
property and offspring, ensuring happiness and prosperity. She was a
gift from the gods, a power given by them to mankind to overcome the
difficulties of life – comparable to the Roman *Genius*. The binding of fate
took place at birth and accompanied one until death, largely determining
ones life and personality. Dola was invisible, but sometimes it could
appear in the form of a woman or a man, as well as a dog, cat or mouse.
Dola's kindness ensured success in life. She could even watch over a
careless and wasteful person. Presumably, besides Dola, there was also its
negative variant (the concept of misery) but reversing this force could be
secured by a sacrificial meal.

# Domovoy

In Russia and other Slavonic countries the *Domovoy* (pl.: *Domovuie*),
also: *Domowik, Domownik, Domowy, Domowoj*, is a very important
household-spirit. He guarded the house and the farmyard, helped with
the daily chores, also took care of farm animals. He was identified with
the spirit of the original householder. This householder or Domovoy was
treated by the inhabitants of the house as a member of the family and it
was necessary to leave some food for him. When moving from one place
to another, the Domovoy was asked to move to the new house together
with its hosts. A neglected Domovoy took revenge on his hosts (e.g. by
breaking plates, scaring the inhabitants, beating children) or by moving
out of the cottage. He could also send evil forces, bane and *Ghouls*. He
was believed to prowl around the house at night, living usually behind the
stove (sometimes under the threshold, in the attic, in the pigsty, or in the
barn). He often took the form of a little grandfather dressed in a peasant
way, with long gray hair and a bushy beard. He could also take the form
of a cat, weasel, dog, snake, or rat. Sometimes he also had a companion,

The *Domovia, Domowika, Domowicha* or *Domacha*, most often identified
with a *Kikimora*, which came out at night from under the floor and spun
wool. The Polish equivalent of the Domowika was *Uboże*. The Ruthenian
Domovoy has a wife and daughters, who are beautiful – as were the
Hellenic *Nymphs*, but their favors are deadly to mortal men. In one
district of the Viatka, the Domovoy is described as a little old man, the
size of a five-year-old boy. He wears a red shirt with a blue girdle; his face
is wrinkled, his hair is of a yellowish grey, his beard is white, his eyes glow
like fire. In other places his appearance is much the same, only sometimes
he wears a blue caftan with a rose-colored girdle. Everywhere he is given
to grumbling and quarreling, and always expresses himself in strong,
idiomatic phrases. In Lusatia he takes the form of a beautiful boy, who
goes about the house dressed in white, and warns its inhabitants, by his
sad groaning, of impending woe. When hot water is going to be poured
away, it is customary to give warning to the Domovoy, that he may not be
scalded.

## The Domovoy and the ancestor-cult

Since the introduction of Christianity into Russia, something of a
demoniacal nature has attached itself to the character and the appearance
of the Domovoy, which may account for the fact that he is supposed to be

a hirsute creature; the whole of his body, even the palms of his hands and the soles of his feet, being covered with thick hair. Only the space around his eyes and nose is bare. The tracks of his shaggy feet may be seen in the snow in wintertime; his hairy hands are felt by night gliding over the faces of sleepers. When his hand feels soft and warm it is a sign of good luck: when it is cold and bristly, misfortune is to be expected. These days the Domovoy is supposed to live behind the stove, but in early times he – or the spirits of the dead ancestors, of whom he is now the chief representative – was held to be in even more direct relation with the fire of the hearth. In the 19th century in the district of Oblast Nijegorodskaya along the Wolga, it was still forbidden to break up the smoldering remains of the faggots in a stove with a poker; to do so might cause one's "ancestors" to fall through into Hell. The term "ancestors" is universally applied to the defunct, even in the case of dead children. When a Russian family moved from one house to another, the fire was raked out of the old stove into a jar and solemnly conveyed to the new one, with the words *"Welcome, grandfather, to the new home!"* being uttered at its arrival. This, and the customs following out of this, supposedly point to a time when the spirit and the flame were identified as equal, when some – now forgotten – form of fire-worship was practiced.

On the 28th of January the peasants, after supper, leave out a pot of stewed grain for the Domovoy. This pot is placed in front of the stove, and surrounded with hot embers. In olden days an offering of corn was placed directly on the fire. In some districts, tradition expressly refers to the spirits of the dead, the functions which are generally attributed to the Domovoy, and they are supposed to keep careful watch over the house of a descendant who honors them and provides them with due offerings. Similarly among the (non-Slavonic) Mordvins in the Penza and Saratof District, a dead man's relations offered the corpse eggs, butter, and money. saying: *"Here is something for you: Marfa has brought you this. Watch over her corn and cattle, and when I gather the harvest, do thou feed the chickens and look after the house."* In Galicia (west Ukraine and southeast Poland) the people believed that their hearths were haunted by the souls of the dead, who made themselves useful to the family, and there were many Czechs who held that their departed ancestors looked after their fields and herds, and assisted in hunting and fishing. Directly after a person's burial, according to them, their spirit takes to wandering by night about their old home, and watching that no evil befalls his/her heirs.

## The Domovoy's favorite color

Each Domovoy has his own favourite colour, and it is important for the
family to try and get all their cattle, poultry, dogs and cats of this hue.
In order to find out what it is, the Orel peasants take a piece of cake on
Easter Sunday, wrap it in a rag, and hang it up in the stable. At the end of
six weeks they look at it to see of what color the maggots are which are in
it. That is the color which the Domovoy likes. In the districts of Yaroslaf
and Nijegorod the Domovoy takes a fancy only to those horses and cows
which are of the color of his own hide. There was a peasant once, the story
runs, who lost all his horses because they were of the wrong color. At last
the poor man, who was almost ruined, bought a miserable hack, which
was of the right hue. *"What a horse! There's finally something like a horse!
Quite different from the other ones!"* exclaimed the delighted Domovoy,
and from that moment on, all went well with the peasant.

## The importance of the stove

The Russian Domovoy hides behind the stove all day, but at night, when
all the house is asleep, he comes forth from his retreat, and devours what
is left behind for him. In some families a portion of the supper is always
set aside for him, for if he is neglected he waxes wroth, and knocks the
tables and benches about at night. Wherever fires are lighted, there
the Domovoy is to be found; in baths, in places for drying corn, and in
distilleries. When he haunts a bath (banya) he is known as a *Bannik*; the
peasants avoid visiting a bath at late hours, for the Bannik does not like
people who bathe at night, and often suffocates them, especially if they
have not prefaced their ablutions by a prayer. It is considered dangerous,
also, to pass the night in a corn-kiln, for the Domovoy may strangle the
intruder in his sleep. In Poland it is believed that the Domovoy is so loath
to quit a building in which he has once taken up his quarters, that even
if it is burnt down he still haunts it, continuing to dwell in the remains
of the stove. In Galicia and Poland the invisible servant who lived in the
stove, was called *Iskrzycki* (Iskra being Polish for "spark"), who most
zealously performs all sorts of domestic duties for the master of the house.
In Belarusia the Domovoy was called *Tsmok*, a snake. This House Snake
brought all sorts of good to the master who treated it well and gave it
omelettes, which were placed on the roof of the house or on the threshing-
floor. When this was neglected, the snake would burn down the house.
It rarely showed itself to mortal eyes, but when it did, it generally was to
warn the heads of the family to which it was attached of some coming woe.

## Domovoy as guardian of herds and stables

It is said that the Domovoy does not like to pass the night in the dark,
so he often strikes a light with a flint and steel, and goes about, candle in
hand, inspecting the stables and outhouses. Hence he derives a number
of his names. Sometimes he appears as *Vazila* (from *vozit'*: to drive), the
protector of horses, a being in shape like a man, but having equine ears
and hoofs; at other times as *Bagan*, he is guardian of the herds, taking
up his quarters in a little crib filled for his benefit with hay. On Easter
Sunday and the preceding Thursday he becomes visible, and may be seen
crouching in a corner of his stall. He is very fond of horses, and often
rides them all night, so that they are found in the morning foaming and
exhausted. Sometimes, also, he goes riding on a goat. When a newly
purchased animal was brought home for the first time, it was customary in
several places to go through the following ceremony. The animal was led
to its stall, and then its possessor bowed low, turning to each of the four
corners of the building in succession, and said, *"Here is a shaggy beast for
thee, Master! Love him, give him to eat and to drink!"* And then the cord by
which the animal had been led was attached to the kitchen-stove.

## Domovoy as Banshee

The Domovoy often appears in the likeness of the proprietor of the house,
and sometimes wears his clothes. He is industrious and frugal, he watches
over the homestead and all that belongs to it. When a goose is sacrificed
to the *water-spirit*, its head is cut off and hung up in the poultry-yard, in
order that the Domovoy may not know, when he counts the heads, that
one of the flock has gone. For he is jealous of other spirits. He will not
allow the *forest-spirits* to play pranks in the garden, nor *witches* to injure
the cows. He sympathizes with the joys and sorrows of the house to which
he is attached. When any member of the family dies, he may be heard
(like a *Banshee*) wailing at night; when the head of the family is about to
die, the Domovoy forebodes the sad event by sighing, weeping, or sitting
at his work place with his cap pulled over his eyes. Before an outbreak of
war, fire, or pestilence, the Domovoys go out from a village and may be
heard lamenting in the meadows. When any misfortune is impending
over a family, the Domovoy gives warning of it by knocking, by riding
at night on the horses till they are completely exhausted, and by making
the watch-dogs dig holes in the courtyard and go howling through the
village. And he often rouses the head of the family from his sleep at night
when the house is threatened with fire or robbery.

*Domovoy* (1934) by Ivan Yakovlevich Bilibin (1876-1942)

**Quarreling Domovuie**

The Russian peasant drew a clear line between his own Domovoy and
his neighbor's. The former was seen as a benignant spirit, who would do
him good, even at the expense of others; the latter as a malevolent being,
who would very likely steal his hay, drive away his poultry, and so forth,
for his neighbor's benefit. Therefore incantations were provided against
him, in some of which the assistance of *"the bright gods"* was invoked
against *"the terrible devil and the stranger Domovoy"*. Domestic spirits
of different households often engage in contests with one another, as
might be expected, seeing that they are addicted to stealing from each
other's possessions. Sometimes one will vanquish another, drive him
out of the house he haunts, and take possession of it himself. When a
peasant moved into a new house, in certain districts, he took his own
Domovoy with him, having first, as a measure of precaution, taken care
to hang up a bear's head in the stable. This prevented any evil Domovoy,
whom malicious neighbors could have introduced, from fighting with,
and perhaps overcoming, the good *Lar Familiaris*. It was a terrible
thing for a family when a strange Domovoy got into a house and turned
out its friendly spiritual occupant. Fortunately there was a means of
expelling him, which was to take brooms, and with them to strike the
walls and fences, exclaiming, *"Stranger Domovoy, go away home!"* and
on the evening of the same day to dress in holiday array, go out into
the yard, and call out to the original tenant of the hearth, *"Grandfather
Domovoy! Come home to us – to make habitable the house and tend the
cattle!"* Another means was to ride on horseback about the yard, waving
a fire-shovel in the air, and uttering an incantation. Sometimes the shovel
was dipped in tar. When the Domovoy rubbed his head against it he was
disgusted, and left the house.

**Domovoy's alter ego**

Sometimes a man's own Domovoy takes to behaving unpleasantly to him,
for the domestic spirits have a dual nature, answering to that which the
old Slavonians attributed to the spirits of the storm. The same forces of
nature which fattened the earth and made it bring forth harvests, often
manifested themselves as destructive agents; so the Domovoy, although
generally good to his friends, sometimes does them harm, just as fire
is at one time friendly to man, at another hostile. Every now and then,
the peasants believe, a house becomes haunted by *Teazing*, absolutely
malicious beings, who make terrible noises at night, throw about sticks

and stones, and in various ways annoy the sleeping members of the
family. When the regular Domovoy does this, usually all he needs is a mild
scolding. Various stories prove the truth of this assertion. Here is one of
them. In a certain house the Domovoy took to playing pranks. *"One day,
when he had caught up the cat and flung her on the ground, the housewife
expostulated with him as follows: 'Why did you do that? Is that the way
to manage a house? We can't get on without our cat. A pretty manager,
forsooth!' And from that time on, the Domovoy gave up troubling the cats."*

## The Domovoy as Alp

One of the many points in which the Domovoy resembles the *Alps*
or *Mare*-type spirits is his fondness for plaiting the manes of horses.
Another is his tendency to interfere with the breathing of people who
are asleep. Besides plaiting manes, he sometimes operates in a similar
manner upon men's beards and the hair of women, his handiwork being
generally considered a proof of his goodwill. But when he plays the
part of our own nightmare, he can scarcely be looked upon as benign.
The Russian word for such an Alp is *Kikimora* or *Shiskimora*. The first
half of the word is probably the same as the provincial expression *shish*
"Domovoy", "demon", etc. The second half means the same as the German
*Mar* or our *mare* in *Nightmare*. In Servia, Montenegro, Bohemia, and
Poland *Mora* means the demoniacal spirit which passes from a witch's
lips in the form of a butterfly, and oppresses the breathing of sleepers at
night. The Russians believe in certain little old female beings called *Marui*
or *Marukhi*, who sit behind oil stoves and spin by night. No woman in
the Olonets district thinks of laying aside her spindle without uttering a
prayer. If she forgot to do so, the Mara would come at night and spoil all
her work for her. The Kikimori are generally understood to be the souls
of girls who have died unchristened, or who have been cursed by their
parents, and so have passed under the power of evil spirits. According
to a Servian tradition the *Mora* sometimes turns herself into a horse, or
into a *Dlaka*, or tuft of hair. Once a Mora so tormented a man that he
left his home, took his white horse and rode away on it. But wherever
he wandered the Mora followed after him. At last he stopped to pass the
night in a certain house, the master of which heard him groaning terribly
in his sleep, so he went to look at him. Then he saw that his guest was
being suffocated by a long tuft of white hair which lay over his mouth. So
he cut it in two with a pair of scissors. Next morning the white horse was
found dead. The horse, the tuft of hair, and the Nightmare, were all one.

**The 30th of March the Domovoy turns malicious**

The Domovoy generally turns malicious on the 30th of March, and remains so from early dawn till midnight. At that time he makes no distinction between friends and strangers, so it is as well to keep the cattle and poultry at home that day, and not get near the windows more than necessary. It is uncertain whether his short-lived fury at that season of the year arises from the fact that he is then changing his coat. Some believe that a kind of mania comes over him then, others that he feels a sudden craving to get married to a witch. Anyhow it is considered wise to propitiate him by offerings. These gifts can take almost any edible shape. In the Tomsk district, on the Eve of the Epiphany, the peasants place on a certain part of the stove little cakes made expressly for the Domovoy. In other places a pot of stewed grain is set out for him on the evening of the 28th of January. Exactly at midnight he comes out from behind the stove, and snacks on it. If he is neglected he waxes wroth, but he may be appeased with the help of a wizard, who kills a rooster and lets its blood run on to one of the whisks used in baths. With this in hand he sprinkles the corners of the cottage inside and out, uttering incantations. While unclean spirits fear the crowing of roosters, it never in any way affects the Domovoy. Another way of pacifying the irritated domestic spirit is for the head of the family to go out at midnight into the courtyard, turn his face to the moon, and say, *"Master! Stand before me as the leaf before the grass, neither black nor green, but just like me! I have brought thee a red egg."* Thereupon the Domovoy will assume a human form, and, when he has received the red egg, will become quiet. But the peasant must not talk about this midnight meeting. If he does, the Domovoy will set his cottage on fire, or will induce him to commit suicide.

**Slavic variations of the term Domovoy**

The Slavic languages and their local forms have variations of the term Domovoy and use alternative names to describe the household god, including:
- *Děd, Dědek, Děduška* (names of this form convey the concept of "grandfather")
- *Did, Didko, Diduch, Domovyk* (Ukrainian)
- *Damavik* (Belarusian)
- *Dedek, Djadek, Skřítek* (Czech)
- *Šetek, Šotek* (Bohemian)
- *Škrata, Škriatek* (Slovak)

- *Škrat, Škratek* (Slovenian)
- *Skrzatek, Skrzat, Skrzot* (Polish)
- *Chozyain, Chozyainuško* (Russian, meaning "master" and "little master")
- *Stopan* (Bulgarian)
- *Domovníček, Hospodáříček* (Bohemian)
- *Domaći* (Croatian)
- *Zmek, Smok, Ćmok* (snake)

The female counterpart Domania can appear as:
- *Domovikha Kikimora, Marukha, Volossatka* (Russian)
- *Damavukha* (Belarusian)



## Dousheta

In Bulgarian folklore the *Dousheta* is a *Vampire* born of a deceased child. Tradition has it that if a child dies before it can be baptized, it will continue to exist as a vampiric demon. The roots of the Dousheta, however, must go back beyond the Christening of Bulgaria, as in European lore there are several samples of vampiric or demonic creatures who evolved from dead children, like the Scandinavian *Myling* e.a.

## Drak

The *Drak* (also called *Fürdrak, Drakel, Alf, Stöpke* and *Glüswanz*) is a flying house spirit that looks like a dragon, but has nothing in common with it. It is known in some Slavic regions nut because it is mainly a creature of northern and central Germany it is described in more detail in *Spirit Beings in European Folklore* – Compendium 2.

## Drekavac

*Drekavac, Drekawatz* or *Drekavats* (Serbo-Croatian: *Drekavac* – howler, screamer), also known as обезьян-ревунов (howler monkeys) is a ghostly being from South Slavic folklore, commonly believed to be the soul of a dead unbaptized baby. It is believed that the one who hears the Drekavak shouting outside from his house, will die. The same fate strikes a person on whom the shadow of the creature falls. Usually a Drekavac has a very thin spindly body with a disproportionately large head, but it may also look like an animal or like a normal child. When the Drekavac enters in the appearance of a baby, it foreshadows the death of a human, while its appearance as an animal foreshadows the death of an animal that belongs to the household. It may emit the bleat of a goat, the cry of a child, meow, or scream like a bird. What all descriptions have in common, however, is the creature's piercing, terrifying scream. It is believed that the Drekavac can be seen at night, especially around the time of the Twelve Days of Christmas (the period between 25 December to 6 January – known in Serbia as the unbaptized days) and towards the beginning of spring, when evil spirits and demons are said to appear most frequently. It is noteworthy that the creature in the form of a child announces the imminent death of a person, but in animal form is held responsible for the perishing of livestock. The Drekavac usually spares its parents, and it is very afraid of dogs, which can be used to scare it away. It is not very fond of light either.

Some believe that the species of Drekavac varies from region to region. Usually it is described as being over one meter tall and quadrupedal. In some legends, the creatures live in packs, or hide in caves and tunnels. There is a belief that the Drekavac cannot be killed or overcome. One can only baptize it if the creature cried out in the form of a child, to redeem it. In parts of Serbia and the Balkans, it is believed that before meeting the being, one will first see the Drekavac in a dream. A person who has harmed the child in life, is at risk of getting strangled by it while asleep. The Drekavac is usually the scary hero of children's horror stories, but in remote areas (such as the mountainous Zlatibor in Serbia) even adults believe in this creature. In 2003, residents of the village of Tometino Polje occasionally reported strange attacks on their cattle. The nature of the wounds: the throat was cut and the body was completely drained of blood. It was difficult to determine what kind of predator could have caused it, but the villagers claim they had heard several eerie screams before the attacks, so there must have been a Drekawac involved. More than 200 sheep were slaughtered here in a couple of years. In Serbia, the village of Svoynovo, under Mt. Juhor and the town of Paracin, are said to have a Drekavac and according to the locals the screams are sometimes unbearable. On October 5, 2011, a strange creature, remotely resembling a dog and emitting terrible screams, was seen near the village of Drvar in western Bosnia, after which streams of curious tourists and explorers came to visit the place.

**Similar creatures**

- *Bukavac* from Syrmia, Serbia – a six-legged beast with gnarled horns that lives in the water during the day and comes out at night with a great roar and then strangles people and animals.
- *Jaud*, a Drekavac from an unborn child afflicted with vampirism.
- *Plakavac* from Herzegovina, a newborn strangled by its mother, which rises from the grave at night and returns to its parents' house. It just screams there, but cannot do any harm.

# Drioma



In Slavic folklore, *Drioma* (in Russian Дрёма) is a spirit of the evening and night. It takes on the appearance of a benevolent-looking old woman with soft hands, or that of a small man with a soft, lulling voice. A Drioma walks under the windows in the evening, and when the darkness thickens, enters the house through the cracks and crevices. She comes to see the children, puts them to sleep by closing their eyes, arranges the blanket, caresses their hair. This spirit is less kind to the adults, to whom she sometimes inspires nightmares.

# Dschuma

The *Dschuma* is a witch-like demon from Romanian folklore, looking like either a young virgin or an old hag, and infected with cholera that it spreads wherever it goes. At night, it can be heard wailing in pain, as the disease is worse then. The Dschuma cannot be destroyed, but it can be made to leave an area by giving it a scarlet shirt, which has to be created by seven old women in one night. If seven old women are not available, seven maidens can do the job. The shirt has to be left in the woods where the creature dwells and she will put it on as she is very sensitive to cold and usually naked. She then leaves the village out of gratitude, however, she herself decides when exactly.

# Dvorovik or Dvorovoi

The *Dvorovik* (yard keeper) is spirit of the courtyard. It was associated with a farmstead's grounds, cattle shed and possessions, a servant of the housekeeper in Ukrainian folklore. In Poland he was called *Dworowy*. The Dvorovik protected the farm, all the property and the animals in the yard

from floods, fires, robbery etc.. He also brought wealth, prosperity and a
good harvest, looked after stables, pigsties, cowsheds, orchards, apiaries,
chicken coops, blacksmith shops and home gardens. He also patronized
work in the field. The Dvorovik is a subordinate of the *Dovokhoviks*, as
well as the *Dovykovik*, they can both help the owners of the property,
and maliciously demand a bounty (preferably: candles, bread, and
sheep's wool). He could appear in various guises, but like other tutelary
household-spirits he often took the appearance of a small grandfather,
dressed in a peasant way with a long beard. He distinguished himself by
his multi-colored hair, however. He also took the form of a snake with
a cocked head. The Dvorovik lived in a cowshed or a pigsty and was
constantly roaming around the house. He had a peculiar relationship with
domestic animals: he was always on friendly terms with the goat and the
dog, yet he disliked other animals, and birds are not approved of by him
at all (they are in the power of another household-spirit, the *Kikimory*
or *Kikimora*.) The Dvorovik especially disliked white animals: cows, cats,
dogs and white horses. However, the animals he loved he looked after
very well, ensuring their beauty and health and even braiding the horse's
manes. Unloved animals were haunted and tortured. They were ridden at
night, their tails and manes were torn. Small children could be in danger
by the creature as the Dvorovik could asphyxiate them. It was believed that
a Dvorovik could be killed by hanging a piece of a magpie on a strategic
place. Also, unloved animals could be prevented from being harassed,
tortured, or killed by keeping a goat around. Traditionally, the Dvorovik
was hanged on Malakhy (16 September) and Pilipov's Eve (27 October),
asking him not to be cruel anymore and depriving him of his faculties.

## Dwojedushnik or Dvudushnik

*Dwojedushnik* (Russian Двоедушник; transliteration *Dvoedušnik*
or *Dvudushnik*) literally mean *Two-soul*. In Slavic folk belief the
*Dwojedushnik is* a human being capable of combining two souls, one
of which is demonic, and the other, human. Sometimes it was about
combining two hearts in one person. In this context, one of the two hearts
carried in itself shades of supernatural, dangerous, devilish or "impure"
sensations. A Dwojedushnik or Two-soul could be a person of any gender,
both male and female; they included wizards, *Vampires*, *Bosorkans*,
*Volkolaks*, *Vitryaniks*, witches, pestilence atmospheric elements, and even
showers and hail clouds. In the Polish part of the Carpathians, Two-souls

included people with the *evil eye, Watermen (Topelniki)* and various mythological characters associated with the atmospheric elements, like showers and hail clouds. The folk tales report that during the daytime the Dwojedushnik did not differ from the average citizen, but at night, he or she immediately fell into a very deep sleep, and in such a way that it was impossible to wake the person. During this sleep the person was outside of the physical body, and could keep his or her external appearance, or take the form of an animal (a dog, a horse, a hare, etc.). For example, a witch who was a Dwojedushnik had an opportunity to turn into a bat, a dog, a mouse, a cat, or any object: a poker, a wheel, an axe, etc.

The wandering soul of such a person could do harm to ordinary people, send them spoil, bad weather, drought, make them drink blood, etc. At the same time, if someone tried to detain a Dwojedushnik, it could kill either by its own force, or by the power of the elements, like a storm from which it is impossible to escape. Folklore noted that the destructive motive in the actions of such a soul did not depend on the personal will of its owner, who could not even remember what happened to him/her during sleep. The soul of such a creature leaves and returns to its body through the mouth in the form of a mouse, fly, etc. So after that had happened, a Dwojedushnik could be quickly awakened by changing position by way of bringing the head to the position of the feet. However, it was generally believed that any sleeping person should not be awakened quickly and unexpectedly, especially not the case of a Dwojedushnik, as the soul, traveling through the astral world, would not have time to return to its body, which could cause at least two weeks of illness, or in the worst case scenario, even death.

The reasons for the birth of a Dwojedushnik were most often attributed to the improper behavior of the parents, for example, people who were conceived when the mother had her period could become a Dwojedushnik. If someone was born to a woman in labor, who looked at a clergyman holding a cup during the "great exit", that child could also become a Dwojedushnik. In some places it was believed that the seventh girl in a family, who was born in a row of only girls, was bound to become a Dwojedushnik. It was possible to recognize a Dwojedushnik by some signs which distinguished it from ordinary people: Dwojedushnika are born with teeth, talk to themselves, have a red neck, on top of their head they have two curls, etc. In Poland Dwojedushnika referred to people suffering from sleepwalking.

*Dziwozona* (1864) woodcut by Jan Styfi (1839-1921) after engraving by Henryk Pillati

**Dwojedushnik's after-death state**

People believed that a dead Dwojedushnik became the cause of a strong storm, downpour or hail. After the death of a Dwojedushnik his or her pure soul was sent to the other world, and the unclean soul became a dangerous *Ghoul* or vampiric being who lived on in the grave, under water, in the thickets, in remote places, etc. This creature could not only drink blood, but also cause disease in children, cause pestilence, the death of livestock, drought, etc. Folklore preserved a number of means to disarm these restless souls. The dead were buried with precautions, at the edge of the cemetery, as far as possible from any path or road. Various objects were put inside the coffin, so that the soul would be busy playing with them. Poppy-seeds were scattered on the grave, which forced the soul to collect all of them. If the deceased continued to harm the living or cattle after death, the grave was opened, and in the most drastic version, the head was cut off, the body was turned upside down with its back up or feet to where the head was, and a linden, aspen, or hawthorn stake was driven into the heart.

# Dydko

*Dydko* (also: *Didko, Ditko, Dytko, Dydo*) is a spirit of Polish folklore, originally a demon of Slavic belief, who was later degraded to a *Bogeyman*. The character of Dydko derives from the well-known Russian *Household-spirit*, the *Domovoy*. After Christianization it degraded to the role of a devil, especially a forest devil, before it was forced into the role of a night terror, used to scare children into obedience. The Dydko was imagined as a clumsy figure with a large head, usually on straw legs similar to spider legs. According to later beliefs, the Dydko would appear in a mirror – to maidens who spent too much time in front of it.

# Dziwożona

*Dziwożona* appears as a female demon and a goddess in ancient Slavic beliefs. The word "dziwożona" (wilderness/wild wife/woman) is in Polish a loan from Slovak: *Diva lena/Divá žena* meaning "wild woman". The Polish equivalent was popularized by the novel *Dziwożona* by Zygmunt Kaczkowski, published in 1855. In Czech, the word appears as *Diva žena*, in the Hucułów there was *Dykaja żena*, in the Sorbs *Vodna žona*. In Red Ruthenia, on the other hand, the word *Bohynie* (goddess) fits the description of *Dzvozhona*. *Dzwożona* was particularly used by the Tatra highlanders, while the word *Diva lena*, but also *runa* (a reference to *Mamuna*) was used by the Slovakian highlanders. The term Dziwożona is exclusive to mountain regions; in different places, a similar demon was called *Mamuna* or *Boginka*, although there are also tales suggesting that they are different entities. In later folklore all three figures became *Rusalka*.

Dziwożony were depicted as ugly, hunchbacked women, with long tangled hair, sometimes with a red cap decorated with ferns on their heads and with long breasts or pathologically elongated nipples, which they threw on their backs and with which they even washed their underwear. They lived in rocky outcrops, in lakes (e.g. Lake Żabie) or in mountain caves (e.g. a cave near the village of Łopuszna). They fed on the sweet herb *słodyczka* (Polypodium vulgare, the common polypody). It was believed that Dziwożony kidnapped young girls and young married women. Apart from that, they kidnapped babies from their cradles, swapping them for their own ugly *changelings* with physical distortions or mental disabilities. Such a changeling could be recognized by its uncommon appearance – disproportionate body, often with some kind of disability – as well as its wickedness. It had a huge abdomen, an unusually small or large head, a hump, thin arms and legs, a hairy body and long claws; it also prematurely lost its first teeth. Its behavior was said to be marked by a great spitefulness towards the people around it, a fear of its mother, noisiness, reluctance to sleep and exceptional gluttony. As an adult (which was in fact rare, as nearly all changelings were thought to die in early childhood), it was disabled, gibbered instead of talked, and mistrusted people.

To protect a child against being kidnapped by a Dziwożona, the mother had to tie a red ribbon around its hand (this custom is still preserved in some regions of Poland, although without the original meaning), put a red hat on its head and shield its face from the light of the moon. Under no circumstances should she wash its nappies after sunset nor turn her head away from the child when it was asleep. Another method of deterring a Dziwożona was to keep a St. John's Wort flower at home or to grab it when the danger was direct. This practice is also prescribed in sources describing *Boginki*. The descriptions of the creatures' behavior and methods of protection against them are identical with the records of beliefs from different areas related to daemons. The way to get ones child back, was to take the changeling to a field, a border, or a garbage dump, and to beat it with a rod, additionally sprinkling water over it with an egg shell or forcing it to drink water from an egg shell: *"Take back yours, give back mine"*. Then the Dziwożona, moved by her own child's crying, would return for it, giving back the kidnapped newborn.

# E



## Eretik

In Russian folklore the *Eretik* ("heretic"; also: *Eretich, Elatomsk, Erestan, Erestun, Erestuny, Eretica, Eretich, Ereticy, Eretiku, Eretitsa, Eretnica, Eretnik, Eretnitsa* (female) or *Xloptuny*) is interpreted in several ways. It emerges from a dying person that becomes possessed while passing away, and is "reanimated" by a witch or sorcerer. One could also become an Eretik by being deemed a heretic, selling one's soul to the Devil, sleeping on a grave, or making inappropriate noises in a bath house. Although in some descriptions the Eretic is a weird Satanic *Vampire* creature, preying on flesh and blood, most active at night in spring and fall, and living in dry riverbeds where it routinely performs Black Masses. In contrast to other Slavic *Vampires* or *vampiric Revenants* it is however regarded as a living person – although the way of destroying it is akin to the way it is done to its undead relatives, the Vampires. It was believed it caused a person to wither away, eventually dying, but it could also glare at a person with such hatred and malice that it could kill with a mere look. This feature would place the creature in the spectrum of the *Jettatori*, persons with the Evil Eye, who – willingly or not – cause havoc, accidents or other negative situations, merely by their presence or gaze.

# F

## Fajermon

*Fajermon, Fajerman* or *Fajermón* is a vicious demon from folk beliefs of Cieszyn Silesia. He was supposed to have the form of a tall man without a head and from the place where the head should be, a bright flame was burning. He could be summoned by three whistles. It was either the soul of a penitent – in a legend from the Stonava area – doing penance for not having thanked anyone for anything in his earthly life, or the soul of a person who had harmed animals, especially horses, for which he did penance for a long time, by which he often took the form of a horse while waiting for salvation. He ran across the fields and meadows, where the peasants plowed the land. When one farmer thanked him for his help with the harvest, the Fajermon would turn into a figure dressed in a white robe and was freed from further punishment.

## Fene



*Fene* is a demon of illness in Hungarian folklore. Today, a common saying still uses its name: *"A fene egye meg!"* (Let it be eaten by the fene!), which is uttered as a form of swearing when something does not go as one wishes. Fene is also considered the place where demons roam in general, i.e. the popular Hungarian curse *"Menj a fenébe!"* is an equivalent to the English *Go to Hell!* Fene is a word with an unclear meaning, probably developed in folk medicine, with infinitive and adjective meanings. According to the *Pallas Nagy Lexikona* (Pallas's Big Dictionary), it means *wild, cruel, wicked, horrible, contagious.* Fene is used as a collective noun for various skin diseases with ulcerative, rashy sores, *"eating, gnawing at the bod"*. The lexicon suggests that the word once had a mythological meaning: *"Mint ilyen a betegségeket okozó, gonosz démonok sorába tartozhatott"* (As such, it may have belonged to a line of evil demons that caused disease). The *Magyar Néprajzi Lexikon* (Hungarian Ethnographical Encyclopedia) considers the word to be of Finno-Ugric origin. The encyclopedia points out that Fene was often used to signify a *wolf*. Modern Hungarian language also used "fene" in names of several diseases:

- *hidegfene* "cold fene" (disease of the bone)
- *melegfene* "warm fever" (skin disease of the extremities)
- *rákfene* "crab-skin" (skin disease of the face)
- *farkasfene* "wolf's mane" (herpes)
- *lépfene* "anthrax" (as a disease of pigs)

According to a 1798 note – quoted in the *Magyar Néprajzi Lexikon* – a fene is *"a hard swelling, and the pain is very great"*. In addition, the *Pallas Nagy Lexikona* mentions the diseases *holtfene, fövene, fészkesfene, feketefene, fityfene, fittyögösfene, fütykösfene.*

## Fext

A *Fext* is a mythical undead creature in Slavic folklore. Its origins are found in the terrors of the Thirty Years' War (17th century) in central Europe. It is said that bullets cannot harm the Fext, except bullets made of glass. Some of the great generals of that time were called Fexts because of their assumed immortality.

# G



## Gierach

The *Gierach* (also *Gierhals*) is often mentioned in German folklore from the sixteenth to the eighteenth century. It is also known in northern Poland, but mainly a creature from Germany. See under *Gierach* in *Spirit Beings in European Folklore – Compendium-2*

## Gnieciuch

*Gnieciuch, Gniot, Gniotek, Gnietek, Gnocek, Gnotek, Wiek* is a Slavic demon from the category of *Alps* and *Nightmares*, who try to suffocate people in their sleep. In Malopolska (Little Poland) he is depicted as a small, fat boy with a big belly, who wears a red cap and has a lot of money. He strangles people in their sleep, but before he does so, he takes out his own intestines from his belly in order not to crush his victim to death with his own weight while strangling. First he sat down on his victims legs, then he moved up towards the upper body. When he sat on the chest, he would then strangle with his arms and legs, holding his victim by the throat, completely incapacitating him. He could even strangle a person to death, if the victim did not wake up in time. According to the inhabitants of Zbydniowice, the Gnieciuch would first sit on the stomach, then on the chest, and then suck out the blood and vital forces so that the person would wake up weakened. The people of Ropczyce and the surrounding area imagine the Gnieciuch as a small boy who is always cold and coughs before he approaches a person in order to crush him. He also wears a red cap and if someone managed to take this cap from him, he asked it back and offered as much money as he could to regain his cap, or he took some sort of revenge. Lasowiaks believed that the Gnieciuch was invisible to sober people. He usually tormented drunkards. He was small in height but very heavy, with a big belly, and his legs and arms were thin, with long fingers, ending in crooked claws. On its thin neck was a disgusting head with large ears and bulging eyes, and its wide mouth had teeth protruding forward. Inhabitants of Ocice compared this demon to a small heavy doll with a golden cap and shoes, and three sacks of money. The inhabitants of Mielec, on the other hand, believed that Gnieciuch kept his money in a red cap; taking it away from him ensured great wealth, but it was impossible to achieve. He resided in the hallway, where the quern usually stood and would locate himself in its hollows. He eavesdropped on the conversations of the household members, and he could even make mischief during the day. He would enter the rooms through a knot hole in the ceiling, leaving his entrails behind.

## Gornapshtikner

The *Gornapshtikner* (горнадапне́р *Gornadapner,* хортылакне́р *Khortylakner*) is a kind of *Uruakan* (phantom, ghost) – specific the evil spirit of a dead foreigner, suicide or villain in Armenian folklore. It has much in common with the German *Aufhocker.* A Gornapshtikner may appear to people in anthropomorphic or zoomorphic appearance – for instance in the form of a cat, dog, wolf, bear, donkey or other animal. At night, it stands along the roads (especially near cemeteries) or it roams around the houses, scaring passersby, jumping on their backs, or onto their horses or carts. By dawn, they return to their graves.

## Grad

*Grad* (hail) is a male Slavic demon, personifying dangerous meteorological phenomena. He was imagined as a man bringing hailstones.

## Graniecnik

*Graniecnik* – a penitent soul, that after violating land-boundaries turned into a field demon, native to the vicinity of Nowy Targ, Little Poland. The Graniecnik appeared at night on the borders of the villages. He had no interest in people unless he encountered them on the road. He transformed himself into various forms: a peasant with his head cut off and a flame bursting from his neck, or a skylight fluttering over the fields.

## Grobnik

A *Grobnik* is a Bulgarian *Vampire* of the Kukush, Ohrid, and Struga districts. The name literally means "grave shadow" or "shadow from the grave". It is also known as the *Gromlik* and was described as having only one nostril.

## Grzenia

In the Kashubian folklore of Pomarania, north Poland, the *Grzenia* is a benevolent spirit that acts as the protector of sleep and dreams. He puts tired people to sleep and makes them wake up refreshed.



## Guta

In Hungarian folklore the *Guta* is a demon who gives his victims strokes, heart attacks, or a sudden paralysis. His name translates as "apoplexy". The Hungarian saying *"He has been beaten by the Guta"* means that the person has died suddenly of a stroke.

## Gveleshapi

In Georgian folklore, the *Gveleshapi* (გველეშაპი, in ancient sources გველ-ეშაპი – Snake-whale) is an evil serpent shaped water demon that ruled and lived in lakes, rivers, and water sources. The creatures were associated with water-related disasters.

## Gwizdek

*Gwizdek* (Whistle) is the name of a Silesian demon that brings wealth. It was believed that Gwizdek had the power to bring back spent money, and makes itself known by whistling when it is encountered by a person who does not know how to handle it.

Christian propaganda image of *Chort, Khors, Czart, Czort* (1698)

# H

## Habernitsa

*Habernitsa* (cornflower) is a female noon demon in Slavic mythology, especially of Silesia, near Prudnik. She is referred to as *Chabernica* in Polish and *Хаберница (Habernitsa)* in Russian. She has her English equivalents in the *Cornflower Wraith, Lady Cornflower* or *Cornflower Witch* and *Lady Midday*. She was usually pictured as a young slim woman dressed in azure with cornflowers in her hair, that roamed field bounds during midday, where she made sure that children did not trample the corn and ran between the crops in search of flowers. She was angered by people who trampled the grain, used sharp tools, or when the harvesters did not wear their hats. Those, who she thought deserved punishment, were put to sleep with her whisper, after which she caused them headache, paralysis or low back pain. Sometimes she attacked her victims by breaking their arms, legs or neck. To avoid the wrath of the *Habernitsa*, a worker had to take a break from work during the midday of Angelus (at 12:00 AM). Angelus is a Catholic prayer, traditionally recited in Roman Catholic churches, convents, and monasteries three times daily at 06:00, 12:00 and 18:00.



## Hozjajka mednoj gory

*Hozjajka mednoj gory* (Хозяйка медной горы – Mistress of the Copper Mountain), also known as *Malakhitnitsa* (Malachite maid), *Azovka-devka* (Azov Girl). Malakhitnitsa is a beautiful mountain spirit with typical Venusian features, in legends of Ural miners. In the national folktales and legends, she is depicted as an extremely beautiful green-eyed young woman in a malachite green gown or as a lizard with a crown. She has been viewed as the patroness of miners, the protector and owner of hidden underground riches, the one who can either permit or prevent the mining of stones and metals in certain places.

The Copper Mountain is the Gumyoshevsky mine, the oldest mine of the Ural Mountains, which was called "The Copper Mountain" or simply "The Mountain" by the populace. It is now located in the town of Polevskoy, Sverdlovsk district. In some regions of the Ural Mountains, the image of Hozjajka mednoj gory is connected or identified with another female creature from the local folktales, the *Azov Girl* (Russian: Азовка, tr. Azovka), the enchanted girl or princess who lives inside Mount Azov. The Mistress of the Copper Mountain became a well-known character from her appearance in P.P. Bazhov's collection of the Ural Mountains folktales called *The Malachite Box*.

## Hurbóż

In south-east Polish folklore the *Hurbóż* or *Hurbusz* is a Slavic demon that suffocated people, a kind of *Alp* or *Nightmare*, believed to have originated in the Sanok and Krosno regions. He had the appearance of a cat, that could strangle you with his soft paws, and was sometimes also accused of tormenting horses by tangling their manes.



# I

## Iele

The *Iele* (usually translated as *Fairies*) are supernatural female spirits or *Vâlve* from Romanian folklore, a kind of *Fairy-Maidens*, with great powers of seduction and magical abilities. Iele accumulate some of the attributes of *Nymphs*, *Naiads*, *Dryads*, and sometimes *Sirens*. They are similar to the *Samodiva* of Bulgarian folklore. The myth of the Ieles is of uncertain origin. The speculative etymologies of the folklorists are somewhat fanciful, since Iele is not a name, but a noun having a phonetic pronunciation close to that of the personal pronoun, in the feminine third person, pl. ele. The real name of these creatures remains a mystery, tacit and inaccessible, and is replaced by attributive symbols usually classified in epithets: *Albe, Dânsele* (Goddesses), *Drăgaice* (the Nice), *Domniţe* (Ladies), *Fetele Codrului* (Girls of the Woods), *Frumoase* (the Beautiful or Nice), *Împărătesele Văzduhului* (possibly Empresses of the Garden or Empresses of the Air), *Irodiţe* (Herodias), *Măiestre* (Mistresses – or possibly the Artistic), *Miluite, Muşate, Vâlve* (*Vâlve*, the plural of Vâlvă means: female spirits), *Vâlva Băii* (Spirit of the Bath), *Vâlva Pădurii* (Spirit of the Woods), *Rusalii, Nagode, Vântoase* (Windy, Wild, Woody?), *Şoimane* (Falcons).

Iele appear mostly at night by moonlight, in secluded places (glades,
woodlands, ponds, riverbanks, crossroads, deserted greenhouses,
on lonely cliffs, in the mountains or even in certain trees, such as the
walnut tree), dancing naked, or only wearing a shawl, or wrapped in
transparent veils, with bells at their feet. The clearing in the wood or the
field on which they danced looks afterwards as if it had been scorched
by a wildfire. The number in which the Iele appear is either unlimited, or
reduced to seven, or sometimes three. In the last case legend considers
them to be the daughters of Alexander Macedon and names them
*Catarina*, *Zalina* and *Marina*. The Iele are not evil inclined. They only
retaliate when they are aroused, offended, or spied on when they dance,
and then punish the culprit. According to the most common global
characteristics, the Iele are immortal, beautiful, a-corporal, voluptuous
and seductive, excellent dancers and choral singers; they wear their long
hair unfurled and dress in fragrant garments of silk or linen, usually
translucent or even shimmering; invisible by day, they can be seen at
night, at great risk to the observer; though often winged, they can also fly
by levitation, at terrific speeds (in one night crossing nine seas and nine
countries), but sometimes they travel by fire-horse carriage.

# İye

*İye* (also: *İne* or *Eğe*; Chuvash: *Ийĕ, İyĕ*; Tatar: *Ия, İyä*; Yakut: *Иччи, İççi*;
Turkmen: *Eýe, Эе*; Tuvan: *Ээ, Ee*; Uzbek: *Ega, Эга*; Russian: *Ийе, Ije*) is
a tutelary spirit or demon of a place, person, nation, natural element,
or animal, in the shamanistic beliefs of Turkic peoples. As such, they
function as deities of the particular thing attributed to them, but are not
necessarily the object of worship. İye are hidden powers transmitted to the
respective objects. Many items, especially those to which great importance
is attached, have an İye. They expect it to be treated respectfully, otherwise
they become angry and may cause harm to people. The İye live separately
from the İye of other elements. The term means "owner, master, lord,
possessor" in Turkic languages. *Ezen* (familiar spirit, protector spirit) has
the same meaning (owner, possessor) in the Mongolian language.

## Creation myth

Even if the shamanistic worldview of the Turks does not have a canonized
creation story, research of folklorist Verbitsky Vasily's in the Altai revealed
a story about the origin of these spirits. According to it, the first man

had created his own world. However, when he became arrogant towards God, *Ülgen* banished him to the underworld. In the process, *Erlik*, and the spirits he created, were banished from heaven and fell to earth. They became demons of the respective elements they fell into. Henceforth, the fallen Erlik is also counted among the İye. The İye who had fallen into the underworlds are, with Erlik, considered *Kara İye* (Dark Spirits) and are comparable to devilish spirits.

**Various İye**

Famous İye are, for example, *Su İyesi* (water-spirit) and *Od İyesi* (fire spirit). The fire-spirits can then be divided, according to their element, into further weaker spirits. Thus, *Od Anası/Atası* (mother/father of fire) is considered the tribal father/mother of the further spirits of fire and would have arisen directly at the separation of Heaven and Earth and is thus considered the son/daughter of *Yer Tanrı* (Earth God). Depending on their power, the İye have different influences on the elements. The water-spirits would have the power to break dams, drown people and animals, or drag them under water. More powerful water-spirits can also cause diseases associated with their respective element. The *Su Dedesi* (water-grandfather) had the ability to cause water sickness, in which blisters appear on the body. Benevolent İye can also help people and give rain. Some Iye are close to people's daily lives. As the spirit of the house, the *Ev İye* protects the property. Good manners please the Ev İye, and reward the inhabitants, while bad behavior and disorder bring misfortune. His favorite place to stay, he says, is doorways, the basement, or the center of the house. Some even count the Ev İye as part of the family. According to one rite, it is given food, (e.g. milk) at night, while it protects the house. In Anatolia, when a new house is built, the Ev İye is invited.

**Overview of main İye:**

| | |
|---|---|
| *Su iyesi*: | water-spirit |
| *Od iyesi*: | fire-spirit |
| *Ev iyesi*: | household-spirit |
| *Yel iyesi*: | wind-spirit |
| *Dağ iyesi*: | mountain-spirit |
| *Orman iyesi*: | forest-spirit |
| *Irmak iyesi*: | river-spirit |
| *Abzar iyesi*: | courtyard-spirit |
| *Yer iyesi*: | earth-spirit |

*Bulut iyesi*:     cloud-spirit
*Kara iye*:       dark-spirit, comparable to a demon

**Overview of specialized İye**

| | |
|---|---|
| *Aran iyesi, Damız iyesi, Kitre iyesi*: | stable-spirits |
| *Avul iyesi, Köy iyesi, Bucak iyesi*: | village-spirits |
| *Ağaç iyesi, Yığaç iyesi*: | tree-spirits |
| *Bulak iyesi, Pınar iyesi, Çeşme iyesi*: | fountain-spirits |
| *Değirmen iyesi*: | mill-spirits |
| *Ekin iyesi, Arış iyesi*: | wheat-spirits |
| *Ergene iyesi, Urkay iyesi, Şahta iyesi*: | spirits of mine pits |
| *Mal iyesi, Sığır iyesi*: | spirits of cattle |
| *Kıla iyesi, Hayvan iyesi*: | spirits of animals |
| *Otağ iyesi, Çadır iyesi, Çerge İyesi*: | tent-spirits |
| *Söğök iyesi, Gur iyesi, Gömüt İyesi*: | grave-spirits |
| *Tarla iyesi, Basu iyesi, Etiz İyesi*: | field-spirits |
| *Toplak iyesi, Mescid iyesi*: | spirits of the mosque |
| *Yol iyesi, Yolak iyesi*: | road-spirits |
| *Yunak iyesi, Hamam iyesi, Cağlık iyesi*: | bath-spirits |
| *Ören iyesi, Peg iyesi, Çaldıbar iyesi*: | spirits that dwell in ruins |
| *İn iyesi, Mağara iyesi, Ünkür iyesi*: | cave-spirits |



# J

## Jablón

In the Kashubian folklore of Pomerania the *Jablón* or *Jablon is* a spirit
who lives in orchards and takes care of trees, fruit bushes and gardens, as
well as the alleged culprit of fruit and vegetable thefts.

## Jaroszek

In Silesian folklore *Jaroszek* is a *field-demon* that lives in muddy fields,
fooling people in the shape of a partridge, pheasant or hare. Attempts
to catch Jaroszek may end in drowning in the mud, but if caught
successfully, he then transforms into a household demon who becomes a
helper in domestic matters.

## Jasiek-Ptasiek

*Jasiek-Ptasiek* (German: *Vogelhannes*) is a legendary phantom living under the Bird Mountain (now Smolna, in the forest Pokrzywno outside Polanica-Zdroj). Jasiek-Ptasiek in his lifetime was called Johann Schmiedt and was a brewer, who in the second half of the 17th century leased Tawernę, a Kłodzko winery with traditions dating from 1418. (today there is a bank in that place in the Kłodzko Market Square). He cursed and cheated terribly, until once when he slandered a widow, he was punished by God: he had apoplexy (a stroke) and died. He then gave a terrible scare in the Tavern, as when his coffin was opened, it turned out that the body had disappeared. For a reward of hundred guilders, promised by the town councilors, the executioner from Klodzko managed to catch Jasiek in a leather sack and carried him off to the Pokrzywno forest. Since then, Jasiek – always eager to mischief – has been prowling around, scaring people passing by and confusing the way for stray travelers, especially between Ptasia Góra and Łomnicka Równia. Many legends about his mischief were created, fusing his mischievousness with the folk humor of the Kłodzko county, with stories like: *Jasiek-Ptasiek dokucza babom* (Jasiek the Bird teases women), *Jasiek-Ptasiek i żołnierska dziewka* (Jasiek the Bird and the soldier maiden), *Jasiek-Ptasiek nawraca niewierzącego* (Jasiek the Bird converts an unbeliever), *Jasiek-Ptasiek i kataryniarz* (Jasiek the Bird and the organ grinder), *Jasiek-Ptasiek i kobiety koszące trawę* (Jasiek the Bird and women mowing grass). In Poland there is also a beer brand called *Jasek-Ptasiek.*

## Jaud

In Serbo-Croatian folklore the *Jaud* is a small *Vampire* which appears in the form of a child. The Jaud comes from the soul of a baby who died before it was born and is related to the southern Slav *Drekavac,* the Scandinavian *Myling* etc.

## Jędza

*Jędza,* (also: *Jęza, Jęga, Zła baba, Jędza baba, Jędzyna*) is an Old Slavic demon, originally an evil goddess, representing illness and wrath, who after Christianization degraded to a wrathful, emaciated witch, with the character of a *Ghoul.* Thus Jędza became an old, tall, skinny, evil woman

who lived in the wilderness. She would steal children from their mothers,
put them in cages, feed them, and then eat them – baked or raw.


# Jigrzan

*Jigrzan* is a good Kashubian spirit, guardian of games, parties, dances and
all kinds of entertainment. This benevolent happiness bringing spirit used
to be accompanied by celebrations in honor of the sun, light and fire. It
was said that Jirzan makes someone happy, and that someone who is very
happy is as cheerful as Jigrzan.




# Jikhar'

*Jikhar'* (or: *Jikhar'ko, Jikhar'ka, Jikhor'ka*; Russian: Жихарь, Жихарько,
Жихарька, Жихорька) is the individual or generic name of a character
who appears in some eastern Slavic folk tales. It has several distinct
aspects. The outdated term Jikhar' seems to be understood differently
depending on the region of Russia. A Jikhar' can be an old man or a
young man, a "native" inhabitant, a rich landowner or a peasant living in
the country, or an evil spirit or animal – especially a rooster. The *Baiennyï
jikhar'* (баенный жихарь) is a wicked spirit that resides in the baths,
which is of course better known as the *Bannik*. Jikhar' is also the name
of a river, and a family name. The Ukrainian form, Жихор (*Jykhor*, in
the sense of hermit rather than house spirit) is probably the origin of the
name of a station on the southern network of Ukrainian railroads, near
Kharkov. In the Pudoga region the Jikhar' was an evil spirit close to the
*Domovoj*. In the north of the Pudoga region we find a household-spirit
called *Jikhar'ko*. He is small in stature, disheveled, has a large beard, and
is benevolent though also a prankster. However, it is believed this Jikhar'
sometimes steals children from their cradles while their mothers are
away.


# Julki

*Julki* are dwarves, and probably souls of deceased ancestors in the faith
of the Pomeranian population from the area of Łabusz and Jamno. They
live in the underground hills and burial mounds and favor people that in
times of famine are sharing some food supplies with them.

# K

## Kaji

*Kaji* (ქაჯი) are a race of spirits in Georgian folklore, that are often portrayed as magic-wielding, demonic metal-workers. They lived in Kajeti (ქაჯეთი) and had magic powers that they used against humans. *Land Kajis* were malevolent, while *river* and *lake Kajis* were friendly to humans. Female Kajis were beautiful, and they either seduced heroes or helped them in their quests. They appear prominently in the *Vepkhist'q'aosani* (ვეფხისტყაოსანი) (lit.: One with the skin of a tiger), a Georgian medieval epic poem, written in the 12th century by Georgia's national poet *Shota Rustaveli*. In this poem the Kajis abduct Princess *Nestan-Darejan* and fight the heroes at Kajeti fortress. Although Rustaveli portrays them, not as a race of supernatural beings, but as a tribe of human wizards (albeit wizards of awe-inspiring power). The Kajis also feature in *The Snake-eater* by another celebrated Georgian poet, *Vazha-Pshavela*, in which they appear as the preparers of a stew of snake-meat that confers occult wisdom on the hero, Mindia. Their name is related to the Armenian storm and wind-spirits, the *Kaj* (Armenian: քաջ, k'aj; pl.: քաջք, k'ajk').

## Karakondjul

The *Karakondjul* is a Bulgarian demon (also: *Karakondjol*). It is reputed to dwell in caves, or rivers, or an abandoned water mill, and come out at night. The description of the creature varies a lot. It is described as being human-like except for having a hairy body, a tail, and a large head with horns on it, or a one-eyed being standing on a single leg, or a horse-headed man. It is considered a shapeshifter which may also appear as a dog, a human, a sheep or a calf. An ancient Bulgarian exorcism-custom, rooted in Tracian antiquity, and using special costumed dancers, called *kukeri* or *koukeri,* is performed to scare away the evil creature (among others) and avoid contact with it.

## Karakondžula

According to tradition, when a *Karakondžula* found someone outdoors during the night of an unbaptized day, it would jump on the person's back and demand to be carried wherever it wanted. This torture would end only when roosters announced the dawn; at that moment the creature would release its victim and run away.

In Serbian Christmas traditions, the Twelve Days of Christmas were previously called the "unbaptized days" and were considered a time when demonic forces of all kinds were more active and dangerous than usual. People were cautious not to attract their attention, and did not go out late at night. This last precaution was especially because of the Karakondžula (Serbian Cyrillic: караконцула; also *karakondža* / *караконца*, *karakandža* / *караканца* or *karapandža* / *карапанца*), imagined as heavy, squat, and ugly creatures. The Karakondžula is also known to punish and torment people who commit adultery. Adulterers were known to sneak out of their homes while their significant other would sleep, and then visit the person they were cheating with or a prostitute. The Karakondžula would sit and wait on the top of the door-frame of the front door to the house, jump on the back of the adulterers and lash them with a stick or scratch, or dig its sharp nails into the persons back and neck and force them to run through the nearby forests all night. Like most nocturnal creatures the Karakondžula would flee at the sight of first dawn.

## Karankoncolos

The *Karankoncolos* is a malevolent creature in Northeast Anatolian Turkish folklore. It is a variety of the *Bogeyman*, usually merely troublesome and rather harmless, but sometimes truly evil. It is believed to have thick hairy fur like the legendary Yeti. The name is most likely derived from *kara-kondjolos* (*Vampire* or *Werewolf*). According to late Ottoman Turkish myth, they appear on the first ten days of Zemheri (the dreadful cold) when they stand on murky corners, and ask seemingly ordinary questions to passers-by. The legend states that in order to escape harm, one should answer each question, using the word kara (Turkish for black), or risk being struck dead by the creature. It was also said in Turkish folklore that the Karakoncolos could call people out during the cold Zemheri nights by imitating voices of loved ones. The victim of the Karakoncolos risked freezing to death if he or she could not awake from the charm.

# Keshalyi

*Keshalyi* (also: *Kešali*, *Keshali*) are Roma *Fairies* of destiny and *Forest Nymphs*, known only to the Romani tribes of the Danube countries, Transylvania and southern Russia. Possibly they are distantly related to the *Fates*. The name Keshalyi comes from the word *kesh* (silk) and means "the silken one". Their hair is said to be as soft as *"the finest silk"*. As real forest-spirits they sit, usually in threes, on lonely rocky rifts high up in the mountains and often let their miles-long hair blow down into the gorges and valleys, which creates the fog, which is called *nebulo* in Romani language, and also *bal Keshalyakri* (hair of the Keshalyi). If they shake their heads, this creates the hail, which the gypsies call *jiuva Keshalyakri* (lice of the Keshalyi) in addition to *paho*. The whole winter they sleep in inaccessible caves in the rocks and only appear again at the beginning of spring. When the gypsies hear the cuckoo cry for the first time, they say: *"Palekode Keshalya uprushcen!"* (Soon the Keshalyi will rise!). It is said that the cuckoo is the messenger of the Keshalyi, with whom it spends the winter and who send it out early in the year to find out whether it is already spring. When it is quite warm, the cuckoo returns, tired and sick, with his message to the Keshalyi. The Gypsies believe that the cuckoo is healthy only in the spring, but spends the rest of the year with the Keshalyi sick and frail; therefore it is called *ciriklo nasvalo* (sick bird).

According to present-day folk belief, the Keshalyi are favorably disposed toward humans only while still a virgin and exert an influence on people's fate. When someone offends them, they take heavy revenge on that person and punish their whole clan and wreak havoc in their place of residence. Each Keshalyi is allowed to love only one man, with whom she produces only one child, which dies soon after birth. Then the desolate mother flees even higher up into the mountains; grief furrows her hitherto "snow-white" face and her "mist-gray" robe turns black. Soon the man of her love also dies (usually in autumn), and then the Keshalyi pulls out her hair in grief, which then float over the fields as "summer threads", the shimmering threads of the field spider in autumn, also called "old woman's summer" (*Briga Keshalyakri*: Grief of the Keshalyi).

Childless women of the gypsies who wish to have children, collect such threads and consume them together with their spouses during the waxing of the moon, while murmuring:

89

K

> *"Keshalyiya lisperpen,*       (You Keshalyi are spinning, spinning,
> *!in pani hin andre len!*       As long as the water runs in the streams!
> *Mangavas pal bolyipen,*       We invite you to the baptism of children,
> *Kana lolo sheloro*       When the red thread of luck
> *Monde turnen lisperpen*       You spun, you spun
> *Vash raklesko, ko avla*       For the child we received
> *Monde, oh Keshalyiya!*       Received from you, oh Keshalyi!)

This "red thread of luck" is identical with the "rope of fate", which is, for example, in German folklore the *drei Mareien* (to be compared with *Norns* or Fates) spun for human beings at their birth, and which we find in the folklore of many different peoples. When a Keshalyi wants to give a child "good luck" in its life, she spins the "red thread of luck", which she then makes appear as a red braid on the neck of the favored one. But only as a virgin – as already mentioned – she can do such a thing.

### The nine demons of disease

According to legend, once upon a time the Keshalyi came into conflict with a class of demons, the *Loçolico*, which ended in a blackmail-treaty in which the Keshalyi queen *Ana* married the demon king. Later both made a new contract, resulting in the Loçolico-king leaving her forever. Since that time she has lived alone in her palace, except for the children she had with her former husband; the disease-demons. They went out into the world, mingling with each other and creating many new disease-demons. The nine demons of disease, born from the marriage of the Keshalyi queen with the Loçolico king, are called:

1) *Melalo* (the dirty one); he is the most feared of all, and brings upon mankind not only sickness, misery and sorrow, but he also drives them to frenzy, murder and robbery. Melalo has the form of a small, two-headed bird of gray color. With his sharp claws he rummages through *trupos te vodyi* (body and heart) of people. Its name comes from the dirty gray color of its plumage.

2) *Lilyi* (the slimy one) is the name of the sister and wife of *Melalo*. From her marriage come many lesser demons, which have no special names. Wherever Lilyi sends one of her children, *lilye nasvalipena* (snotty diseases) break out, like mucus fever, dysentery, catarrh, and so on. Lilyi has the form of a *Lilye maci* (slimy fish).

3) *Tculo* (the fat one) is especially feared by pregnant women, into whose wombs he enters and causes terrible pain. He has the shape of a small ball, which is densely covered with spikes; if he rolls around in the body, he causes terrible abdominal pain. His wife is called *Tcaridyi.*

4) *Tcaridyi* (approximately: the hot, glowing one). She also preys on pregnant women, in whom she produces hot fevers, especially maternity fever. She has the shape of a small worm, whose body is densely covered with hair. She leaves some of her hairs in the body of the human being, which causes the "heat". From her marriage with her brother *Tculo* come innumerable little demons, all of them possessing the characteristics of their parents. No Romani tribe or family is sure not to harbor in its circle one or more members of this gaggle of demons, each of which has different powers.

5) *Shilalyi* (the cold one) produces the "cold fever". She has the form of a small white mouse, which possesses innumerable feet. Her bile is her younger brother, *Bitoso.*

6) *Bitoso* (the fasting one). He is the most innocent of all his brothers and sisters; for he produces only headaches and stomachaches, cough and loss of appetite. He has the shape of a many-headed worm. The same form is possessed by its children, who also produce less dangerous diseases.

7) *Lolmisho* (from lolo and mishos: the red mouse) has, as its name indicates, the shape of a red mouse. He runs over the body of a sleeping person, who then gets a skin disease. His wife, the eighth child of Ana, is called *Minceskre.*

8) *Minceskre* (the one of the female pubic), because she especially produces syphilis and suppurating bumps, when she crawls at night as a hairy beetle over the body of a sleeping person. Its numerous children also produce individual skin diseases, such as smallpox, frizzles, measles, and so on. The ninth and last child of Ana, at the sight of which even his father, the Loçolico king himself, was frightened, is the grayish fiend *Poreskoro.*

9) *Poreskoro* (approximately: truant). He has four cat heads and four dog heads, furthermore a bird body and a slender tail. It is a hermaphrodite

that fertilizes itself, which is also the case with all its numerous offspring. Rarely he/she and its children appear, but wherever they fly, cholera, the plague and all other possible serious epidemic diseases break out.

These are the names and descriptions of the disease-demons among the Turkish and Serbian Gypsies. Among the Hungarian and Transylvanian Gypsies, they are summarized only under the collective name *Misec* (evil, demon), although they also know about the nine disease-demons. Only the name of Minceskre, which produces skin diseases and especially syphilis, has survived among them to this day. In Galicia and Russia, the Gypsies also believe in nine disease-demons, although these do not appear as children of the Keshalyi queen Ana, but are created by the "supreme devil", an eight-footed goat. From each foot of the goat a disease-demon sprang forth, the ninth came from its tail.



## Khovanets

In Ukranian-Carpathian folklore, the *Khovanets* (hider; from Ukrainian *khovaty,* to hide) is a *household-spirit* that guards the home and helps the householders, but can also turn against them. He is also known as the *Pohatnyk* (a derivative from "house") or *Hodovanets* (a derivative from "to feed") and there are many different descriptions of his appearance. He is mostly depicted as a dwarfish creature, hairy, sometimes with horns; he could shapeshift into a hen, frog, cat or other animal and change his size. The spirit was believed to be born from a *znosok* (a little hen egg with an unformed yolk) which was carried under an armpit for nine days, during which a person couldn't cut his or her nails, pray, speak, or greet anyone. This was a very risky enterprise. If everything was done right, then on the ninth day this person would get a servile house spirit, but if one of the rules was broken, the Khovanets turned into a demon and could even torture this person to death. The Khovanets brings his master and family wealth and prosperity, takes care of the cattle, works on the field, protects the house from thieves and foretells the future. Because of the latter, as well as his kindness to children, some folklorists relate the Khovanets – like many other Slavic household-spirits – to dead ancestors.

Usually the Khovanets lives in the attic, and is fed with unsalted food, mostly wheat bread, milk and sugar. Several Khovanets can live in one

place without any problems, distributing different types of work among themselves. If a Khovanets got offended by something, for example if he was given salted food, he would crush all the plates at home, roister in the household and could leave the place for good, taking happiness with him, or he could torture the host so much that he'd hang himself. A Khovanets also doesn't like it when people cut down fruit trees that grow in the yard or on the border with a neighboring house. The Khovanets can be killed by thunder; or after slapping him hard with one hand, but if one hit his head with a beech stick, he'd come back to life.

## Kikimora



Most folklorists regard the *Kikimora* (Russian: кикимора: *Kikímora*, шишимора: *Shishímora*) as a leftover of an old pagan deity, that was transformed into a female poltergeist-like house and swamp-spirit after the Christianization of the Slavs and Ugrians. The Kikimora (or similar creatures) are known in the East and West Slav pantheon – among Russians, Polacks, Czechs and Ugrians – and also has analogues among the South Slavs, but is mostly a Russian and, to a lesser extent, Belarussian figure. She appears in the 17th century as Kikimora in relation to the trial against and torturing of a supposed male witch-doctor, Mitroshka (Nikifor) Khromy from Galitsky County, accused of sending evil spirits to people, which did "mischief" in the house, ruined horses and scared away the cow herd. Folkloric predecessors of the Kikimora ultimately seem to lead back to the East Slavic goddess *Mokosh* or *Mokosha* (Russian Макошь, Мокошь), associated with spinning, wool, patronage of women and the home. Also, the image of the Kikimora may be connected with the image of the deity of destiny and with the cult of the souls of deceased ancestors. There is a suggestion that *Mara-Kimora* is the most ancient name of this *householdspirit*. On the other hand, the Kikimora combines traits that also makes an independent origin possible. One option is that the "predecessor" of the Kikimora was the "nasty" *Kachitsa*, mentioned in the *Word of Saint Vasily on fasting* from the *Golden Chain* (14th century). Folk beliefs derive the Kikimora from those who died a "wrong" death (unbaptized or murdered children, suicides, etc.), or from children cursed and kidnapped by unclean forces. It was also believed that disgruntled builders and sorcerers could put a magic object into the house – usually a doll – which would come to life afterwards.

*Kikimora* (1934) by Ivan Yakovlevich Bilibin (1876-1942)

Kikimoras were described as a short, curled, untidy, strangely dressed, usually invisible or ugly old woman, a long-necked girl or woman, a little girl or even a man or an old man. According to various other descriptions the Kikimora can be very small and thin, with a large head, long arms, short legs, with bulging eyes, furry paws, horns, a tail, and/or she is covered with feathers or wool. She could also appear in the image of an animal. Kikimoras are usually invisible. They are restless and run fast and can communicate with people by human speech and by knocking. According to folk-beliefs, Kikimoras live in dwellings, less often in outbuildings, in baths, in empty houses. The appearance of Kikimora was considered a sign that the house was not clean and did not have good luck. In most regions Kikimora activity was not tied to a specific time of year, only in some places it was counted among the Christian evil spirits. During the daytime Kikimora hides from people in the secluded places of buildings.

**Behavior and features**

At night she comes out of her hiding place and does her favorite things, in the first place spinning and similar kinds of women's work. But this work was of poor quality, and usually the housewives had to redo everything afterwards. It was commonly believed that Kikimoras cause various troubles: they disturb people while sleeping and scare them by different sounds, annoy little children, behave like *Alps* and suffocate sleepers, throw various objects around, drop and break things, pluck or cut the hair of people or cattle, plucks the feathers of domestic birds. They do everything to drive the inhabitants of a house mad with noises, until they leave. There are stories about Kikimoras destroying people. Her role in the house is usually juxtaposed with that of the *Domovoy*, where one of them is considered a "bad" spirit, and the other a "good" one. When the Kikimora inhabits a house, she lives behind the stove or in the cellar, and often produces noises similar to those made by the mice in order to obtain food. She usually brings bad luck to whoever sees her – not infrequently, such an incident ends in the death of a housemate. But she also steals the house poultry or prevents them from laying eggs. According to popular belief, to ward off the evil influence, the cut-off neck of a jug, or a stone (called *Kuriny bog:* Russian: куриный бог; chicken god) with a natural hole in it, should be hung above the nests or in front of the stables. Kuriny bog refers in the Slavic language area not only to perforated stones, but also to other objects used as talismans against the Kikimora – such as vessels with a lined bottom, or old things, for example worn-out bast shoes, which were used in the same way as perforated stones. Occasionally, the Kikimora and the Mara have been identified with each other. Conversely, the Kikimora has sometimes been interpreted by the Russians as the wife of the Domovoy. The folklore of the Kikimora never achieved a strong outline, as under this name, besides an independent house-spirit, could also be understood a number of other characters. As the wife of the Domovoy, the Kikimora could also be seen as a useful house-spirit, which helps a good mistress with spinning, housework, and care for children and animals. In modern culture, more often the forest-Kikimora or marsh-Kikimora starts to appear, covered with grass and moss; an ugly old woman, scaring and hitting people and kidnapping children.



**Demographic varieties**

Beliefs about Kikimora are common among Russians except the South Russian ethnographic group and, to a lesser extent, among Belarusians, who also know her as *Kikímar*. Other names for Kikimora or similar spirits are: *Kikimorka, Kikimmra, Kukimora* (North Russia), *Kikimor, Kikka, Kyka, Mara, Mora, Maruha, Chuchumora, Shishimora, Shushimora, Mokosha, Mokusha, Mokrukhha, Ogiboshna, Samopryakha, Pustodomka, Susedka,* and *Veshchytsa* (Vitebsk province, Belarussia). The Ukrainians, in the Kyiv province, have recorded beliefs about creatures called *Nichki,* who have features similar to Kikimoras. The word Kikimora, without a corresponding set of representations, is also used in other Slavic languages; in dialectal Polish for instance, *Kicimora* is a ghost, a spirit that chokes at night; the Czech and Slovak know the *Kykymora* as the house ghost of the ancient Slavs. The Bulgarian Kikimora is a female evil spirit, and *Werewolf* is called *Serbohorv* (terrible ghost). Similar representations of evil domestic spirits are also observed among peoples with whom Russians had lived side by side for a long time and thus were under mutual influence, such as the *Komi* and the *Veps.*

**Complex etymology**

The word Kikimora is regarded as a compound word. The origin of the first part kik- remains controversial. It is derived, according to one version, from the Balto-Slavic root *kik / kuk* (kyk) / *ktsk* (kuk) / kъkъ ("humpy, bent over", later also "hump, mound, grave mound, grave" as well as "swamp, marshy valley"). Furthermore Kikimora could be derived from the Indo-European *keuk / kouk,* meaning: "to bend"or "to curve". The names of several demons are probably related to the same roots, like the Russian *Kuska*, *(bath-spirit)*, the *Kukan*, *(marsh-spirit)* and the *Kukaska* (devil). Belarus and the Kashubs have a kind of Bogey named *Kuka* (*"something terrible, living in the dark, what scares children"* or *"an evil spirit, which is given to people by a witch"*), while the Lithuanians have their *Kaukas*, that is closely related to the Prussian and Latvian *Kauks* (house-man, Gnome, devil, dwarf).

According to another version, the first part comes from *kykati* – "to shout (like birds do), to make a loud noise, to cry, howl, wail, chuckle, hiccup, wheeze, cluck, cackle, cuckoo". Kika also translates as "the cry of a bird".



According to a third version, Kikimora comes from *kika* (kyka) – "a chub, strand, braid; a female headdress with horns, sometimes resembling a bird". The first part of the word Shishímora comes either from the Russian dialect words *shishit* (to rummage, to move) or from the words *shish, shishko, shishiga*, which were used to name an indefinite unclean force. The second part in the majority of Slavs acts as a separate word *mara/mora*, under which a number of heterogeneous mythological characters – often not personified – appear: something vague, "strange and incomprehensible, that which seems to appear in dreams, mental confusion, oblivion and other altered states of consciousness, ghost, apparition, obsession, deception of the senses". The same root is probably included in the English *Nightmare*, French *cauchemar* (mara, nightmare). It is possible that the first part was added to the word *mora* as a result of the taboo of calling demons by their "real" name among the Slavs, so due to the fear of calling them in this way.

### Music and literature
The Russian composer Anatoly Lyadov (1855-1914) portrayed Kikimora in 1905 in his symphonic poem of the same name, op. 63. The figure of Kikimora has also found its way into Russian literature on various occasions, for example in the stories of the same name by Albert Likhanov, Ludmila Milevskaya or Orest Somov.

## Kłobuk
The *Kłobuk*, *Kolbuk* or *Kaubuk* in Slavic beliefs is a (usually) benevolent household-spirit which takes care of peoples possessions and the stove/ fire place. The spirit was identified with the soul of a dead foetus. He

usually took the shape of a large chicken, but also of a duck, goose, magpie, crow, cat and even a man. Belief in the Kłobuk was mainly alive in the southern (Polish-speaking) regions of the former East Prussia, primarily among the Warmians (from southern Warmia), and to a lesser extent among the Mazurians. The Warmian Kłobuk is feathered and is said to mostly resemble a large chicken (or other bird, such as the magpie or duck).

A Kłobuk can be brought into the house, which it will then accept as its own if tempted with food – including its favorites; boiled eggs and noodles – or by the owners hugging a chicken. It is also possible to 'grow' a Kłobuk, by burying a miscarried fetus under the threshold of the house, which after seven days, seven months or seven years will turn into the chicken-like spirit. The Kłobuk cared for multiplying the wealth of its host. However, he did so by stealing from the neighbors. Melchior Wańkowicz describes the Varmia people's belief in a Kłobuk in his 1935 report *Na tropach Smętka*. The Kłobuk appears in the novel *Once a Year in Skiroławki*, by Zbigniew Nienacki.



## Kocmeuch

*Kocmeuch* (nickname: *Kocmołuch* – dirty one, slob), a malicious demon from the Lasowiaks' beliefs, witch harms people by stealing milk from cows. During the day Kocmeuch sat hidden in a stable under the threshold, and at night he invisibly crawled under a cow's udder to milk it. He was imagined as a small, deformed man, without clothing, with a large egg-shaped head set on a thin neck, with large and sagging ears, slanted eyes, and a strongly bloated belly and protruding belly button, equally bulging buttocks and thin arms and legs armed with bird claws. The presence of this demon in a stable was detected by the gradual decrease in each milking. The Kocmeuch could only be chased out of the stable by placing sacrificial objects in it.

## Koshchei

*Koshchei* (Russian Кощей; also called *Koschtschei*, *Kashchei*, *Kashchey* or *Koschei*) is a demonic figure of Russian mythology. He appears as an ugly old man who threatens mainly young women. He is also often referred to by the epithets Кощей Бессмертный, which literally translates as

"Koshchei the Deathless," more freely translated as "the Immortal" or (incorrectly) "the Eternal". In other Slavic languages (e.g., Polish) his name may be derived from the word *kość* (Polish for bone), which may suggest a skeletal personification.

The peculiarity of Koshchei is based on the fact that he is very difficult to kill, due to the habit of keeping his soul outside his body. His soul is hidden in a needle, which is in an egg, which is in a duck, which in turn is in a rabbit, which is in an iron box buried under an oak tree on the island of Bujan, which is far out in the sea. To defeat Koshchei, one must reach his soul. When the box is dug up, the rabbit escapes, from which, if killed, the duck escapes. If you kill it and take the egg from it, you have power over Koshchei. He loses his magic and weakens. Koshchei will die if the needle is broken (some stories require it to be broken on his forehead). Many different stories have been created around this folkloric figure.



## Korgorusze

*Korgorusze* (коргоруши) or *Kolowiersze* (коловерши), in the beliefs of eastern Slavs, were spirits who acted as helpers of the householder. It was believed that they appeared in the form of cats, or as a phantom appearance that symbolized the householder.

## Krasnoludek

*Krasnoludek* or *Krasnal* is a Polish mythological type of *Gnome* or *dwarf*, common in many Polish and translated folk tales (for example, Brothers Grimm's *Snow White and the Seven Dwarfs* is translated into the Polish language as *Królewna Śnieżka i siedmiu krasnoludków*). They resemble small humans and wear pointy red hats like the *Kabouter* of the Netherlands. Due to the popularization of fantasy literature, they are now differentiated from both Gnomes (Polish: *gnom*) and dwarfs (Polish: *Krasnolud*), both of which are used in fantasy literature context, while the word Krasnoludek still remains mostly the domain of older folk tales. The word *krasnal ogrodowy* is also used to describe garden Gnomes. In folklore, *Krasnoludki, Zwane także kraśniętami, Skrzatami, Ubożętami, Podziomkami* or *Inkluzami*, are small, caring household-spirits. They were derived from the souls of ancestors or deceased infants. The source of the name is debatable. The word Krasnoludek comes from the old Polish *krasny*, *kraśny*, usually translated as "red, colorful", "nice-looking" or "good", but it can mean "fat" or "bulky" as well, combined with a Polish *ludek* (small person or human-like creature). During the day, Krasnoludki hide under the threshold, behind the stove, in mouse holes or nooks in the smithy or the stable. At night, when the household members have gone to bed, they come out and walk around the farmyard before the rooster crows, finishing the finished household chores and guarding the children against evil spirits. Occasionally there are also folk-tales of evil dwarves, who harm people.

# Kresnik



The *Kresnik* (Croatian and Slovene: *Krsnik, Kresnik, Kršnjak, Krisnik, Skrisnik, Grišnjak*) is a special person in South Slavic mythology, a *Vampire* hunter and a shaman, whose etheric double wanders from the body in the form of an animal, capable of fighting with evil forces to protect the society (community) from misfortune and crop failure. The Kresniks can be compared to the North-Italian *Benandanti*, described by Carlo Ginsburg. A Kresnik (female: *Kresnica*) turns into an animal at night to fight off the *Kudlak*, its evil vampiric antagonist, with the Kresnik appearing as a white animal and the Kudlak as a black one. The Kresnik's double leaves the body, either voluntarily or due to a higher power, to fight evil agents and ensure good harvest, health, and happiness.

A Kresnik is born in an ordinary family, but with characteristic attributes: wearing a white "shirt" or a red "cap". Since the shirt and cap are considered to be a source of power – without which he loses magical powers – they were dried and ground up and eaten with food. Growing up, the young Kresnik or Kresnica lived as an ordinary person until the age of 18-20 and then underwent initiation with the help of the oldest or most powerful Kresnik. The Kresnik was also taught magic and traditional medicine by *Vile (Fairies)* and developed the ability to heal people and cattle. After Christianization, a fable was launched, claiming the Kresnik instead was taught magic at the "School of Black Magic in Babylon", but he nevertheless retained benevolent traits as a generous and powerful friend of the poor. The origin of the name may be from the word *krst*, which means "cross", and which in Serbia is the word for a stone sign denoting village boundaries. It may also be derived from the same root as the Slav word for "resurrection," so that the word itself means something approximating "resurrector." Kresnik (or rarely Kersnik and Krsnik) is also a Slavic god associated with fire, the Summer Solstice, and storms. His mythical home, a sacred mountain at the top of the world, represents the Axis Mundi.

## Krvoijac

In Bulgaria *Krvoijac* (also: *Kropijac*, *Krvopijac*) is a generic term used to describe a *Vampire*, but it is also used to describe a specific and rather unusual type of vampiric entity, whose coming into existence was correlated to the Orthodox Christian period of Lent. It was believed that if a person drinks wine or smokes during Lent, he/she will become a Krvoijac when he/she dies. The body that the spirit occupies, after having undergone some transformation during 40 days in its grave, looks like a person who has only one nostril. It also has a barbed tongue to allow it to drink blood from its victims, but it prefers not to attack humans. The Krvoijac does not have fangs like many other Vampires and it can eat regular food. When it moves, it creates sparks. Although not regarded as very harmful to humans, a *Djdadjii* could be hired. A Djdadjii carried a bottle of blood and protected himself with pictures of Jesus and Mary and captured vampiric spirits in this bottle. This bottle was then destroyed by throwing it in a fire.

Great Lent, or the Great Fast, (Greek: Μεγάλη Τεσσαρακοστή or Μεγάλη Νηστεία, meaning "Great 40 Days," and "Great Fast," respectively) is the most important fasting season in the Church year of the eastern Orthodox Church. Great Lent officially begins on Clean Monday, seven weeks before Pascha (Ash Wednesday is not observed in eastern Christianity), and runs for 40 contiguous days, concluding with the Presanctified Liturgy on Friday of the Sixth Week.

## Kudiani

In Georgian folklore the *Kudiani* (კუდიანი) is a type of hideous hunchbacked witch-like demon, having large teeth and a tail, from the latter her name is derived (*kudi*, კუდი, "tail"). *Kudianis* can disguise themselves as humans in order to bewitch them. The leader of the Kudianis, *Rokap* (როკაპი), often summons them to a special mountain (compare other witch-mountains as the *Brocken* (Germany), *Łysa Góra* (Poland), *Lysa Hora* (Czech Republic)) where they hold a festival similar

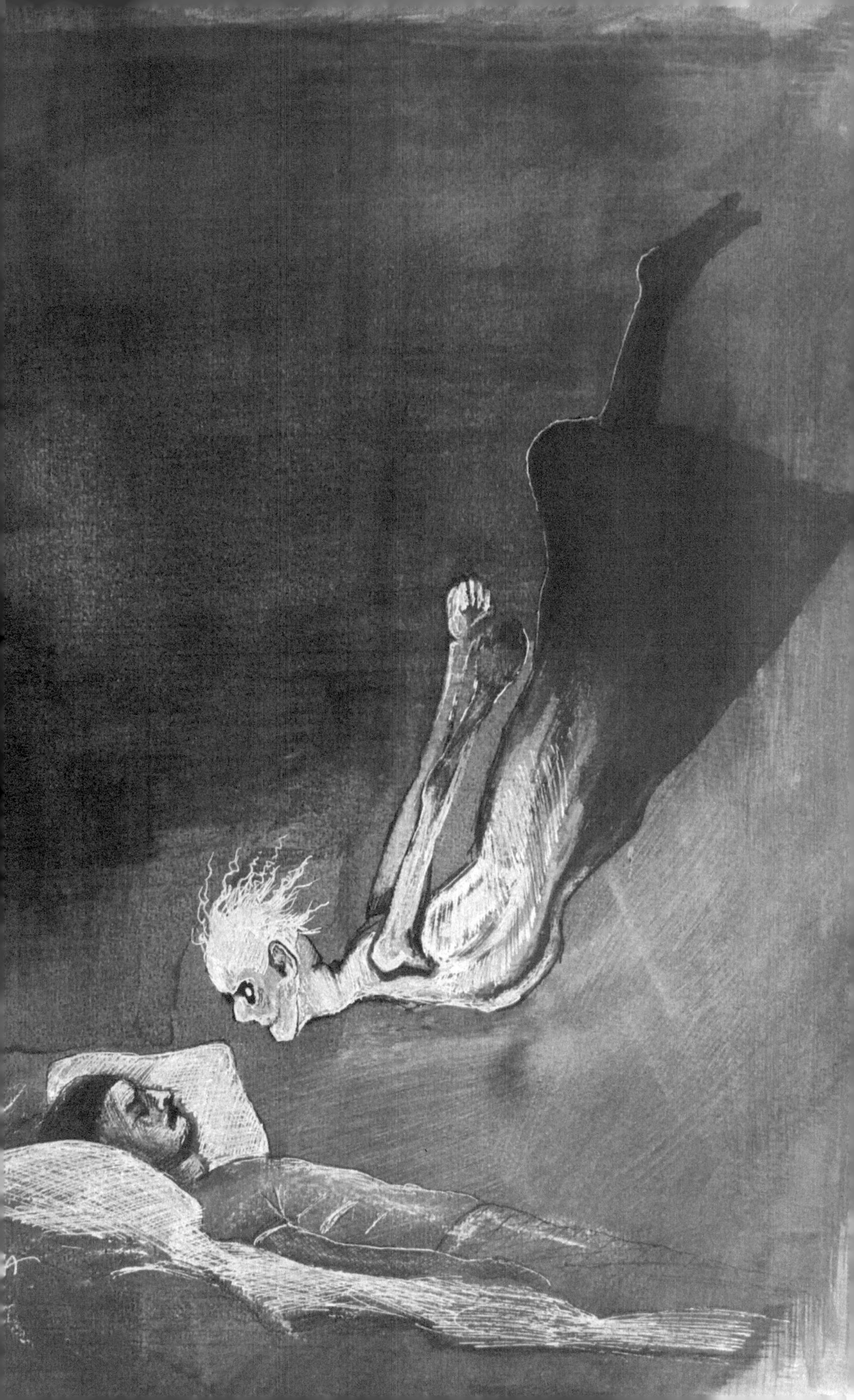

to the European *Walpurgis Night*. In Georgian mythology *Ghmerti*, the creator god, punished Rokab by chaining him to a column under the earth, where he devours human hearts brought to him by the Kudiani. Every year, he tries to free himself, but he always fails.



## Kudlak

In Croatian and Slovenian lore, a person born with a caul was destined to become either a *Kudlak* or a *Kresnik*. When destined to become a Kudlak this person would already begin a career of evil while still alive; his soul would leave his body at night in animal form and fly through the air to attack people or to magically do other kinds of harm to the community he lived in. When he died, he became an undead *Vampire* who was then an even greater threat to the community. But if a person born with a caul became a Kresnik, he became a champion of the community. While he lived, his soul left his body in animal form at night to fight against both living and undead Kudlaks. Where the Kresnik was the representative of goodness and light, the Kudlak symbolized evil and darkness. Their astral battles remind us of the *Benandanti* and *Malandanti*. The Benandanti (Good Walkers) were members of an agrarian visionary tradition in the Friuli district of northeastern Italy during the 16th and 17th centuries. The Benandanti claimed to travel out of their bodies while asleep to struggle against malevolent witches (Malandanti – Bad Walkers) in order to ensure good crops for the season to come. Between 1575 and 1675, in the midst of the Early Modern witch trials, a number of Benandanti were accused of being heretics or witches under the Roman Inquisition.

## Kukudh

The *Kukudh*, also *Kukudhi, Kukuvriq* or *Kukuthi* is an undead creature in Albanian mythology. Kukudh is most probably a derivative of Albanian *kuku* (to mourn, lament), as its synonym Kukuvriq suggests. Alternatively from Greek κούκουδον (core), related to κουκούδι (lump, bubo, plague). In Tosk and Gheg folklore, the Kukudh is associated with nightmares and death, and connected to the nocturnal bird, the owl, and the cuckoo (Albanian: *qyqe*), which are considered to be bad omens. In some versions the Kukudh is a Revenant, a miser's poor soul that haunts his house after his death. For this reason, people feared the house of a miser and would avoid staying overnight out of fear of being killed. Only a brave boy may defeat the creature and bring eternal peace to its damned soul, being appointed his heir in reward. In some areas, the Kukudh appears as a stocky and short-legged man with a goat's tail. He is invulnerable and may only be strangled with a noose made of vine. Because he brings mayhem, an evil man is also commonly referred to as a Kukudh. In some Albanian lore the Kukudh is more linked to a merchant than a miser and known for its wanderlust. The traveling Kukudh seldom needs to feed, and when it does, it takes only a small amount of blood from its victim, in almost every case leaving the person alive, who after a brief recovery period, will regain his/her full health. A Kukudh can be a vicious combatant and it is well advised not to provoke one into a physical confrontation. Under normal circumstances the Kukudh is invulnerable to any sort of attack, unless it is facing a wolf, its only natural enemy. Wolves hate the Kukudh as well as the other species of Albanian Vampires, and only wolves can damage or destroy one. If a Kukudh should manage to escape from a wolf attack, it will retreat to a grave and if so much as a single limb is destroyed, the Vampire will never rise again. In and around Tomorr, there is a legend that a *Lugat* who is not burned in due time will become a Kukudh. The Lugat is seen as some kind of vampiric-Revenant which matures within a certain amount of days into a Kukudh, its definite form.



The term Kukudh, and *Karkanxholl* (etymologically related to *Kallikantzaros*, Greek: καλικάντζαρος also known as the *Karkançoli)*, are also used for undead "gypsy" corpses, who go around in January, laden with chains and effusing a deadly breath, known notably among Calabrian Albanians. According to another version, the Karkançoli is vested with iron clothes, which is why chainmail armor is known as *këmish karkançoli* in Albanian. In southern Albania the Kukudh is a blind female demon of sickness, carrying the plague. Kukudh is also the name of a sickness like cholera, but worse. Alexander the Great is said to have brought it, after having raped the corpse of an Epirote princess, who would not return his love during her lifetime.

## Kulshedra

The *Kulshedra* or *Kuçedra* is a water, storm, fire and chthonic demon in Albanian mythology and folklore, usually depicted as a huge multi-headed female serpentine dragon. The *Kulshedra* is believed to spit fire, cause drought, storms, flooding, earthquakes and other natural disasters against mankind. According to folk beliefs, the Kulshedra's earlier stage is the *Bolla*, which has the appearance of a chthonic water serpent. The Bolla's eyes remain shut for the whole year except on Saint George's Day, when it gazes at the world and will devour any human on sight. The Bolla will go through a series of metamorphoses and eventually morph into a Kulshedra, but only if it lives many years without being seen by a human. The name Bolla or *Bullar* (southern Albania) also signifies "serpent". In some regions the Kulshedra is depicted like a female eel, turtle, frog, lizard or salamander. The Kulshedra can also appear in the guise of a woman, who keeps her true nature hidden. As a semi-human divine figure she holds also positive qualities that emerge indirectly from Albanian folk tales, beliefs and rituals. It is said that the village where the Kulshedra lives has great prosperity in agriculture and livestock. Indeed she absorbs by her breath foodstuffs from everywhere, and her village thrives, while the affected villages become poor and do not prosper. People used to practice sacrifices to her so she could bring them good and stop any harmful action.

# L

## Łapiduch

The people of the Sandomierz Forest, one of the largest forests in southern Poland, believed in the *Łapiduch,* a soul torturing demon, who lurked for penitent souls and tormented them. Łapiduch looked like a bulbous ball, supporting itself on five-fingered, clawed feet, with short hands and long fingers armed with sharp claws. He was based in the wilderness, where he kept a watchful eye out for penitent souls, and when he managed to capture them, he abused them and made them weep. He never attacked living people.



## Latawica

*Latawica* (kite; male version: *Latawiec*; pl.: *Latawce*) – a demon from Slavic beliefs, identified with the souls of aborted children (later unbaptized). Latawce were imagined as black birds and identified with the wind and whirlwinds. At first they were regarded as negative demons, although not very harmful to humans, or as demons that protected the home (especially in Mazovia and Pomerania). After the adoption of Christianity they were redefined as devils who had sexual relations with people. The female Latawiec, or Latawica, is described as a *Succubus* of a spectacular beauty. Her aim was to seduce and destroy her male victim and take possession of his soul. A man bewildered by the demon's appearance and sexual prowess found himself heading for a fall. He would lose interest in anything but her night visits and eventually wither and die, unless he would drink a concoction made of marigold and some other herbs. Only this could break the evil spell and save him. Carrying garlic was used as a precaution to discourage any approaches by the creature. In time, the words "latawiciec" and "latawica" came to be used to describe promiscuous people. According to other legends, a Latawiec (or a *Lataniec*) was a flying fiery spirit raised from cockerel eggs, which brought people money and grain. It resembled a viper. The belief was found in Poland and the western outskirts of Belarus and Ukraine. The name of a children's toy is probably derived from this meaning. Latawce were not completely immortal as they could be killed by lightning.

## Lazavik

The *Lazavik* (Belarusian: Лазавік) is a creature of Belarusian folklore. It is regarded as a benevolent character that lives amidst the vine bushes (*laza* in Belarusian). In folk tales the Lazavik is described as a small creature with one eye, a long beard and a very long whip in his hand. Belarusian people used to say that when Lazavik walks through the marshland, his one eye shines like a light. The Lazavik prefers to stay unnoticed by people, and will often hide himself in his small house with no windows and or doors. The Lazavik was the guardian of the Belarusian marshes. If its marshes were drained, the Lazavik died with them, just like a Hamadryad died when her tree was cut down, or died from natural causes. With its whip, Lazavik drives away small, harmful, and noisy *Lozniks* (immature swamp- or water-demons) through the vine bushes. A special feature of the Lazavik was that he could free a person out of jail. He could also torment people, but usually no-one got angry at him, because the spirit was much more of a helper then a nuisance to people.

## Leshy

The *Leshy* or *Lyeshy* (Belarus: лясу́н *Lyasun*, лесавік *Lesovik*; Ukranian: лісовик *Lisovik*; Polish: *Laskowiec*) is a forest-spirit, widely known among Russians (especially in the North), and to a lesser extent representations of him were common among Eastern Belarusians and Eastern Ukrainians. Written data on the creature appear no sooner than the late 18th and early 19th century. Many unique details were collected by W.R.S Ralston in his *Songs of the Russian People* – see most of the text below. The Leshy usually appears as a solitary creature, though in some accounts he is described as having a wife (*Leshachikha, Leszachka, Lesovikha* and also, the *Lisunka* or the *Kikimora* of the swamp) and – sometimes kidnapped – children (*Leshonki, Leszonky, Leshachata*). A Little-Russian story, closely resembling one told in Germany of a *Holzweibchen*, tells how a woman one day found a baby Leshy lying naked on the ground and crying bitterly. So she covered it up warm with her cloak, and after a time came her mother, a Lisunka, and rewarded the woman with a potful of burning coals, which afterwards turned into bright golden ducats. Sometimes the Leshies carry off mortal maidens, and make them their wives. But whether they intermarry or not, their weddings are always attended by noisy revels and by violent storms. If the wedding procession traverses a village, many of the cottages will be injured: if in a forest, a number of its trees will fall. A peasant will rarely dare to lie down to sleep in a forest path, for he would be afraid of a wood-demon's bridal procession coming that way and crushing him in his slumbers. In the district of Archangel a whirlwind is said to be caused by the wild dancing of a Leshy with his bride. On the second day after his marriage the Leshy, according to the custom prevalent in Russia, goes to the bath with his young wife, and if any mortal passes by at that time, the newly-married couple splash water over them, and drench them from head to foot.

As the *Vodyany* haunts the waters, so does the Leshy make the *lyes* (forest) his home. In Slavic beliefs he is the demon and master of the forest,and the ruler of all the animals living in it. He is also revered as a demon of the souls of dead people. The Leshy is often malicious, and to those who do not treat him with respect, he often does much mischief. One of his tricks is to suck the milk from their cows. In the Olonetsk district it is believed that every summer a herdsman ought to give one cow to the Leshy. If he fails to do so, the revengeful spirit will destroy the whole herd. In the district of Archangel it is held that if the herdsmen succeeds in pleasing the Leshy, the Leshy will see to the pasturing of the village cattle. In Belarus, on the other hand, he is supposed to be the protector of the wolves. In the districts of Kiev and Chernigov the peasants divide the Leshies into two classes; those belonging to the woods and those who belong to the cornfields. The ones in the woods are giants with an ashen hue; the other ones are, before the harvest, of the same height as the growing corn, and after it, dwindle away till they are no higher than the stubble.

## Appearances

Although a forest-demon, the Leshy was supposed by some 19th century critics to be one of the spirits that belong to the realm of the clouds and storms, and they hold that their hypothesis is confirmed by the fact that it can assume different shapes; whirlwind, humanoid, plant or animal, or as a faceless spirit, and alter his stature at will, at one time making himself taller than the trees of the forest, and at another shorter than the grass of the field. He often appears as a peasant dressed in a sheepskin, but ungirdled – as is always the case with evil spirits – and with the left skirt crossed over the right. One of his peculiarities is that he never has any eyebrows or eyelashes. Sometimes he has but one eye. When he appears in his own shape, and without clothes, he greatly resembles the medieval pictures of the Devil. From his forehead spring horns, his feet are like those of a goat, his head and body are covered with shaggy hair, which is sometimes as green as that of the *Rusalkas*, his fingers are tipped with long claws. In mythological stories – and depictions by artists – the Leshy also appears as a phyto-anthropomorphic creature. It happens that it is entirely a plantlike object – a tree (pine, spruce, birch, oak, aspen), bush, stump, leaf, moss, fungus, etc. Further on, he begins to show human characteristics: his shape, with branches like hair. On the other hand, anthropomorphism may dominate and the connection with vegetation may appear in considerable detail: long disheveled green hair as branches of a tree or bush, a lichen beard, moss-covered clothing of wood color and structure, a moss-covered face, skin thick as bark. Finally, plant features can be reduced to attributes: a club or baton in his hands, a green beard, eyes or clothes. The association with the forest is supplemented by the ability of a Leshy to whip a person with rods, to make noise, to hum, to crack the trees. Sometimes the Leshy personifies the whole forest, and fills its entire space.

## Behavior

Leshies frequently quarrel among themselves, using huge trees and pieces of rock as their weapons. The devastation usually attributed to hurricanes, are in reality, the peasants say, due to these mighty combatants of the forest world. When the Leshy goes round to inspect his domains, the forest roars around him and the trees shake. By night he sleeps in some hut in the depths of the woods, and if by chance he finds that a belated traveler or sportsman has taken up his quarters in the refuge he had intended for himself, he strives hard to turn out the intruder, sweeping over the hut in the form of a whirlwind which makes the door rattle and the roof heave, while all around the trees bend and writhe and a terrible howling goes through the forest. If, in spite of all these hints, the uninvited guest will not leave the hut, he or she runs the risk of being lost in the woods the following day, or swallowed up in a swamp.

All the birds and beasts which inhabit the forest are under the protection of the Leshy. His favorite is the bear, his only servant, who watches over him when he has taken too much of the strong drink he loves so well, and guards him from the assaults of the *water-sprites*. When the squirrels, field-mice, and some other animals go forth in troops upon their periodical migrations, the peasants explain the fact by saying that

the Leshies are driving their flocks from one forest to another. In 1843
a great number of migrating squirrels appeared in certain districts of
Russia, and the local peasants said that it was because a Leshy in the
Vyatka district had gambled away all his squirrels to a brother demon
that lived in Vologda, and the lost property was on its way to their new
master. Similar gambling transactions are frequent among the water-
sprites. Fishermen know at once why it is that certain fish suddenly desert
particular spots. They have been staked and lost by the local Vodyany. But
neither the Leshy nor the Vodyany will use a pack of cards in which any
clubs occur. Anything that resembles the sign of the cross is distasteful to
Slavic demons.



## Lord of the Forest

A sportsman's success in the woods depends, to a great extent, on his
treatment of the Leshy. In order to please that wayward spirit, he makes
an offering of a piece of bread, or a pancake sprinkled with salt, and lays
it on a tree stump. The Perm peasants offer up prayers once a year to
the Leshy, presenting him with a packet of leaf-tobacco, of which he is
very fond. In some districts the hunters make an offering to the Leshy
of whatever animal they first bag, leaving it for him in an oak forest.
One of the incantations intended to be used by a hunter calls upon the
"Devils and Leshies" to drive the hares into his power, and its magic force
is supposed to be so great that the *wood-demons* must obey. The Leshy
is very fond of diverting himself in the woods, springing from bough
to bough, and rocking himself among the branches as if in a cradle,
whence in some places he is called *Zuibochnik*, (*zuibka* = a cradle). At
such times he makes all manner of noises, clapping his hands, shrieking
with laughter, imitating the whinnying of horses, the mooing of cows,
the barking of dogs. So loud is his laughter, say the peasants, that it may
be heard for versts around (1 verst = 0,66 mile). In their opinion, when
the winds make the woods resound, the voice of the Leshy may be heard
in what ignorant people might think was the crashing of branches or the
creaking of stems; the sounds, also, which are erroneously attributed to
an echo are in reality the calls of demons, who wish to allure an unwary
sportsman or woodcutter onto dangerous ground, with the intention of
tickling him to death if they can get hold of him. For in this respect the
Leshies resemble their sisters the *Rusalkas*. In olden days, when forests
were larger and denser than they are now, the Leshy used to be constantly
deluding travelers, and making them lose their way. Sometimes he would

*Ovinnik* (1934) by Ivan Yakovlevich Bilibin (1876-1942)

*Leshy* (1906) by Pyotr Dobrynin taken from the 1906 Journal *Leshy*

alter the landmarks, or would assume the likeness of some tree by which the travelers were accustomed to steer. Sometimes he would himself take the form of a traveler and engage a passer-by in conversation. His victim would chat away unconcernedly, till all of a sudden, he found himself in a swamp or ravine. Then a loud laugh would be heard, and looking round, he would see the Lyeshy at a little distance grinning at him. Sometimes by night a forest-keeper would hear the wailing of a child, or groans apparently proceeding from someone in the agonies of death. His only safe course under such circumstances was to go straight onward, without paying any attention to those noises. If he followed them he would probably fall into a foaming stream, which rushed along where no stream had ever been seen before. Wherever the Leshy goes, he always tries not to leave any tracks behind, covering the traces of his footsteps with sand, or leaves, or snow. If by any chance a passer-by strikes upon the Leshy's recent trail, he becomes bewildered, and does not easily find his way again. His best plan is to take off his shoes and reverse their linings, and he may as well turn his shirt or pelisse inside out. Besides making travelers lose their way, the Leshy amuses himself in many ways at their expense, blowing dust into their eyes and their caps off their heads, freezing their sledges tight to the ground, and so forth, so that a popular saying conveys this advice, *"Don't go into the forest; the Leshy plays tricks there!"* Worse than that, he often brings illness upon people wandering the woods, so that when anyone falls ill after returning from the woods, their friends might say, *"He has crossed the Leshy's track"*. In order to get cured he takes bread and salt, wraps them in a clean rag, and carries them to the forest. On his arrival there he utters a prayer over his offering, leaves it as a sacrifice to the Leshy, and returns home with the firm conviction that he has left his illness behind him.

**Invoking the Leshy**
If anyone wishes to invoke a Leshy, one should cut down a number of young birch-trees, and place them in a circle with their tops in the middle. Then one must take off one's cross, and, standing within the circle, call out loudly, *"Dyedushka!"* (Grandfather!) and the Leshy will appear immediately. Or one should go into the forest on St. John's Eve and fell an aspen, taking care that it falls towards the East. Then one must stand upon the stump, face turned eastward, bend down and say, while looking between one's feet, *"Uncle Lyeshy! Appear not as a gray wolf, nor as a black raven, nor as a fire for burning: appear just like me!"* Then the leaves of the aspen will begin to whisper as if a light breeze were blowing

over them, and the Leshy will appear in the form of a man. On such occasions he is ready to make a bargain with his invoker, giving all kinds of assistance in return for the other's soul.

**Alternative names**

The Leshy is known by a variety of names and spellings, including the following:

- *Borovoi* (Russian: Боровой, Polish: *Borowy*) "(He) of the forest"
- *Dedushka-lesovoi* or *Lesnoi dedushka/ded* (Russian: Дедушка-лесовой, Лесной дедушка/дед, Belarusian: Лясны дзед, Polish: *Leśny dziad*) "forest grandfather"
- *Gayevoi* (Russian: Гаевой, Polish: *Gajowy*) "(He) of the grove"
- *He* (Russian: он) also used for the Devil, based on superstition – prohibiting invocation of evil
- *Les chestnoi* (Russian: Лес честной) "Honorable one of the forest"
- *Les pravedniy* (Russian: Лес праведный) "Righteous one of the forest"
- *Leshak* (Russian: Лешак, Serbo-Croatian: *Lešak*, Лешак)
- *Leshy* (Russian: Леший, Belarusian: Лешы, Polish: *Leszy*, Serbo-Croatian: *Lešij*, Лешиј)
- *Lesnik* (Russian: Лесник, Polish: *Leśnik*, Bulgarian: Лесник, Serbo-Croatian: *Lesnik*, Лесник)
- *Lesnoi dukh* (Russian: Лесной дух) "forest-spirit"
- *Lesnoi dyadya* (Russian: Лесной дядя) "forest uncle"
- *Lesnoi khozyain* (Russian: Лесной хозяин) "forest master"
- *Lesnoi zhitel'* (Russian: Лесной житель) "forest dweller" or "woodsman"
- *Lesny muzhik*, "forest man"
- *Lesovik* (Russian: Лесовик, Belarusian: Лесавік, Ukrainian: Лісовик, Serbo-Croatian: *Lesovik*, Лесовик)
- *Lesovoi* (Russian: Лесовой, Serbo-Croatian: Lesovoj, Лесовој)
- *Lesun* (Russian: Лесун, Belarusian: Лясун)
- *Mežainis*, "Forester"
- *Miškinis*, "Woodsman"
- *Miško velnias*, "forest devil"
- *Vir'ava* (Erzya: Вирьава) "forest mother"

## Liczyrzepa

*Liczyrzepa* is the same *mountain spirit* as *Rübezahl*, described in detail in *Spirit Beings in European Folklore – Compendium 2*

# Lidérc

A *Lidérc* is a unique and complex supernatural being of Hungarian folklore. It appears in three known varieties, which often borrow traits from one another: a miracle chicken or *Csodacsirke* (the most traditional form); a temporal devil or *Földi ördög*; and a Satanic lover, *Ördögszerető*. There may even be a fourth variety: the *Lüdérc*.

### • *Csodacsirke*

The first, more traditional form of the Lidérc is a miracle chicken, *Csodacsirke* in Hungarian, which hatches from the first egg of a black hen kept warm under the armpit of a human. Some versions of the legend say that an unusually tiny black hen's egg, or any egg at all, may become a Lidérc, or that the egg must be hatched by placing it in a heap of manure. The Lidérc attaches itself to people, in order to become their lover. If the person it attaches itself to is a woman, the being shifts into a man, but instead of pleasuring the woman, it fondles her, sits on her body, and sometimes sucks her blood, making her weak and sick after a time. From this source comes a Hungarian word for nightmare *Lidércnyomás*, which literally means "Lidérc pressure", from the pressure on the body while the being sits on its victim. Alternate names for the Lidérc are *Iglic*, *Ihlic* in *Csallóköz*, *Lüdérc*, *Piritusz* in the South, and *Mit-mitke* in the East. The Lidérc hoards gold and thus makes its owner rich. The victim can dispose of this stealing Lidérc, it must be persuaded to perform an impossible task, such as haul sand with a rope, or water with a sieve. It can also be destroyed by luring it into a hollow tree.

### • *Földi ördög*

The second variety of the Lidérc is as a tiny being, a temporal devil, *Földi ördög* in Hungarian. It has many overlapping qualities with the miracle chicken form, and it may also be obtained from a black hen's egg, but more often it is accidentally found in rags, cardboard boxes, glass bottles, or in the pockets of old clothes. A person owning this form of the Lidérc suddenly becomes rich and is capable of extraordinary feats, because the person's soul has supposedly been given to the Lidérc, or even to the Devil.

### • *Ördögszerető*

The third variety is as a Satanic lover, *Ördögszerető* in Hungarian, quite similar to an *Incubus* or *Succubus*. This form of the Lidérc flies at night, appearing as a fiery light, a *Will-o'-the-wisp*, or even as a bird of fire.

In the northern regions of Hungary and beyond, it is also known as *Ludvérc, Lucfir*. In Transylvania and Moldavia it goes by the names of *Lidérc, Lüdérc*, and sometimes *Ördög* (lit. the Devil). While in flight, the Lidérc sprinkles flames. On Earth, it can assume a human shape, usually the shape of a much lamented dead relative or lover. Its footprints are that of a horse. The Lidérc enters homes through chimneys or keyholes, and brings sickness and doom to its victims. It leaves the house with a splash of flames and dirties the walls. Burning incense and birch branches prevent the Lidérc from entering one's dwelling. In the eastern regions of Hungary and beyond, it is said the Lidérc is impossible to outrun. It haunts cemeteries, and it must disappear at the first crow of a rooster at dawn.

### • *Lüdérc*

The *Lüdérc* is sometimes regarded as different in nature from the Lidérc or even as an altogether different being. It acts as a helping spirit that appears in the shape of a flame and has a sexual character, as some kind of "hybrid" between the *Will-o'-the-wisp* and the *Incubus/Succubus*. The Lüdérc is often male, but can be female as well, depending on its relation with the opposite sex. Also, like it is the case with the Lidérc, these creatures may appear as a person's deceased fiancé or past lover. So in a confusing way the properties of the Lüdérc overlap those of the Lidérc, but as a separate entity the Lüdérc lacks the evil nature of the Lidérc. However, as the "characteristics" of folkloric beings are seldom fixed, the Lüdérc may also represent a less manifested feature of the Lidérc, which makes the latter creature somewhat less evil and even more complex.

## Likho

*Likho* or *Liho* (Russian: Лихо, Belarusian: ліха, Polish: *Licho*) is a personification of bad luck and misfortune in Slavic mythology and tales. The Likho wandered the world in search of places where people lived happily. It usually set fire to buildings, brought hunger, poverty, and disease, and then left. She also whispered bad thoughts in people's ears, sent plague on fruits and vegetables, harassed livestock, and destroyed possessions. There was no way to protect oneself from the Likho, the only way was to endure it patiently and wait for it to go away. She rarely appeared in visible form. When she did it was a frightening creature with only one eye (Лихо одноглазое, One-eyed Likho), often described as an emaciated old or terribly skinny woman, dressed in black, or as a *Forest-Goblin* who could cling to someone's neck. In some respects, she somewhat resembles the Cyclops of Greek mythology, but usually Likho is a bad spirit creature and one of her features is that she can be received by or passed on to another person with a gift. Rather than being included in the major canon of the Slavic belief system, the Likho is mostly found in fairy tales.

Likho is not a real proper name, but a noun, meaning bad luck in modern Russian and the odd number in Polish (obsolete). Several proverbs utilize this term such as the Russian "Не буди лихо, пока оно тихо", meaning *"Don't wake Likho while it is quiet"*, *"Let the sleeping dogs lie"* and the Polish "Cicho! Licho nie śpi", translated as *"Quiet! Evil does not sleep"* and "Licho wie", literally *"Licho knows"*, used to mean that a given piece of information is known by no one else. The British Slavic scholar William Ralston points out in his collection *Russian Folk-Tales* that the Russian adjective *likhoi* has two meanings: on the one hand "bad, harmful", etc., but on the other hand also "brave, courageous". He also notes that in Polish, *licho* originally means "odd", and that Polish housewives considered it imprudent, for example, to let hens hatch an odd number of eggs. The word is likely to be related to Indo-European *leikw*, meaning *"something to remain"*, *"to leave behind"*. The derived adjective *likhoy* can be used to describe someone who is a bit too daring or brave. In Czech, *lichý* means odd (number), idle, vain. The Polish, *lichy* means shoddy, poor, flimsy. In Belarusian, лiхi means bad, evil (like in prayer), odd (side of clothing). In the Ukrainian language it denotes bad luck or incident.



## Likhoradka

*Likhoradka* (Russian: Лихорадка or лихоманка "fever", трясавица "shakes", Serbian: Милоснице or Milosnice) or *Tryasavitsa* is a female spirit in Slavic mythology. The Likhoradka was purported to be able to possess a person's body and at first cause chills, then fever. In some tales she is considered a creation of the dark deity *Chernobog*. Later Russian legends describe twelve *Likhoradkas*, with individual names associated with special illnesses. The Russian words for fevers were indexed by Alexander Nikolaevich Afanasyev (1826-1871) as: *Tryaseya – Ogneya – Ledeya – Gneteya – Grynusha – Gluheya – Lomeya – Purnea – Jaundicea – Korkusha – Glyadea – Ognejastra*. The very number twelve and the sharply negative semantics of the "shaking sisters" are connected with the apocryphal motif of King Herod's daughters. The Herodian maidens

in Slavic mythology are plain-haired women of devilish appearance
(bat wings, various deformities). In some plots they are seven, ten,
forty, or seventy-seven. The word *likhoradka* is of Old Russian origin.
It was formed with the suffix *-ka* from *likhoradit* (to wish evil), derived
from *likho* (evil, harm or bad luck) and *radit* (to wish). In the Russian
language of the 11th to 17th centuries the word is known in the meaning
of "purulent abscess, crust", "chills and fever". As a mythological figure,
Likhoradka was related to *Chuma*, which in modern Russian is the term
for plague. Likhoradka was sometimes portrayed as a tall woman with
disheveled hair, a pale face and a white dress, who brought sickness to the
people she tried to touch or to kiss. To expel a Likhoradka, the back of a
feverish patient was massaged heavily with an object which had previously
been placed on chicken litter (roosting place). The patient could also be
made to drink a concoction of chicken droppings, or one could put a
dead chicken under their pillow. According to some beliefs, on January
2 (Gregorian calendar)/15 January (Julian calendar) the fevers came out
of their dungeons, hiding from the frost. On this day the transoms were
sprinkled with be-spelled water. It was believed that the Likhoradka was
afraid of the rooster's cry, of barking dogs and bells ringing.

## Liogat or Sampiro

In Albanian folklore the *Liogat* or *Sampiro* (also: *Liougat, Liugat,
Ljugat, Ljuna, Ljung, Llugat*) is a *vampiric Revenant,* of Turkish descent.
At the time this entity had a very strong correlation with a Christian
scapegoating and demonizing policy towards Muslims and Turks in
Albania. A sixteenth century church decree declared that all Albanians
of Turkish descent would become a *Vampire* after their death, no matter
how good or spiritual a life they may have led. Attending a Muslim
religious service, consuming meat handled by a Turk, or being a habitual
liar or professional thief in life was also not done. And finally this curse
befell upon any Albanian who had committed an unnatural act, such as
bestiality, homosexuality, prostitution, transvestism, or having sex with a
Turkish person. Later, in 1854, the name of the vampiric Revenant known
as the Liogat was officially described as meaning *"dead Turks in winding
sheets"*. The Liogat or Sampiro returns from the grave three days after its
death, with its burial shroud wrapped around its body and wearing high-
heeled shoes upon its feet. His eyes are large and glow brightly. A small
amount of dirt from its grave is inexplicably kept in its navel. Every night

he rises from his grave but the creature is particularly fond of nights with heavy fog. Once he finds a victim, it follows the person, making "kissing" sounds that can be heard clearly over the click of his high-heeled shoes. When he finally attacks, he drains a survivable amount of blood from the person and then flees the scene as quickly as his high heels can carry him. On nights when he does not feed, the creature will visit the countryside and peek into the homes of people. His glare alone will spread a disease that infants are particularly susceptible to. The Liogat was also considered to be a death omen when seen. Like every *Vampire*-Revenant he is afraid of wolves and sometimes he flees back to his grave as a *Corpse candle* or *Will-o'- the-wisp*. In other versions the soil on which he walks is always loose, and a blue ball of light will be hovering above his head. In order to kill a Liogat or Sampiro, a stake made of yew wood, had to be driven through its heart in a single blow.



## Lioubgai

According to *Le Musée des Vampires* (a museum located in Les Lilas, France) the *Lioubgai* or *Lioubgaï* is one of the many kinds of Albanian *vampiric Revenants*. The word Lioubgai is specifically reserved for a *Vampire*-Revenant who is created when a person dies on the battlefield and his body is badly burned, but not wholly destroyed. Rising up as a Lioubgai, he will return to the battlefield at night, where he will feed on the blood of dying men.


## Lisna

The *Lisna* or *Lisnytsia* (She of the forest) is a kind of Ukrainian *Huldra* or *Skogsrå*: a female forest-spirit with the typical hollow back. The Lisna develops from an illegitimate baby who has been killed in the forest by its unwed mother. For seven years, the soul of the baby wanders around in the forest, begging to be Christianized. If no one hears its crying and blesses it by the end of seven years, it turns into a Lisna. The Lisna is a sort of *Niavka (Wood-Nymph)*, very attractive, except for this hole in her back. She and her companions dance in open circles in the meadows and clearings in the woods. She is however also often seen in the uplands. Her hobby is playing havoc with young men in love. She appears in her victim's dreams for nine nights in a row and if he does not tell his dreams to anyone she visits him and tries to seduce him, just like a *Nichnytsia* (Ukrainian night-demoness). She assumes the form of his beloved woman who is temporally or permanently absent. It is difficult to get rid of a Lisna. The victim must steal the sash that has been worn by a priest during mass and bind the Lisna with it, holding her by force until the rooster crows, at which time she should vanish. During this act the young man has to mobilize all his willpower, as the Lisna wil use every seductive trick possible. During the next nine nights he has to avoid the bed in which he first encountered the Lisna. If he does not succeed and remains under her spell, she will sexually exhaust him up to the level where he may die. Her favorite prey consisted of young shepherds, whose vital energies, in a mysterious way were passed on to their herds: while a young shepherd that is under the spell of a Lisna, is getting weaker and weaker, his sheep will get healthier and flourish as never before.



## Lisovyk

The *Lisovyk* is a figure of Ukrainian folk demonology that controlled the forests and their riches: the trees, birds and other animals, especially the deer. Every forest had its own Lisovyk, who appeared in the form of a humanoid being covered with pelt and hooves instead of feet, a giant with horns, a tree, or an animal. He could be recognized by the absence of a shadow. He lived in the woods or in inaccessible places and in winter inhabited caves or deserted shepherds' huts, where he whistled and sang. He could lead people astray in the forest or could help hunters by sending animals into their paths. The Lisovyk was notorious for kidnapping women who stray in the forest. He took them to his lair to mate with them. He occasionally exchanged human babies for his own offspring, or stole children who were cursed by their parents. According to folk-belief he sat on a tree in the forest on the eve of Saint John's Holiday and laughed and shouted joyfully, his peals of laughter echoing through the mountains. In the Hutsul region, the Lisovyk was represented as a shepherd. The *Chuhaister* is a variation of the Lisovyk, but unlike the latter he is a friendly creature. After Ukraine's conversion into Christianity, Saint George also became a protector of animals and cattle.

## Lisunka

In Russian folk-belief the *Lisunka* (pl.: *Lisunki*), are *forest-women*, akin like the *Holzweiber* or *Wilde Frauen* etc. in German speaking regions. They are described as hairy and hideous, and often regarded as female Leshies.

# Lubia

*Lubia* or *Ljubi* is a female *water-* and *storm-demon* in Albanian mythology and folklore, usually depicted as a huge multi-headed serpentine dragon, similar to the *Kulshedra*. In Southern Albanian beliefs, she is a *storm-deity*. She is also referred to as *Mother Lubia*. Lubia is believed to live in a wonderful vegetable garden. She can cause the waters to dry up unless a virgin is sacrificed to her. Her multiple heads remind us of the *Lernaean Hydra* of Greek mythology, the monster killed by Heracles as the second task of his *Twelve Labors*. Just like in the Greek myth, when one of the heads of Lubia was cut off, another grew in its place. The demon was also known to have an irresistible taste for flesh, especially that of little girls. The Kulshedra and Lubia are very similar in both appearance and function and could only be placated by a human sacrifice. The Lubia however was the one accredited with more power and notoriety within Albanian culture.

# Lubiczk

In the folklore of Pomarania the Kashubian *Lubiczk* is the guardian spirit of love and sex. It is believed that Lubiczk attaches himself to people in love, and makes that they cannot live without each other anymore.

# Lugat

In Albanian folklore the *Lugat*, sometimes confused with the *Liogat*, is a *vampiric Revenant* and in some versions an "unripe" *Kududh(i)* – in other words a Kududh(i) in its first stage. A Lugat could emerge from a person who died suddenly, like in a murder, suicide or due to a sudden illness. Sources vary as to how long it took for a Lugat to mature into a Kududh(i). Some sources claim it is a mere 30 days, but according to others it takes 40 years. Most commonly however 40 days was given as the length of time. When the Lugat arose from the dead, it was very strong and it looked like a normal person that was somewhat bloated, more so after it had just fed itself. Its skin was reddish but showed no signs of decomposition. It preyed nightly on those it knew in life first, before moving on to animals and other people. For discovering the grave of a Lugat a white horse was used and guided over the cemetery. When it came to a grave that it would not walk over, this indicated the *Vampire* was resting beneath. The Lugat then had to be exhumed and burned to ash. Wolves could also kill a Lugat. In other versions the Lugat seems to have been a more autonomous creature that abided in shadows and darkness, especially places that never saw the sunlight, such as inside water wells, old ruins, and caves. He had a frightening appearance and was extremely violent. This Lugat could fly and ride the winds, and assailed his victims in their sleep. He also lured people, especially children, to himself while he was concealed in darkness. In Albania, the word *lugat* is also used to simply describe a wicked or frightening person.

## Lutk

*Lutken* or *Ludken* (from the Sorbian for "little people") are *Kobolds* from the Lusatian saga world, usually dwelling in the earth. In Sorbian they are called Lutki and in the Mark Brandenburg they are called Lutchen. The singular Lutk is usually only used in the sagas where an individual Lutk comes into contact with a human, mostly from the peasant class. The Lutken are said to have been mostly friendly to people and often frequented their homes. They are small people who once lived on the earth and with the invasion of Christianity, frightened by the sound of church bells, fled into the earth's interior. In the north of Lusatia, they were associated with the old urns and clay jars people sometimes found, which were thought to be the household goods of the Lutken. Their residential mounds were called *Ludkowa gora* (Ludkenberg: Ludken mountain) or *Ludkowa gorka* (Ludkenhügel: Ludken hill). In Upper Lusatia, *dwarf* legends are also known, which tell of *Querxen* and *Veensmännlein*, especially in southern Upper Lusatia.

*Vampire sucking the blood of his victim* (1910) from the magazine *La Vie Mysterieuse*

# M

## Macica

In Mazurian Polish folklore the *Macica* (Worm) is a demon and *Bogeyman* from the region of Dzialdowo (German: Soldau), who causes stomach cramp and gastric colic. Macica is understood as a manifestation of the influence of something evil, stuck in the human body. The demon was imagined as a worm with strong claws and pincers, with which it pinched and jerked human intestines when aroused and irritated. Every human being had a Macica within his or her body that could inflict great suffering. However, when it departed from the body, the person would die. This demon had a spherical body and countless legs and was the size of a thaler – an old large silver coin with a diameter of (1+1⁄2 inch) / 4 cm.

## Mamuna

*Mamuna, Mamona* is a female demon from ancient Slavic beliefs, also known as *Czarcicha, Dekla, Łanucha, Oćwiara, Odmienica, Osinauczycha, Pałuba, Paniuńcia, Płaczka, Siubiela* and *Zamianica*. In later times the *Boginka*, once a unique spirit, and *Dziwożona* became identified with the Mamuna. She is also often identified as Dziwożona. Mamuna is derived from the verb *mamić/omamiać* (to deceive). Ethnographers and linguists have noted various variants of the name of this demon, including the names *Mamuny, Mamony, Mamóny, Mamonie, Manie* in the Lesser Poland region, and *Mamuny* in the Przemyskie and Sanok-Krośnieńskie regions and in Silesia. One theory states the name is derived from the Hebrew demon *Mamon* or *Mammon*. During the Middle Ages, Mammon was commonly personified as the demon of wealth and greed. In some areas (e.g. Mazovia) the name *Sibele* also appeared.

*Mamuny* (pl.) were believed to be the souls of women who died during pregnancy or confinement. There were no uniform ideas about their appearance. They were depicted as:
• old women covered with hair all over their bodies (e.g., the Slovak *Runa*)
• half-women-half-animals, *Wild Women* (Slovakia, Czech Republic)
• beautiful, naked or clothed women

- a kind of witches (Pieniny highlanders)
- forest demons (Silesia).

They were sometimes reported to be the souls of:
- penitent women, girls who had miscarried or killed their children
- suicides
- perjurers
- midwives or more specific midwives who died in childbirth
- girls who died during the "announcement", i.e. between the announcement and the wedding
- old maidens, witches



Mamuna sat on river banks under bridges and washed her underwear while noisily playing with tadpoles. In other versions, she inhabited caves and ravines. She used to harass pregnant women and midwives, and abduct or swap newly born children. A *changeling* placed by a Mamuna was detected by its underdevelopment. Usually the swapped or abducted children were unbaptized infants. Quite often Mamuny stayed close to the mother's house in order to perform the swap at the right moment. For this purpose they tried to call the mother of a newborn baby out of the room for some imaginary reason. Sometimes they tempted her with singing and music, or with the false sounds of partying and dancing that supposedly came from the tavern, to lure her out of bed and go outside to join the people having fun. In other cases the Mamuna would even try to swap the baby by force – she would try to kidnap the child by beating and scratching it. A baby swapped in this way was called an *Odmienkiem* (changeling) *Podrzucem lub płonkiem* (toss or fling), *Bobakiem* or *Bobem*. Such a changeling did not move from its cradle, spoke little and ate almost nothing. The death of a retarded child was explained by the fact that the Mamuna's offspring never grew well among humans and always died within a short amount of time. Contradicting to this picture of a sad and helpless creature, the demon's child could also survive and become a personification of cunning and malice.

In Slovakia, Mamuny used to steal food from woodcutters and green peas from the fields of the Pieniny highlanders. In Leczyce, there is a belief that Mamuny kidnap children from the fields at high noon. The Pieniny highlanders believed that Mamuny appear during the new moon and in winter.

## Marchołt

In Poland *Marchołt* is a literary character in a medieval text based on the
story of King Solomon, as well as a generic term for *demon*, originating
from a Jewish-Aramaic dialect, meaning "cauldron" or "vessel". The
Jewish kabbalistic term for demon is the feminine word *Qlippah* (pl.:
*Qlippoth*), also meaning "vessel", "empty shell", etc.

## Marțolea

*Marțolea* is a demonic *Faun*-like entity in Romanian mythology
(especially in the regions of Bukovina and Maramureş). Its gender is
unclear as it can shape-shift at will, but the male version predominates.
It lives up in the mountains and descends on Tuesday nights to lure
with its singing and punish the women caught working. Called also
*Marț Sara* (the old Romanian words for "Tuesday Evening") it demands
the semi-holy day of Tuesday to be respected and forbids four women's
chores: spinning of the wool, sowing, boiling laundry and baking bread.
Marțolea's punishments for breaking its rules are ridiculously harsh, like:
killing by ripping the woman's belly open, hanging her guts on nails to
the wall, and around the dishes in the case of unmarried women. For the
married women the punishments are killing or possessing their baby, or
their husband if he is far from home. Marțolea usually appears as a goat
with a human like head, horns and hooves. He can however shape-shift
into a big, old, ugly woman dressed in black, a soldier, or a handsome
man. To married women the demon shows itself as an old woman, to
married men as a virgin and to unmarried women as a young charming
man. In some regions, there is a different character called *Joimârița*,
another form of the Romanian word for Thursday. This demon however
punishes lazy children instead of women. Marțolea repays the women
who keep the Tuesday sacred by leaving them eggs on their doorstep or
flowers from the highest mountains in Bukovina. On the first night of
March, young women that wear March Trinkets (Mărțişor) are repaid by
Marțolea with a silver coin that the girls will have to keep all year.

## Marudą

*Marudą* (meaning: a dull, grumbling, sluggish, tardy, troublesome,
tedious or clumsy person) is a demonic female figure of Polish folklore,
that torments children in their cradles, prevents them from falling asleep,

and makes them cry. In the 19th century, to protect children from the Marudą, special magical procedures were used, such as placing a bowl with water in the room where the infant slept, and in it a ball of thread, a spoon and a spindle. The demon, occupied with these accessories, would leave the child alone. Another method was to make nine dolls out of knobbly twigs, and they were put on the baby's cradle, starting from the head. Or a ball of thread, a needle, some poppy seeds, and a piece of bread were placed under the child's head, and an incantation was pronounced. In some areas of the Lublin region, girls were forbidden to play with dolls, because they believed that the doll could contain a Marudą that would suffocate the child.



## Matsil

*Matsil* (მაცილი) are evil spirits from the underworld that plague travelers and hunters in Georgian folklore. Folk tales refer to Kopala's efforts to defeat them. Kopala (Georgian: კოპალა) is a traditional hero or demigod revered to in the highlands of Pshavi in Georgia.

## Mavka or Miavka

The *Mavka* or *Miavka* (*Majka, Mauka, Mawka, Nawka, Nejka, Niauka, Niavka, Śpiewnica, Tanechnica, Wyniwka*) is a female Ukrainian and Lemko *vampiric* field demon and *water-spirit*. More or less equivalent to the *Rusalka*, and depicted as a charming young woman, dangerous to humans, luring passersby to secluded places to tickle them to death. Poland, Bulgaria, Servia and Macedonia also have their variable of the Maivka. The word *mavka* (*navka*) was formed from the common Slavic *pavj/pavj/pavja/pavje* (the dead, evil spirits, pitchforks). In the Ukrainian language, the name *Mavka* is synonymous with the word *Mermaid*. It was believed that *Miawki* annually descended to the fields when the crops were shedding their ears. They were the dead unbaptized children, small as cats, hence the origin of their name: the cat's miau. They danced on the grass. They were of great beauty, cheerful and lively, but cruel. They attacked strays in the midst of ears of grass. By various tricks they put the victims in a good mood, and then by tickling them they forced them to laugh most violently, until they died, and then fed on the blood of their victim. Miavki had no reflection in water, did not cast shadows, and had "no back", meaning that their insides could be seen. (Those were more often called *Nyavka* and they were believed to live in western Ukraine, which has more dangerous mountain rivers than Central Ukraine, while *Mavkas*, who were believed to live in Central Ukraine, had their backs.) In some accounts, they were also said to help farmers by looking after cattle and driving out wild animals. Mavkas were believed to live in groups in forests, mountain caves, or sheds, which they decorated with rugs. They made thread of stolen flax and wove thin transparent cloth for making clothes for themselves. They loved flowers, which they wore in their hair. In the spring they planted flowers in the mountains, to which they enticed young men, whom they tickled to death. On Pentecost (known as Mavka's Easter, Ukrainian: Навський Великдень) they held games, dances, and orgies. A demon accompanied them on a flute or pipes.

In Poland the spirit is mentioned in the legends of the people of southern Malopolska. They had modish eyes and wove cornflowers, ears, and poppies into their fawn-colored hair for decoration. They were less cruel than the *Południce*. In the southern Slavic regions it was also believed that the souls of deceased unbaptized children became *Mavkas*. In western Bulgaria and eastern Serbia, people believed that they appeared in a flock of birds and were especially dangerous for mothers with children. The idea of dead unbaptized children appearing as birds goes back to the pre-Slavic notion that the dead visit the world of the living as birds. In southern Serbia and Macedonia, the *Navi, Nave* or *Navoi* appear in the form of women (Samovil) – they arrive in a whirlwind, and if the whirlwind hits a woman in labor, she will immediately fall ill.

**Kostroma the first Mavka**
It is believed that the first Mavka (or Rusalka) was the fertility goddess *Kostroma*. According to legend, as siblings Kostroma and Kupalo once ran into a field to listen to songs of bird Sirin, but Sirin kidnapped Kupalo and carried him into the river Nav. Many years later, one day, Kostroma walked the shore of the river and made a wreath. She boasted that the wind would not blow the wreath off her head. According to the belief, that meant that she would not marry. This boast was not approved of by the gods. The wind became stronger and eventually blew the wreath from Kostroma's head into the water, where it was later picked up by Kupalo, who was nearby in his boat. According to Slavic customs, the one who picks up the wreath must marry the girl who made it. Kupalo and Kostroma fell in love and shortly after they were married – without any knowledge that they were brother

and sister. After the wedding, the gods told them the truth. Because they could not be together, Kupalo and Kostroma committed suicide. Kupalo jumped into the fire and died, while Kostroma ran to the forest, threw herself into the forest lake and drowned. But she did not really die, and became a *Mermaid* (Mavka). Walking around that lake, she seduced the men she met on her path and dragged them into the watery abyss. She always mistook them for Kupalo, and found out that the caught young man was not her lover only when he had already drowned.

## Mężyk



*Mężyk* (also: *Mały mąż*, *Mały człowiek*, *Mały* mężczyzna, names all denoting "a man", "a small husband", "a small man", etc.) is a male demon in the beliefs of the Pomeranian people. He is the equivalent of the female *Dziwożon, Mamun, Sybieli, Boginek*, etc. With a long beard that touches the floor, he would grab a baby from its cradle, throw it on a bench by the chimney, and if someone did not protect it in time, he would kidnap it and take it with him to the underworld. To prevent this from happening, a steel object was placed in the cradle.

## Mjertovjec

In Belarusian folklore we find stories about a vampiric creature whose appearance is very inconsistent with the traditional Slavic *Vampire*, which in most cases can switch between the *Revenant-Vampire*-type and an etheric blood or energy sucker. The *Mjertovjec* has much more in common with a so called *floating head-Vampire*, mostly appearing as a head with a piece of upper body and part of the spine. These are common in Southeast Asia, but with this one exception: they are completely unknown in Europe. The Malaysian *Penanggalan* for example is an intact woman by day and a segmented monster by night, her disembodied organs twinkling in the darkness like fireflies. Thailand's *Krasue* is a similar monster, one who will feed on feces and carrion, if blood is not available. Vietnam's *Ma Cà Rồng* also detaches its head and spine, but is less vampiric, feeding exclusively on cow dung (but if a human interrupts its feeding, it will kill them). Like its Asian cousins the Mjertovjec's head and upper chest rip from the rest of its body when it launches its nighttime search for blood. In Belarus the Mjertovjec was thought to be the offspring of a dead bridegroom, or more generally accepted, the son

of a *Werewolf* and a witch, showing both human and wolfish features. In
Belarus it was believed that when a *Werewolf* or witch dies, the spirit does
not dissipate or 'move on'; instead it returns to Earth as a very powerful
*Vampire* that terrorizes people from midnight till morning. Apart from
birth or death, an individual can transform into a Mjertovjec by following
the path of an apostate; someone who deliberately abandons faith or
defies the Church, or someone who commits other crimes against God.

**Destroying a Mjertovjec**
The Mjertovjec is a night-hunter and must return to its grave before the
rooster has crowed three times. If it does not, it loses its ability to fly and
then flops to the ground, where anyone with a torch and some kindling
can kill it. The creature is only susceptible to fire, but a sharpened iron
spike driven through its heart can immobilize it in the grave for a short
while. The Mjertovjec has in common with other types of European
Vampires that it shares the obsessive-compulsive urge to stop and count
seeds. So, small seeds were spread on a grave where the Belarusians
suspected a Mjertovjec, to prevent him from leaving the cemetery at night
or hinder its return, thus making it vulnerable.

# Moroi

In Romanian folk beliefs the *Moroi(ul)* (pl.: *Moroii*) is thought to be a
vampiric creature which usually emerges from a baby that died before
being baptized, or was killed, or buried alive, or from a corpse of someone
who was not given proper religious service. It was believed that the
Moroii cry at night and ask for their baptism. The Moroii are said to leave
their graves at night as ghosts who prey on humans and animals. Beyond
the Carpathians, in most of the ethnographic areas of Transylvania,
especially in the Țara Moților and in the forest area of Hunedoara, the
Moroi (and its feminine form, *Moroiniță*) are understood exclusively as
witches who steal the milk and vital energy of cows, as a unique example
of vampirism which nurtures itself with the abundance of food and
energy provided by domestic animals. In Oltenia and Teleorman, on the
other hand, the Moroii are purely identical with the undead. In these
areas the locals are convinced that if someone was during his or her life a
person with a "bad heart", with a grudge against his/her relatives, and if
this person behaved harshly and mercilessly, then – inevitably – he or she
became a Moroi or Moroiniță.

Moroi are often associated with other figures in Romanian folklore, such as the *Strigoi* (another type of *Vampire*), the *Vârcolac* (*Werewolf*), or *Pricolici* (another sort of *Werewolf*-like creature). As with most concepts in folklore, the exact characteristics ascribed to Moroi are variable from source to source. Heinrich von Wlislocki, reported in *Quälgeister im Volksglauben der Rumänen* (1896) the belief that the child of a woman impregnated by a *Nosferat* (a sort of *Incubus-Vampire*) would be extremely ugly, covered with thick hair, and very quickly becoming a Moroi. The origins of the term "moroi" are unclear, but it is thought by the Romanian Academy to have possibly originated from the Old Slavonic word *mora* (nightmare) – cf. Russian *Kikimora*. Moroi is used more often in the southern Romanian languages, especially in Wallachia, while Strigoï (whose etymology is close to *Stryge*) is used throughout the country, but more so in the northern Romanian languages, especially in Transylvania and Moldavia.



## Moryana

*Moryana* is a Slavic mythological character and feminine Elemental spirit. According to Russian belief – she is the daughter of the Морского царя (*Morskoy Tsar*: Sea Tsar) and personification of the cold and sharp wind, blowing from the sea to the land. She was also known as the Морскáя царéвна (Sea Tsarevna) and the Царь-девицá (Tsar Maiden). It was believed that Moryana often swam deep in the sea, taking the form of a big fish and playing with dolphins. She came ashore only on quiet evenings. At this time of day she swayed on the waves, splashed in the water and fingered sea pebbles. When a storm was rising, due to the Morskoy Tsar becoming angry, Moryana calmed him down, and the storm began to subside. She also sailed the sea in a golden canoe. Her beauty was so dazzling that it was impossible to look at her for more than a second. In the beautiful image of the Sea Tsarevna or the Tsar Maiden, fairy tales combine the ideas of the goddess *Zorya* and the goddess of thunder. According to another story, Moryana is a very stern, white-clad giantess with disheveled hair. She commands the southeasterly winds at the mouth of the Volga, thus posing a great threat to sailors in the Caspian Sea. Moryana's main rival is *Ded*, Lord of the Northwest winds, who almost always loses from her; when they clash in a duel, the waves pile up to the sky and, twisting, sink ships. The Russian writer Aleksej Remizov (1877-1957) called Moryana the *Goddess of the Sea* and *Lady of the Winds*.

Moryana may be both an individual character or representing a "family" of *sea-spirits* or *Sea-Maidens*, and there are several common features inherent in almost any belief associated with her; her origin from sea waters, her enormous height, long hair and influence on the weather. Sea-maidens are also described as maidens of enormous size. They hide near the coastal cliffs, and as soon as a ship comes near, they surface and rock it so that it is wrecked. Sometimes they attack people, trying to drag them with them under the water, and the only way to defend oneself from the Sea-Maidens is to tear as much hair as possible out of their heads; hair which looks like sea foam. They are most active during storms. Because of the consonance of her name with the name of *Marena*, Moryana was sometimes identified with her and was then called the "goddess of death".

## Mullo

*Mullo* (also *Milos*; "one who is dead"; female: *Muli*; male: *Mulo*) is an undead, *Revenant*, or *Vampire* of Roma folklore. When someone dies suddenly of some unnatural cause, or does not get the proper funeral rites, he or she can become a Mullo. Mullo's are described as wearing white clothes, with hair reaching to their feet, and one physical oddity, a trait which varies from geographic region to region. Mullo's seem to haunt people they did not like during their lifetime and harass them. The Mullo can attack these people, strangle them or suck their blood (usually it is a relative who had caused its death, or hadn't properly observed the burial ceremonies, or who kept the deceased's possessions instead of destroying them as was proper). To get rid of a Mullo, people would hire a *Dhampire* (the son of a Vampire and his widow) to detect the vampiric creature. To ward off Vampires like the Mullo, Romani people drove steel or iron needles into a corpse's heart and placed bits of steel in the mouth, over the eyes, ears and between the fingers at the time of burial. They also placed hawthorn in the corpse's socks or drove a hawthorn stake through the legs. Further measures included driving stakes into the grave, pouring boiling water over them, decapitating the corpse, or burning it. In the lore of the Balkan Gypsies, a *Lampijerovic* (little *Vampire*) is the child of a human woman and a Mullo. Born a natural enemy to Vampires, this fated hunter can see a Vampire for what it is, even if the Vampire is invisible. Sometimes this is an innate ability of the person; other times he must first perform a ritual to temporarily gain the ability.

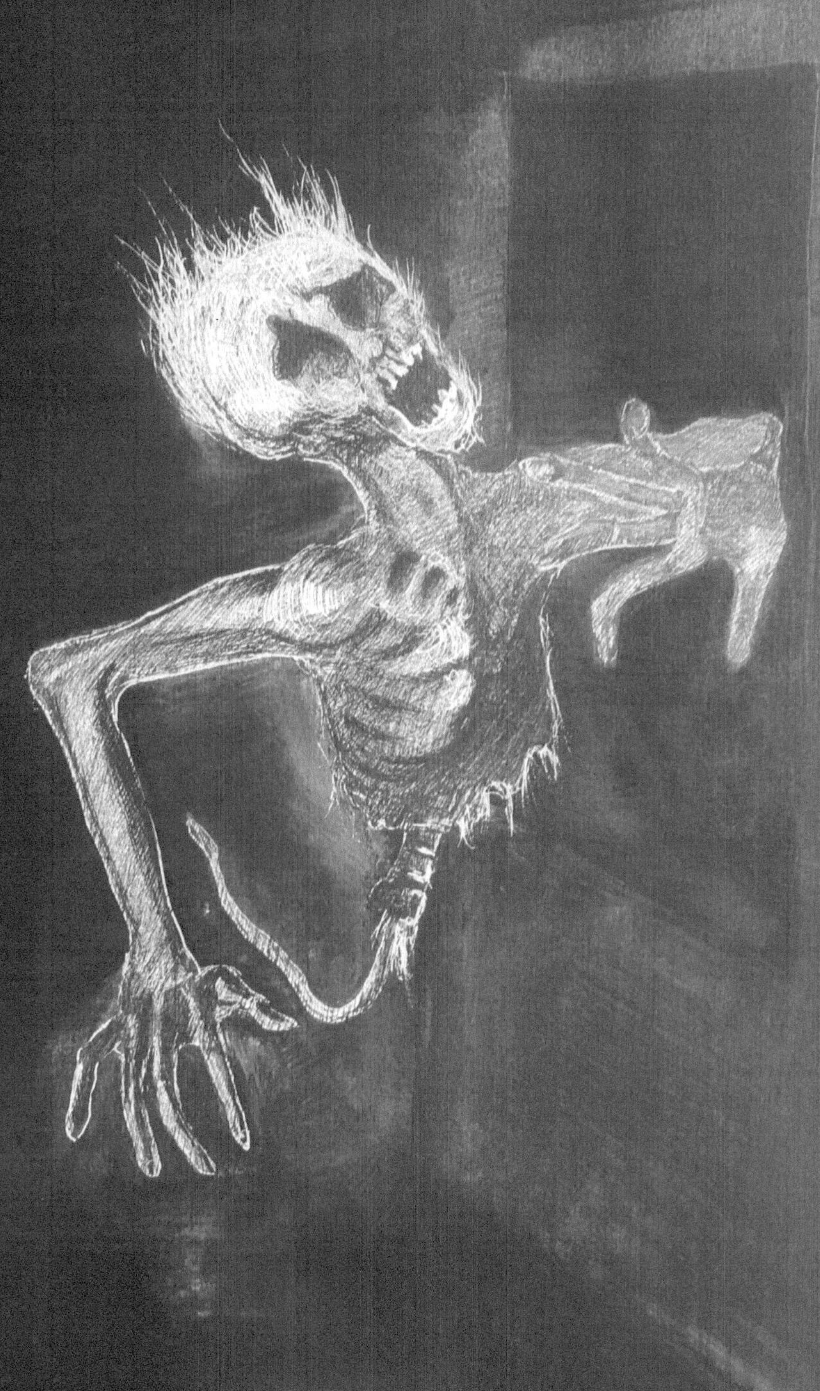

## Muma Pădurii

In Romanian folklore, *Muma Pădurii* (Mother of the Forest) appears
as an ugly, mischievous or mad old woman, living in the heart of virgin
forests, in a dark, dreadful, hidden little house or hut, or an old tree. She
is the opposite of *Fairies* such as *Zână*. However, she is also a protector
of animals and plants, brewing potions and helping injured animals. She
cures the forest if it is dying or sick, and she keeps unwanted trespassers
away by driving them mad and scaring them. Sometimes she has the
ability to change shape. She is thought to attack children and because of
this, a large variety of spells (*descântece* in Romanian) are used against
her. In one popular story, at some point she tries to boil a little girl alive in
her oven. However, the little girl's brother outsmarts Muma Pădurii and
pushes her into her own oven instead, a bit similar to the tale of *Hansel
and Gretel*. Muma Pădurii has features in common with the Russian *Baba
Yaga*.

## Muroï

In Czechoslovakian lore, the *Muroï*, originally considered a demon, is
also a vampiric spirit. His name literally means "destiny", in terms of
meaning closer to fatality than to good fortune. It is said that this demon
is only capable of taking possession of the corrupted corpse of an evil
person, particularly a banker or a politician. Its early medieval legends
make it clear that the Muroï is fiercely opposed to all symbols of faith,
and his birth is in fact preceded by a series of unmistakable signs; one of
them is the appearance of tears of blood on all the images of the Virgin
Mary near his den, which probably expresses pain and offense in the face
of the abomination of his presence. To ensure that this type of *Vampire*
never has the chance to rise from its grave and prey upon the people of its
former community, one must identify the corpse of the possessed person
and remove the heart. If this precaution is overlooked, the help of a rabbi
or a Catholic priest must be enlisted to confront the creature. When
his presence is denounced by the images of the Virgin Mary weeping
blood, the face of the Muroï takes on a rather characteristic red tinge. His
voice disappears; instead, it is replaced by prolonged cries that paralyze
the unwary who have the misfortune to come across him. Certain
demonologists maintain that his wail is not heard by all, but only by those
who are destined to be his victim. Even the death of the Muroï brings no
comfort to his victims. Those who have heard the cry of this demon will

feel it for the rest of their lives as a distant, persistent and terrifying hum
that throbs deep in their ears.

During the day the creature hides in its coffin or in any other lair that
allows him to regain his strength. To discover the precise location of its
hiding place, it is necessary to bring an image of the Virgin Mary and wait
for the bloody tearful outbreak, of which the frequency and intensity are
directly proportional to its proximity to the reprobate. These precautions
have to do with the idea that the Muroï can only be defeated inside its lair,
during the day, and always under the patronage of the Virgin Mary. Once
the heart has been removed, the skin between the thumb and forefinger
of the hands must be cut off with steel scissors. However, the only way to
destroy a Muroï forever is to totally burn the possessed corpse to ashes.



## Murony

The *Murony* or *Muroni* is a *Vampire* in Wallachian folklore. It has the
ability to transform into a variety of different animals. A Murony-attack
does not necessarily leave a mark on the neck of the person whose blood
it sucks and could be very hard to identify and often be thought of as
an animal attack. The only sign that a Murony was there at all, was an
exceptional amount of blood loss. While the Muroni was often thought
to be a Vampire, it can also be considered a shapeshifter, as it could take
on the appearance of animals like a dog, cat, toad, frog, flea, louse, bug or
spider. The Murony is one of many Vampire-species which was believed
to really be a blood-sucking ghost, only taking on the form of other
beings to make feeding easier. These mythical creatures were considered
by Christianity as avatars of the Devil, haunting humans at night to steal
their life force little by little. They could only be destroyed by digging up
their bodies, sticking a needle in their foreheads and piercing their hearts
with a wooden stake before burning them.

# N

## Nav

*Nav* (Croatian, Czech, Slovak: *Nav*; Polish: *Nawia*, *Nawki*, sometimes also referred to as *Lalki*; Russian: Навь; Serbian: Нав; Slovene: *Navje*; Ukrainian: Мавка, *Mavka* or Нявка, *Nyavka*) are plural terms used in Slavic mythology to denote the souls of the dead. According to some scholars (Stanisław Urbańczyk, among others), this word was a general name for demons arising out of the souls of tragic and premature deaths, killers, warlocks, the murdered and the drowned. They were said to be hostile and unfavorable towards humans, being jealous of their being alive. In Bulgarian folklore there were *Navias* that sucked the blood out of women giving birth, whereas in the Ruthenian *Primary Chronicle* the Navias are presented as a demonic personification of the 1092 plague in Polotsk. According to Polish folk tales, the *Nawia* usually took the form of a bird. The words *nawia*, *nav* and its other variants are most likely derived from the Proto-Slavic navъ- (corpse, deceased). Cognates in other Indo-European languages include Latvian *nāve* (death), Lithuanian *nõvis* (death), Old Prussian *nowis* (body, flesh), Old Russian навь or *naú* (corpse, dead body) and Gothic NΛꞴS or *naus* (dead body, corpse).

### As a synonym for the underworld

*Nawia* or *Nav* was also utilized as a name for the Slavonic underworld, ruled by the god *Veles*, enclosed away from the world either by a living sea or river, and according to some beliefs located deep underground. According to Ruthenian folklore, Veles lived in a swamp in the center of Nav, where he sat on a golden throne at the base of the Cosmic Tree, wielding a sword. Symbolically, the Nav has also been described as a huge green plain-pasture, onto which Veles guided souls. The entrance to Nav was guarded by a *Zmey* (benevolent dragon spirit) and it was believed these souls would later be reborn on Earth.

## Nëczk

In Kashubian folklore the *Nëczk* is a *Wassermann* (a kind of *water-sprite*) living in the Baltic Sea, and the Pomeranian lakes and rivers. He is credited with creating whirlpools and water currents that are dangerous to swimmers.

## Nichnytsia

The *Nichnytsia* (night-demoness) is a nocturnal entity of Ukrainian folklore, who shares many characteristics with entities like the *Bohynia* (goddess), *Lisnytsia* (wood-demoness) and *Mamuna* (demoness) and the better known *Rusalka* and *Mavka*.

## Nocnica

The *Nocnica* is a female demonic figure in Slavic demonology, derived from pre-Christian beliefs, described as a posthumous form of existence of the human soul. As a result of the numerous transformations that have taken place in folk demonology, she is usually identified with a *Nightmare* or *Mare*. A reference to *Nocnicach* can be found in the 13th-century *Katalogu magii* (Catalogue of Magic) by Friar Rudolfa, in a sermon by a Polish Hussite from the 15th century, or in the 17th century *Czarownicy powołanej,* a book on witches. In Silesia, Nocnica was seen as a female demon, suffocating people in their sleep – especially infants – and bringing diseases. The name is also used in other regions as a general term for night-demons. Beliefs in Nocnicas have been strongly suppressed, so it is difficult to determine exactly what their origin was. In some parts of Cieszyn Silesia, the name Nocnica was associated with beliefs in a specific class of demons, which were the souls of girls who died during the wedding announcement (or more precisely: after the announcement, but before the wedding). Descriptions of what they look like vary. Sometimes they were described as long-legged creatures living in the woods, dancing in a frenzy, or combing their hair with pine-cones. The folklorist Jan Broda described them as malicious demons of the female sex, dressed in white sheets and black dresses, appearing at night mainly in the wilderness (especially during Advent) and coming out of their hiding places to the sound of church bells, or after being summoned by a whistle. They were considered harmful to humans – they were said to come to cottages at night and harass small children, resulting in their crying and lack of sleep for the family. In the sermons of a Polish huzite we read that when the family was visiting a midwife, they would ask whether the child was a boy or a girl in order to properly protect the child from Nightmares, which pinch and frighten children and do not let them sleep. In the Mazowsze and Lubelszczyzna regions at the turn of the 19th and 20th century respectively, it was said that a child's cry at night was caused by *night-worms*, sometimes also called *Noclicami*.

Bohdan Baranowski reported that they were also credited with deceiving people, leading them into the wilderness, where they had to wander around for a long time, making it impossible or difficult for them to find their way.



## Northnica

*Northnica*, sometimes also *Mara*, or *Nocnica* – the latter a female demon in the Slavs, and also a kind of *Mermaid* known in the former borderlands of Poland. Although often exactly the same creature as the Nocnica, the folklore around the Northnica can also be different. It is a creature characterized by malice and mischief. From the name one can presume that it acts in the middle of the night. Northnica is a demon born from the soul of a deceased sinful woman or a woman who was wronged during her lifetime. A woman could also become a Northnica during her lifetime, for example, through the influence of strong negative emotions. According to some legends, a woman could turn into a midnight witch if she accidentally uttered the words *"zmoraś Mario"* (Mary's nightmare) during baptism or on her deathbed.

## Nosferatu or Nosferat

The earliest known written use of the term is found in 1865, in a German-language article by Wilhelm Schmidt, professor at the k.k. Staats-Gymnasium in Hermannstadt: *Das Jahr und Seine Tage in Meinung und Brauch der Rumänen*:

> *"Hieran reihe ich den Vampyr – nosferatu. Es ist dies die uneheliche Frucht zweier unehelich Gezeugter oder der unselige Geist eines durch Vampyre Getödteten, der als Hund, Katze, Kröte, Frosch, Laus, Floh, Wanze, kurz in jeder Gestalt erscheinen kann und wie der altslavische und böhmische Blkodlak, Vukodlak oder polnische Mora und russische Kikimora als Incubus oder Succubus – zburatorul – namentlich bei Neuverlobten sein böses Wesen treibt. Was hierüber vor mehr als hundert Jahren geglaubt und zur Abwehr geübt wurde, ist noch heute wahr, und es dürfte kaum ein Dorf geben, welches nicht im Stande wäre Selbsterlebtes oder doch Gehörtes mit der festen Überzeugung der Wahrheit vorzubringen."*

(To this I add the vampyr – nosferatu. This is the illegitimate fruit
of two illegitimately conceived persons or the unfortunate spirit of
a person killed by vampyres, which can appear as a dog, cat, toad,
frog, louse, flea, bug, in short in any shape and like the Old Slavic and
Bohemian Blkodlak, Vukodlak or Polish Mora and Russian Kikimora
as Incubus or Succubus – zburatorul – drives its evil nature especially
with newly engaged persons. What was believed about this more than
a hundred years ago and practiced to ward it off is still true today, and
there should hardly be a village that would not be able to present what
it has experienced itself or heard with the firm conviction of truth.)

Claude Lecouteux also regards Nosferat as a Revenant-umbrella-term
under which resort the *Murony*, *Strigoi*, *Muoiu* and *Stafiu*, but not as
a creature as such. *Nosferat(u)* is most likely a distorted derivate of
*Nesuferitu*, which was a euphemism for the Devil (literally: the one not to
be endured/unbearable/to be avoided), composed of the prefix *Ne-* (not)
and *suferit* (infinitive: *a suferi*, to endure). In modern Romanian the term
is still in use, although today it is no longer necessarily associated with
the Devil, but can also simply stand for a cursed person. It has also been
suggested that Nosferat(u) came from the demon *Nosophoros* (plague-
carrier) of Greek folk mythology, but this theory lacks contextual proof.



# O

## Oblakinia

*Oblakinia* or *Obłoczyca* (cloud-goddess) is a female blue skinned Serbo-
Croatian demon of the genus of *Vila*. She is a demon of small build, the
height of half an adult man. The proportions of the body do not differ
from those of an adult woman. She is quite slender, and moves lightly,
often floating in the air. Her face is slim, her head is held high and her
hair is straight and long, blue in color. She has large eyes with a blue
haze. She wears a silver spiral with a blue pebble around one ankle. Her
main occupation is sewing dresses. She makes them from snowflakes,
dewdrops, shreds of clouds, mists, threads of spiderwebs, and decorates
them with various small objects.

## Obot

The *Obot* or *Ubot* is a demon of insatiability in Azerbaijani, Turkish and
Altai folk beliefs. It is a type of *Ubir*. The creature is extremely hideous, with
large bones, fiery eyes and long fearsome teeth. They are never satisfied
with what they eat, as they immediately spit up everything they swallow.
They attract misfortune and cause people to lose all their wealth through
theft or swindling. Obot means as much as "eat, swallow, and destroy".

## Odmieniec

An *Odmieniec* (pl.: *Odmieńce*) also *Podrzut* (Tosser), *Odmienek, Podrzuc,
Podciep* – is a *changeling-child* that was, according to Slavic beliefs, tossed
by demons. Western European folklore includes beliefs in changelings as
children dropped off by *Fairies* or the Devil. In Slavic folklore, however,
an Odmieniec was a changeling-child of the demoness *Mamunas* or
*Dzvozons*, who took a human child, leaving young mothers with their
own. An Odmieniec was a demonic figure that had to be gotten rid of. A
child identified as a Odmieniec was starved, left at crossroads or dumps,
given water from an egg shell or beaten with birch rods. It was hoped that
the goddesses summoned by their crying would return the human child
and take their own. The Odmieniec was described, among other things,
as a *"devil with a big head"*, an ugly individual, loudly and constantly
shouting, with a big appetite, a big belly, not speaking intelligibly,
behaving violently and strangely. This description indicates symptoms
characteristic of various disabilities, for which the village community did
not find understanding and acceptance. There were cases of murder of
"altered" children, e.g. by drowning.

In Upper Silesia, Odmieniec was known under the names *Podciep,
Podciepek*. In the Opole region, it functioned under the name *Mamuna*.
In the Kraków area the name *Bogieniak* or *Bugieniak* was common. In
the villages of Podkarpacie it was common practice to bury a changeling
under a tin tub in the yard – the mother would hit it with a stick to
provoke the child to cry and thus summon goddesses. In the Mielec area,
a child changed by its mother was starved by boiling an egg shell in a
room with straw spread on the floor. The cry of a hungry changeling was
supposed to summon a demon and cause the child to be changed back
again. In the Kraków region, a changeling had to be beaten three times
with a willow rod in order to evoke pity from the *Mamuny* by its crying.

Similarly in the Wrocławia area there was a story of a peasant woman, whose child was swapped by a changeling in the field. After beating the changeling with a rod, the demon appeared with a human infant.

# Omacnica

*Omacnica* is a Slavic demon, a nightshade, moth, night spook, nocturnal parasite and a domestic female spirit. Omacnici were depicted as old women. They walked around in the dark of night. The boys were warned not to eat in the dark, because they could accidentally swallow the phantom, and then they would be insatiable and become gluttonous.



# Ördög

*Ördög* (*Ürdüng* in Old Hungarian and equivalent to *Erlik* in Turkic mythology) is a shape-shifting, demonic creature from Hungarian mythology and early Hungarian paganism, that controls the dark and evil forces of the world. After Christianization, it was identified with the Devil. In Hungarian mythology it is said that God (*Isten* in Hungarian) had help from Ördög when creating the world. Ördög often looks somewhat like a *Satyr* or *Faun*, a humanoid, with the upper torso of a human male and lower portions of a goat; usually pitch-black, with cloven hooves, ram-like horns, a long tail ending in a blade; and he carries a pitchfork. He can also be distinguished by his overly large phallus. He dwells in the underworld or hell (*Pokol* in Hungarian), constantly stirring a huge cauldron filled with souls of those who lived in sin (however, it is uncertain whether the underworld was regarded as a place of punishment in pre-Christian Hungarian mythology, or not, since the naming of it as Pokol developed after Christianization). When he does come to earth, according to some legends, he hides in the walls of its victims homes and makes subtle noises that sound high pitched and even squeaky. In other legends, when he comes to earth, he takes the form of a fox, a dark flame, or a Hungarian shepherd with dark, sparkling eyes. He likes to make bets with humans to see if they become corrupted. His long-term goal is to collect more human souls (*lelkek* in Hungarian).

**Etymology**
*Ördög* is – according to the Hungarian Etymological Dictionary – a word of unknown origin. However, the Altaic word forms *Erlik* and

*Erleg* are clearly related to it, and the sound changes l→d and k→g are phonetically unproblematic. The Turkish name means "emptiness", its original form is *Jerlik*, which is composed of the members *jer* (space, void) and *lik* (something like, -ness), the change *Jerlik→Erlik* fits in with the *je→e* changes common in Old Turkish. It may have been introduced into Mongolian mythology from the Turkic, because the word has no meaning in Mongolian, and is also found there in the form Jerleg. The form *Ürdüng*, which can be read in the funeral oration, confirms that *úr*, *üres* was translated into Hungarian in the sense of "space, empty", or that it underwent the same sound change as *jer→er→úr*.



# Ovinnik

The *Ovinnik (Ovinniy, Ovinniy batyushko, Ovinnushko, Podovinushko, Podovinnik, Zhikhar – Gumiennik* in Polish) is a malevolent male spirit of the threshing houses in traditional folk beliefs of the Eastern Slavs. He protects the harvests from any misfortune, trouble and evil and often gives a good thresh, but is also feared for burning down the threshing houses by setting fire to the grain. To placate him, peasants would offer him roosters and bliny. On New Year's Eve, the touch of an Ovinnik would determine their fortune for the New Year. A warm touch meant good luck and fortune, while a cold touch meant unhappiness. According to Slavic beliefs, the Ovinnik looks like a huge black cat, the size of a yard dog, with eyes burning like coals. However, he may also have other appearances, depending on the geographical location: in the Smolensk region for example, the Ovinnik appears in the guise of a ram, and in the Kostroma region he may take the form of a dead man.

The dwelling place of the Ovinnik is the barn (threshing floor). However, he may take "trips", for example to the bathhouse to visit the *Bannik*, or to any other place of the yard. The Ovinnik never enters the house: he cannot, because the house is the "area of responsibility" of the *Domovoy*, who is stronger than the Ovinnik. In different parts of Russia and Belarus people have different views on the creature's character, but all agree that the Ovinnik is a very complex creature. It is not easy to placate him, and in general he is quite hostile to humans. The Slavs explained this by the fact that stables in which an open fire was used for drying grain often burnt down, depriving peasant families of their subsistence, and sometimes even their home, because the burning stables often started to inflame the neighboring buildings. The Ovinnik is very fond of wrestling. He can wrestle with a Bannik but also with a man, and such wrestling usually does not end in favor of the latter. Despite his pyromaniac tendencies the Ovinnik is nevertheless classified as one of the "house-spirits", albeit the most fierce. His main function remains to manage the "area of responsibility", i.e. the threshing floor. He oversees the order of laying sheaves, how and when to flood the barn. He makes sure that the bread does not dry during long windy periods. The Ovinnik does not allow to flood the stable or barn on special holidays. According to the old country traditions, on those days stables should have a rest. If a peasant woman violates these centuries-old laws, the consequences can be most grievous, including the death of the "guilty" one. However, the Ovinnik also likes to make mischief for no reason. If he manages to hurt a man, he laughs, claps his hands or barks like a dog. People try to avoid quarrels with the Ovinnik. On his birthday pies and a rooster are brought to him. The rooster's head is cut off on the doorstep, blood is sprinkled in all the corners of the barn, and the pie is left in the basement. This method of pleasing the Ovinnik was however not used very often.

## The Ovinnik as a fortune teller

On the night of *Vasiliev Day* (New Year's Eve) girls, eager to know when their family life would start and what it would be like, put their naked buttocks out of the window of a dryer and waited. If the Ovinnik stroked a girls buttocks with a hairy hand their married life would be prosperous, if he stroked their butt with a smooth hand it would be poor and unfortunate. If the Ovinnik did not touch the girls behind at all, it was a sign that she would not be married in the coming year. There was also a less spectacular variant of this divination ritual whereby a hand was put into the drying room, waiting for a stroke, not the buttocks. According to tradition the Ovinnik can be seen during the Light Matins, an Orthodox or Byzantine morning service on Christmas Day, December 25th.

*Polevik* by Ivan Yakovlevich Bilibin (1876-1942)

# P

## Pasichnyk

Ukraine has possibly the highest concentration of surnames associated with honey and beekeeping. There are over a million of Ukrainians whose surnames are *Pasichnyk* or *Bortnyk* (beekeeper and honey hunter). They are descendants from those generations of Ukrainians who dedicated their lives to the noble craft of beekeeping. There is also a nature-spirit called the *Pasichnyk,* whose task it is to protect the bees and help them build their colonies.

## Perelesnyk

The *Perelesnyk* or *Litavets* is a figure in Ukrainian folk mythology and demonology, akin to an *Incubus*. He was believed to fly in the shape of a fiery dragon, or a young man, who enters homes through chimneys, doors or windows, and who seduces women by assuming the appearance of a deceased spouse or lover. The Perelesnyk has a female counterpart, *Perelesnytsia*, but she rarely appears in Ukrainian folk mythology.

## Pereplut

*Pereplut* is a rather mysterious deity or demon of the East Slavs with an unclear function, though it was probably a *water-spirit*. Pereplut appears in the list of gods and demons of the 15th century *Ruthenian Interpolation of the Word of St. Grigory*, as well as in the *Word of St. John*. According to this last source pagan Slavs worshiped deities or daemons like: *Vila, Mokosh, Dziwa, Perun, Hors, Rozhanitsy, ghosts* and Pereplut. Pereplut was most likely a daemon whose task it was to ensure prosperity when crossing a river, hence his identification as a water deity, which is supported by the etymology of the words *pere- "through"* and *pluti- "to flow"*.

## Permonik

*Permoník* (pl.: *Permoníci*) is a dwarfish mine-daemon inhabiting and guarding mines in Czech and Slovak folklore. Especially in mining areas such as Kladno, Příbram, Kutnohorsko and Oslavsko the miners believed in Permoníci. The closest counterparts of Permonik are the various other mountain and mining spirits in other Slavic countries, like the *Karzełek,* or the Polish and Lusatian-Serbian *Ludeks,* sometimes referred to as *Lutkas* in Slovakia. They also merge with *Gnomes* and the German *Kobolds.* Permonik is derived from the German *Bergmännchen* (little mountain men) and appears in a number of variants: *Permon, Perkmon, Pergmon* (Příbram) or *Perkmont* (Jílové). From the German *Berggeist* (mountain-spirit) comes the term *Perjkast,* used in Kladno. Elsewhere there are names that do not derive from German, such as mining spirits in the Ráchymov region, and *Skarbnik, Pustecký, Fantana, Sosna* and *Klimek* in the Silesian Ostrava region.



Permoníci are characterized by their large head, broad shoulders and short legs, they are dressed like miners and carry a lantern in their hand. Their discovery either heralds misfortune or the discovery of a vein of precious metal. Hearing them work brings good luck. When a miner met a Permoník, he was to greet it with a loud and immediate *"Zdař Bůh!"* (Hail God!) and if the creature got in his way and refused to move, he was to creep up between its legs. Permoníci could be pleased and calmed by sacrifices and the observance of mining customs, and angered mainly by whistling and other noises, or by disregarding their commands and prohibitions.


## Pikòn

*Pikòn* is a Kashubian mischievous spirit, the perpetrator of hairballs and disabilities, usually summoned or sent away by witches.


## Pipa

Pipa (from *pipa;* pipe; barrel high and narrow; quill, coil) is the name of a fire-breathing domestic demon or *household-spirit* in Polish folklore (region Baborów).


## Pitsen or Pitsyn

In the folklore of the Siberian Tatars, the *Pitsen, Pitzen* or *Pitsyn* was a *nature-spirit* – the master of the forest. It was believed that the Pitsen could both bring good luck and cause evil, leading travelers off track into the wilderness. He is usually represented as a man (in particular, as a stately old man with a long staff and a bag on his shoulders) or in the shape of an animal, like some sort of ape, although the Pitsen could change itself into all kinds of creatures. Pitsen were thought to live in abandoned hunting huts. They love horses, ride them, tangle their manes and smear resin on them. In the guise of a beautiful woman, the Pitsen may enter into a love affair with a man. One of the stories about the Pitsen tells that once a hunter met a woman in the woods. He married her and lived richly. One day, when he came home early, instead of his beautiful wife, he saw a monster with fangs protruding from her mouth. She took lizards out of her loose hair and was eating them. The hunter cried out in horror, and at once everything was lost – his wife and his wealth.

In the mythologies of other Turkic peoples, Pitsen correspond to the *Arsuri* of the Chuvash, the *Shurale* of the Kazan Tatars and Bashkirs. The Tobolsk and Omsk Tatars are close to the hairy, unpleasant smelling *Yysh-keshe* (forest people), who lure travelers into the woods and marry them.


## Płamęta

*Płamęta* is a mischievous, malicious *House-Goblin*, from 19th century beliefs in the Tarnobrzeg area (Southeast Poland). He is depicted as a small creature in an almost human form, naked, with sparse hair, a large head and a wide laughing mouth. Instead of hands it had bird claws, and instead of feet, hooves. He always hid under a deer broom, the kind made from the stems of the common broom *(Cytisus scoparius)*. He was invisible to humans, and would interfere with their work, for example by putting his foot in the way. He was messy and made a mess on the farm. The broom under which he sat was taken and swung in all directions in order to ward off the fleas; when he continued to fuss, one merely said goodbye with a cross and left the room.


## Plonek

*Plonek* (Old Polish: *plon* – profit, harvest) was a *household-spirit*, resembling a black rooster, who lived in the barn. He appeared in the folk tales of central Poland (Kalisz, Wieluń, Olesno). People believed he multiplied the possessions of his followers by bringing them piles of grain; always the same sort as he never mixed different kinds of grain. A plank was left loose in the gable wall of the building so that the creature would have no trouble entering. It was fed every day and the information about its favorite dish was kept secret and passed down from generation to generation. If treated well, the demon was able to serve for many years. However, like most domestic spirits he disliked lazy and idle farmers. When annoyed he began messing around, made noises or destroyed the crops.

## Plunek



In the folk beliefs of Greater Poland, Sieradz and Pomerania, the *Plunek* is a domestic guardian demon, that could multiply the possessions of the householder. Plunek was usually depicted as a bird.

## Pokuć

In folk beliefs of various regions of Poland, *Pokuć* is a small ghost inhabiting the nooks and crannies of cottages (most often behind the stove or near the threshold), stables and barns. People tried to maintain his friendliness by putting small amounts of food into various nooks and crannies, which would soon disappear (e.g. eaten by mice).

## Polevik

*Polevik, Polevoy* (Belarus: *Palyavík*, Ukrain: *Polovik*) is a *field-spirit*, sometimes nicknamed *Yaroslavl* (field master) in the folklore of the East Slavs. He is described mainly as a humanoid creature with individual animal, plant and demonic features, who is sometimes accompanied by a strong wind and sparks or lights. It was generally believed that there lives only one Polevik in every separate field, which dwells in various irregularities of the terrain. The creature is believed to be most active at noon or sunset and on hot summer-days. The Polevik guarded the field, influenced its fertility and the well-being of the cattle grazing on it. In some places a Polevik was approached with a request to look after the grazing cattle, and in some places gifts were brought to him so that he would favor a good harvest. The Polevik has however a double nature. It could also be very hostile to humans. According to local beliefs they lead wandering people in a field astray or give them diseases. If a person falls asleep on the job after drinking, the Polevik might murder them. Appeasing the Polevik requires two eggs, a rooster, a toad, and a crow placed in a ditch when no one is looking.

The Polevik could appear as a long-legged peasant, covered with fiery fur, with bulging eyes, horns, a long tail with a brush at the end, a beard of ears. Ukrainians also thought he had ears like a calf, claws, large teeth and wings. In Novgorod province it was thought that the Polevik was dressed all in white and that he was gray-haired. Also in Ukraine it was imagined that he was all white as snow, or that he was an old man with a white beard. In Belarus, the Polevik was depicted in long clothes, with booted feet and a cane in his hands. In the Oryol province, on the contrary, he was described as a naked man, black as earth, with grass as hair and multicolored eyes, like a personification of the field itself. In *bylihkas* (real-like stories – *bylichka* means "wonderful encounters with all kinds of super-natural creatures") a Polevik can take the form of both a young person or an ugly little old man, can pretend to be a familiar or an animal (such as a bull or goat) and can change his height depending on the surrounding vegetation. The Polevik is able to speak in a human voice. Like most field-spirits, a Polevik was thought to be accompanied by a strong gusty wind, a whirlwind. Sometimes windy weather was associated with a Polevik blowing or whistling. The Polevik is also associated with the fire element, so in Yaroslavl province it was believed that he whizzes through the village on a troika before a house or barn catches fire. The Polevik can move very quickly, which makes a person think that he sees flying sparks passing by. According to other folklore sources, the Polevik looks like a small man in the daytime, and at night like a flickering fire. M.N. Vlasova and, following her, E.L. Madlevskaya believe that the Polevik is associated with the Fire-element and the movement of the sun, with noon and the time of summer and additional the prosperity of the earth. He personified midday light and heat, contributing to the growth of crops, but could also manifest the destructive nature of fire.

## Pólnica

*Pólnica* is a Kashubian female *field-spirit*, active in the summer. As a beautiful girl, adorned with a garland, she rides a horse around the fields and makes sure that the plants grow well. A man who sees her sometimes dies of longing.

# Poludnitsa

*Poludnitsa* (from Russian: *Polden* or *Poluden*, "half-day" or "mid-day")
is a female Slavic demon, common to the various countries of eastern
Europe and related to *Lady Midday*. She is referred to as *Południca* in
Polish, *Полудница (Poludnitsa)* in Serbian, Bulgarian and Russian,
*Polednice* in Czech, *Poludnica* in Slovak, *Připołdnica* in Upper Sorbian,
and *Полозница (Poloznicha)* in Komi, *Chirtel Ma* in Yiddish. The plural
form of this word is *Poludnitsy (or Poludnici)*. Poludnitsa is a noon
demon in Slavic mythology. She can be referred to in English as *Lady
Midday, Noon Wraith* or *Noon Witch*. She was usually pictured as a young
woman dressed in white, that roamed field bounds. She assailed folk
working at noon causing heat strokes and aches in the neck, sometimes
she even caused madness. Among the Lusatian's, under the name of
*Prezpolnica* or *Pripolnica*, she appears in the fields exactly at mid-day, on
hot summer days, taking the form of whirling dust clouds and holding a
sickle in her hand. She may also appear as an old hag, a beautiful woman,
or a 12-year-old girl, and she was useful in scaring children away from
valuable crops. There she addresses any woman whom she finds tarrying
afield instead of returning home for mid-day repose, and questions her
on the cultivation and the spinning of flax, cutting off the head or giving
her victim a sun-stroke if she is not satisfied with the answers. She seems
to be akin to the demon *Meridianus, "the sickness that destroyeth in the
noonday."* It is worthy of remark that the Russian peasants make use of
a verb, *Poludnovat*, to express the action of drawing one's last breath –
*"His soul in his body scarcely poludnoet"*, they say. There is also a Slavic
tradition that tells of the *Twelve Midnight Sisters (Polunochnitsas)*, who
attack children, and force them to cry out with pain.

## Other Poludnitsa/Lady Midday-varieties

In Wendish mythology, *Přezpołdnica* (in Lower Sorbian) *Připołdnica*
(in Upper Sorbian) she is known as *Mittagsfrau (Lady Midday)* among
German speakers of Eastern Germany's Lusatia and in the now only
German-speaking parts of what used to be the larger region of Old
Lusatia. Further north and west in formerly predominantly Slavic-
speaking areas of Germany, especially in the state of Brandenburg, a
related mythological spirit appears to be the *Roggenmuhme (Lady of
the Rye)* that makes children disappear when they search for flowers
among the tall grain stalks on hot summer days. In the Altmark, it is the
*Regenmöhme* that will abduct ill-behaved children, and in the formerly

Polabian-speaking region around Lunenburg (German Lüneburg) in Lower Saxony, the name of this demon is *Kornwief* or *Kornwyf*, meaning "wheat-woman". In the vicinity of Prudnik in Upper Silesia, people believed in the *Cornflower Ghost* (Polish *Chabernica*), a demon similar to Lady Midday. She was usually pictured as a young slim woman dressed in azure with cornflowers in her hair, that roamed field bounds during midday. She was angered by people who trampled the grain or used sharp tools. Those, who she thought deserved punishment, were put to sleep with her whisper, after which she caused them headache, paralysis or low back pain. Sometimes she attacked her victims by breaking their arms, legs or neck. To avoid the wrath of the Cornflower Ghost, a worker had to take a break from work during the midday and do the Angelus-prayer.



## Poroniec

In Slavic beliefs, the soul of an aborted child or spent fetus, became a *Poroniec*, as well as a child born dead, or killed by its mother shortly after birth, or not buried according to custom. In Scandinavia the creature is called a *Myling*. The Poroniec is a malicious, hostile and extremely powerful demon, due to the potential of unrealized life present in them. Many taboos concerning pregnant women and women in the postnatal period were connected with the belief in the Poroniec and the prevention of creating one. These included the prohibition to look into a well and draw water from it, the prohibition to leave the house with the newborn (especially in the field), and the prohibition to have sexual intercourse while pregnant. A newborn child was subjected to a number of magical practices, such as wiping it with a straw bundle. It was only after the sixth week of life that the midwife left the house of the newborn, and the child became a human being that was given a name. A miscarried child buried under the threshold of a house as a burial sacrifice became a sympathetic Poroniec and did not turn into an abortion victim or evil entity.

## Poświst

In Polish folklore the *Poświst* (also: *Pochwist*, *Pogwizd*, *Poświściel*) is a pre-Christian Slavic nature-spirit personifying wind and whirlwinds. The Poświst drove away storm clouds and dried the fields. After Christianization he was transformed into an evil air-demon.

## Potercha

In Ukrainian folk-belief the *Potercha* is the ghost of a dead (unbaptized) child who's voice sounds like that of a frog. They usually resemble rotting versions of their living selves, dwelling in deep rivers and lakes all across Ukraine and other Slavic territories or fly around – often tormented by other spirits, taking the form of an owl or a stork. They can also appear as the *Will-o'-the-wisp* leading people into swamps as eerie flashing lights.

## Pricolici



In Romanian folklore *Pricolici* (pl. & sing.) were the spirits of evil people who – similar to *Strigoi* – rose from the grave, but always in the shape of a wolf or dog, and less frequently as other wild animals. They could also be living men capable of turning into wolves or dogs for a while, or the souls of dead men or *Revenants* who turned into dogs, which people feared as the Devil, and afterwards became men again. Or they were *demons* that turned into dogs and cats, lynxes or other animals, that could also be evil spirits in the form of wild beasts descended from wolves, that had devoured man (the latter were called *Tricolici*). Children born with a tail or marks on their heads signifying devil horns; one brother of a twin from the ninth childbirth in the family; a person who accidentally drank wolf urine; children of incest between father and daughter or mother and son, were also thought to become a Pricolici.

Pricolici were depicted with a tail, claws and covered with wolf hair, they have a sharp dog face with long ears, front paws longer than hind paws or vice versa, and a gray ruffled withers like a hyena. According to some accounts, one half of their body is like a man and the other half like an animal (dog, bull, bear, badger). They may look like a large black dog with a white chest or like a white wolf with a long tail. They could become leaders of wolf packs, to help them find their prey, and to distribute it among them. Pricolici have some of the traits of *Vampires*, such as their bloodthirstiness. It was believed that if a Pricolici was wounded and he sucked up his own spilled blood, he would become human again, but the wound would remain, and that if a Pricolici was bitten by a dog, he would also become human, but his body would continue to grow a fur. The etymology of the word is unknown; although it probably has Dacian origins. Malicious, violent men are often said to become Pricolici after death, in order to continue harming other humans. Some Romanian

*Werewolf devouring a woman*, 19th century engraving, Mansell Collection, London

folklore delineates that Pricolici are Werewolves in life and after they die, return as *Vampires*. This also gives rise to the legend of Vampires that can turn into animals such as wolves, dogs, or owls and bats. The common theme of all these animals being that they are nocturnal hunters, much like Vampires. Even in modern times, many people living in rural areas of Romania have claimed to have been viciously attacked by abnormally large and fierce wolves. Apparently, these wolves attack silently, unexpectedly and only choose solitary targets. Victims of such attacks often claim that their aggressor wasn't an ordinary wolf, but a Pricolici that has come back to life to continue wreaking havoc. Pricolici are also depicted in Romanian folklore as children with boundless energy, who like to do nothing but mischief and bring harm to other people, and also to animals; making cattle stop giving milk, chickens stop laying eggs, harass dogs, etc.



## Prigirstitis

*Prigirstitis* is a *household-spirit* of the Polish people; he was a special kind of *Domovoy*, believed to have extraordinary fine hearing, enabling him to hear even the slightest murmur.

## Psoglav

*Psoglav* (Serbian: Псоглави, literally "dog head") is a legendary demonic creature in Serbian mythology. The belief in its existence also extended to parts of Bosnia and Montenegro through Slovenia. The Psoglav is depicted with a human body, horse hooves instead of feet, a dog's head with iron teeth, and a single eye located on its forehead. The creature was said to live in caves or dark places without sunlight that contained many precious stones. He was said to be a man-eater that even dug up rotting bodies from their graves to eat them. In Croatian the term is *Psoglavac*, and in Slovene it is *Psoglavec*. There are many legends about these creatures, especially in the Istrian region of Croatia.

## Pùrtk

*Pùrtk* is a Kashubian evil demon of squabbles and quarrels as well as stench, itch and stupidity, residing in cloacal pits, dung and manure pits.

# Pustecki

*Pustecki* (Polish: *Pustecki*; Czech: *Pustecký*) is a spirit from folk beliefs of Těšín Silesia, inhabiting coal mines in the Karviná region. Pustecki acts as a kind of treasurer. He looks like a miner, in uniform, often a foreman with a long gray beard. He has a gold carbide lamp on his helmet emitting red light and holds a silver pickax in his hands. He could also take the form of animals, such as a frog, or turn himself into a mouse which squeals a lot. In character, Pustecki is associated with the *Skarbnik*. Pustecki was a good and caring spirit. In legends he often rewarded poor miners for their good heart and hard work with gold or money, and he also helped those who were lost underground. He also took care of the souls of those who died while working in the mines. However, he did not tolerate certain behaviors, including whistling in the mines, that he punished. Pustecki also appeared on the surface to warn miners on their way to work of impending disasters.

# R

## Raróg

In Slavic mythology and folklore a *Raróg* or *Raraszek* is a demonic spirit of fire, manifesting itself in the form of a predatory bird (most often a falcon), a fiery dragon or a fiery whirlwind. It was believed that a Raróg could hatch from an egg that would be brooded by a human for nine days. Most probably, the Raróg was an incarnation of the Slavic fire and smithing-god *Swarog*, as indicated by the similarity of the name and a similar motif of depicting the demiurge in the form of a bird, found in Baltic and Finnish mythology. In popular culture, the Raróg survived in the form of a tiny demon (able to fit into a pocket), which brought people luck.

## Rétnik

*Rétnik* is a Kashubian demon that deceived people with magical music. He was also known to throw enchanted instruments to musicians or to put a spell on their own instruments. He was particularly active during Lent and Advent, when playing was forbidden.

## Rokita

*Rokita* is the name of a famous devil in Polish folk tales. He is characterized by unimaginable strength, but is not very cunning. He inhabits areas that are associated with gates to the afterlife. These include swamps, forests, and above all, the interiors of old willows. In Silesia, Rokita was called *Wodnegomąż*, a *water demon* who lives in ponds, rivers, wells and other moist places or water reservoirs. In Zagłębie Dąbrowskie, a *water-spirit* (*utoplok*) could take the form of a powerful man, a horse, a fish or a bird. These forms not only coincide with the forms taken by Rokita, but also the forms taken by *Boruta*. Rokita is often treated as the equivalent of the latter, depicted as a general, wearing a golden coat, or a hat and a frock-coat. It was also a popular story here that he appeared in animal forms, such as: a pig, a bird, a fish, a horse, a dog, a mouse. Regardless of the form taken, whether human or animal, he is characterized by hostile intentions towards people.

## Legends

One of the legends says that Rokita was a very generous robber from Domaradz. He lived on the mountain Chyb with other robbers. He would rob merchants coming to Domaradz and give the stolen goods to peasants. According to another legend, Rokita, otherwise known as *Rokietnik*, was an evil soul who lived in the marshes (hence his name, derived from the moss of the rocket plant often found in Central European forests) to drown those who trespassed on his habitat. There is also a legend that describes him as the *Diabłem Kaliskim* (The Devil of Kalisz) competing with Boruta.

One folktale tells a story where Rokita and Boruto are playing a prank on an innkeeper. Rokita, together with Boruta, went to an inn in Łódź to drink beer there. They were really thirsty and drank a lot of beer. The innkeeper was worried about this and wondered if the guests could pay for such an amount. So he told them that he would not serve them another beer until they had paid for the beers they had already consumed. Rokita only laughed and threw some gold coins on the floor and demanded that the innkeeper would bring them more beer. When he returned with more beer and tried to pick up the gold coins thrown by the devils, it turned out that they were burning his skin with fire. The innkeeper screamed in pain and heard the devils' laughter coming from clouds of smoke where his guests had been sitting just a moment ago. The beer he had brought a moment before had already been drunk, and no trace of the coins remained.



## Rokita's death

The village of Błędowy, which belongs to the parish of Chmielnik village, located a mile and a half from Rzeszów, has its own Rokita-legend. In that village there lived a poor peasant who wanted to hide his financial despair from his wife, so one day he left his home and ran to a steep rock. Standing there, he began to talk aloud about how miserable and rotten his life had become. While he was wailing and crying, Rokita rose before him. At first the peasant was frightened by this figure, but after a while he decided that Rokita was not so terrible. The demon offered him a lot of money, without any interest. His only condition was that on a fixed day and time the peasant had to pay him back every penny. If not, Rokita would take his soul. The villager accepted the offer and politely thanked him, after which the devil disappeared. After some time, the farmer made a considerable sum of money. When it was time to repay the debt, he went to the same place where he had met Rokita the first time and started calling him. In response, another devil told him that Rokita was no longer there. He had been killed by the Blessed Virgin. So the villager returned home without having given the money to anyone, as Rokita was already dead. From then on, people started calling the villager and his family "Rokita's family" by the name of Rokita, and this nickname is used by several families descending from his family.

**Folk beliefs**
Rokita was believed to be able to take the form of a cat. The witches' incantations specifically asked him for an abundance of cows so that they would give more milk. This was an extremely important matter for the people because, in the face of the ever-present threat of famine, a lack of milk became a folk obsession. This is why a whole range of beliefs arose on this subject. These included incantations and prayers addressed to Rokita, as the patron saint of dairy products and milk, and also functioned as proverbs for the kitchen. It is known that on *Zielone Świątki* [1] during a dew-gathering ritual, witches would knock on a bushy willow, saying to Rokita: *"Rokita, give me some milk, I'll give you my body and soul because I'm thirsty for milk"*. The incantation resulted in a rhyme which was repeated by the housewives in the kitchen:

*"Był sobie raz diabeł Rokita i przyszła do niego kobita.*
*Oddaje mu duszę i ciało. Bo jej się mleka zachciało."*

(Once there was a devil Rokita and a woman came to him. She gave him her body and soul. Because she was thirsty for milk.)

When Rokita accepted the sacrifice consisting of the woman's soul, he would come out of the swamp in the form of a cat and start purring contentedly.

---

1    *Zielone Świątki* (Green week – Russian: Зелёные святки, Ukrainian: Зелені свята, Polish: Zielone świątki) is an ancient Slavic fertility festival celebrated in early June and closely linked with the cult of the dead and the spring agricultural rites. In Russian villages, the seven weeks after Easter were a time of festivity, and Green Week took place during the seventh week leading up to Pentecost. Green week is followed by Trinity week (Russian: Троицкие святки) in Russia, which is also called Whitsuntide week in Britain. The end of Semik inaugurated the celebrations of Trinity Sunday, which came three days later.

## Rokitnik

According to Kashubian folk beliefs, *Rokitnik* is a mischievous demon
causing winds. He was imagined as a human figure with bat wings. His
name probably comes from *rokicina* (an old term for the rosemary-leaved
willow, *Salix rosmarinifolia*), in which he used to sit, making pipes from
its twigs.

## Rozhanitsy

The *Rozhanitsy* (also: *Narecnitsy, Sudzhenitsy*) are daemons or deities
of fate in the pre-Christian religion of the Slavs and are known by
many regional name variants: Croatian: *Rodjenice, Rojenice, Roženice,
Sudice, Sudjenice, Sujenice*; Slovene: *Rodjenice, Rojenice, Sudice, Sojenice,
Sujenice*; Bulgarian: *Sudženici, Naručnici, Orisnici, Urisnici, Uresici*;
Czech and Slovak: *Rodjenice, Sudjenice, Sudičky*; Polish: *Rodzanice,
Narecznice, Sudiczki*; Romanian: *Ursitoare*; Serbian: *Suđaje, Suđenice,
Rođenice, Narečnici*; Old East Slavic/Russian: *Rožanice, Udělnicy*. The
terms *Rodzanica, Rodjenica* or *Rojenica* come from word *roditi* (giving
birth) and literally mean "woman giving birth". *Sudiczka, Sudica*, or
*Sojenica* come from the word *sud* (judgment, judge, court) and literally
mean "judging woman". *Narecznica, Nerechnitsa, Narucnica* means
"name giving woman". *Udelnica* means "granting woman". The Bulgarian
terms *Orisnici, Urisnici, Uresici* come from the Greek word ὁρίζοντες
(orizontes – "establish") and mean "establishing woman".

Rozhanitsy are female beings who determine the fate of a child at birth
– related to the three manifestations of the goddess *Moira* (*Clotho,
Lachesis* and *Atropos*) of the ancient Greeks. Usually there are three
Rozhanitsy, known mainly among the southern Slavs. Separate mentions
of Suzhonitsya are found in Czech, Slovak and in the western Ukrainian
regions. With the Eastern Slavs the Rozhanitsy were mentioned in church
denunciatory literature directed against pagans. After Christianization
the Rozhanitsy were replaced by the Mothers of God or Saint Women.
In Russia *Parascheva, Anastasia* and *Barbara* are mentioned, and in
Bulgarian folklore *Maria*, Parascheva and Anastasia. Angels or even
*Christ* Himself also took over the functions of Rozhanitsy. In Poland the
sisters of fate were worshipped as the *Zorze*. Medieval Russian teachings
against paganism, together with the Rozhanitsy also mention *Rod*, with
whom they acted as patrons of the family and the giver of fortune to

descendants. Slavists of the late nineteenth and early twentieth centuries were of the opinion that Rod was the proper name of a forgotten Slavic god. In the 1970s-1990s the reconstruction of the pantheon proposed by B.A. Rybakov, Rod becomes the main Slavic deity. However, according to the majority of scientific research, Rod (as well as Rozhanitsy) was an East Slavic deity or spirit-guardian of kin and destiny.

Rozhanitsy are similar and sometimes mixed up with South Slavic *Vilas*, *Samodivas* (Orisnitsa), *Yudas*; West Slavic goddesses, *Veshtitsa*; as well as demons harming women in labor and their newborns, and demons of disease. Often they appear together with other demons. In some folklore traditions it is believed that if the Rozhanitsy would not come, the child could be taken by an evil force. In preparation for the coming of the three women of fate the family prepared a meal three nights in a row, the house was cleaned, candles and flowers were put on the table, and everyone dressed up in clean fine clothing. Various symbols of a prosperous life were placed in the cradle, like money, wine and bread to be nourished, basil to be healthy, etc. It was believed the Rozhanitsy could give the child a gift (a toy) determining its future fate. In some other folklorist traditions however the Rozhanitsy were feared as harmful creatures and measures for protection of the baby were taken. The family would then lock the windows and doors and not go out after sunset. An old woman was to sit by the woman in labor and her baby all night long to protect them from the Rozhanitsy who tried to deceive the women by taking the child to another house and putting a doll in its place.

## Rusalka

The *Rusalka* (Русалка: Mermaid; pl.: *Rusalki*) is a female *water-spirit* of East Slavic mythology. The concept of the *Mermaid* that exist in the Russian North, in the Volga region, in the Urals, in Western Siberia, differ significantly from the Western Russian and Southern Russian ones. It was believed that Mermaids/Rusalki looked after fields, forests and waters. Before the twentieth century, in the northern provinces of Russia, the word русалка was perceived as "bookish", "scholarly". Earlier this character was known as *Vodyanitsa*, *Vodyaniha* or *Vodyantikha* (Russian: водяни́ца, водяни́ха, водянти́ха; meaning: she from the water or the Water-Maiden), *Kupalka* (Russian: купа́лка; bather), *Shutovka* (Russian: шуто́вка; joker, jester or prankster) and *Loskotukha*, *Shchekotukha* or

*Shchekotunya* (Russian: лоскотýха, щекотýха, щекотýнья; tickler or she who tickles). In southern Russia and Ukraine, the Rusalka was called a *Mavka* and the Serbian *Vilas* are also akin to the Rusalki. Specifics pertaining to Rusalki differed among regions with regards to their looks or behavior. In most tales they lived without men. In stories from Ukraine, they were often linked with water. In Belarus they were linked with the forest and field. In Poland and Czech Republic, water-Rusalki/*Rusalky* were younger and fair-haired, while the forest-Rusalki looked more mature and had black hair – but in both cases, if someone looked up close, their hair turned green, and their faces became distorted. In Polish folklore, the term Rusalka could also stand for *Boginka*, *Dziwożona* and various other entities. In some beliefs, Rusalki were attributed the ability to change into *Werewolves* or other were-animals. It was believed, for example, that they could take the form of squirrels, rats, frogs, birds (Ukraine), or appear as a cow, horse, calf, dog, hare and other animals (Poland).

## Ethymology
The origin of the name Rusalka seems to be doubtful. According to W.R.S. Ralston (1828-1889) who is the main source for this Rusalka-paragraph, it appears to be connected with *rus*, an old Slavonic word for a stream, or with *ruslo* (the bed of a river), and with several other kindred words, such as *rosá* (dew), that refer to water. Another theory states that Rusalka derives from *rusalija* which entered the Slavic languages via the Byzantine Greek *rousália* (Medieval Greek: ρουσάλια), from the Latin *Rosālia* as a name for Pentecost and the days adjacent to it. Longstanding, likely pre-Christian, annual traditions resulted in that time of year being associated with spirits (*navki, mavki*) which were subsequently named after this holiday.

## The changing image of the Rusalka
Rusalki are generally represented in the form of beauteous maidens with full and snow-white bosoms, and with long and slender limbs. Their feet are small, their eyes are wild, their faces are fair to see, but their complexion is pale, their expression anxious. Their hair is long and thick and wavy, and green as grass. Their dress is either a covering of green leaves, or a long white shift, worn without a girdle. At times they emerge from the waters of the lakes or rivers in which they dwell, and sit upon its banks, combing and plaiting their flowing locks, or they cling to a mill-wheel; and turn round with it, amid the splash of the stream. If anyone happens to approach, they fling themselves into the waters, and there

divert themselves, and try to allure the person to join them. Whomsoever they manage to get hold of, they tickle them to death. Only witches can bathe with them unhurt. According to folklorist and scholar Vladimir Yakovlevich Propp (1895-1970) the original "Rusalka" was an appellation used by pagan Slavic peoples, who linked her with fertility and did not consider her evil before the 19th century. Rusalki came out of the water in the spring to transfer life-giving moisture to the fields and thus helped nurture the crops. In 19th century versions, a Rusalka becomes an unquiet, dangerous being that is no longer alive, associated with the unclean spirit. According to linguist and ethnographer Dmitry Konstantinovich Zelenin (1878-1954), young women, who either committed suicide by drowning due to an unhappy marriage (they might have been jilted by their lovers or abused and harassed by their much older husbands) or who were violently drowned against their will (especially after becoming pregnant with unwanted children), must live out their designated time on Earth as Rusalki. The initial Slavic lore suggests though that not all Rusalki occurrences were linked with death by drowning; it is accounted by most stories that the soul of a young woman who had died in or near a river or lake would come back to haunt those waters. This undead Rusalka is not invariably malevolent, and can be allowed to die in peace if her death is avenged. Her main purpose is, however, to lure young men, seduced by either her looks or her voice into the depths, where she would entangle their feet with her long hair and submerge them. Her body would instantly become very slippery and not allow the victim to cling on to her body in order to reach the surface. She would then wait until the victim had drowned, or on some occasions, tickle them to death, while she laughed. It is also believed, by a few accounts, that Rusalki can change their appearance to match the tastes of the men they are about to seduce.

**Rusalka as Mermaid and Washerwoman**
In certain districts bordering on the sea the people used to believe in marine Rusalki, who are supposed, in some places, as for instance around Astrakhan, to raise storms and vex shipping. But as a general rule the Rusalki are seen in Russia as haunting lakes and streams, at the bottom of which they usually dwell, in crystal halls radiant with gold and silver and precious stones. Sometimes, however, they are not so sumptuously housed, but have to make for themselves nests out of straw and feathers collected during the Green Week, the seventh week after Easter. If a Rusalka's hair becomes dry, she dies, and therefore she is generally afraid

of going far from the water, unless she has a comb with her. As long as she has a comb – usually a fish bone – she can always produce a flood by passing it through her waving locks. In some places Rusalki are fond of spinning, in others they are given to washing linen. During the week before Whitsuntide, as many songs testify, they sit in trees and ask for linen garments. Up to the present day in Little-Russia, it is customary at that time of year to hang shifts and rags and skeins of thread on the boughs of oaks and other trees, all intended as a present to the Rusalki. In White-Russia the peasants affirm that during that week the forests are traversed by naked women and children, and whoever meets them, if one wishes to escape a premature death, must fling them a handkerchief, or some scrap torn from one's clothes.



**Relation to seasons and holidays**

On the approach of winter the Rusalki disappeared, and did not show themselves again until the next spring. In Belarus they were supposed to appear on the Thursday in Holy Week, a day which folklore stated was dear to them, as well as to many other spiritual beings. In Ukraine the Thursday before Whitsuntide is called the *Great Day* (or Easter Sunday) *of the Rusalki*. During the days called the Green Week at Whitsuntide, when every home is adorned with boughs and green leaves, no one dared to work for fear of offending the Rusalki. Especially women had to abstain from sewing or washing linen; and men from weaving fences and the like, such occupations too closely resembling those of the supernatural weavers and washers. It was chiefly at that time that the spirits left their watery abodes, and went strolling about the fields and forests, continuing to do so until the end of June. All that time their voices could be heard in the rustling or sighing of the breeze, and the splash of running water betrayed their dancing feet. At that time the peasant-girls went into the woods, and threw garlands to the Rusalki, asking for rich husbands in return, or floated the garlands down a stream, seeing in their movements omens of future happiness or sorrow.

It was believed that after St. Peter's day, June 29, the Rusalki danced by night beneath the moon, and in Belarus and Galicia, where Rusalki (or Mavki as they are there called) have danced, circles of a darker green, and richer grass are found in the fields. Sometimes they induced a shepherd to play music for them. All night long they danced to the shepherd's music: in the morning a hollow marks the spot where his foot had been, while

he was playing. Sometimes a man would encounter Rusalki that began
to writhe and contort themselves after a strange fashion. Involuntarily
he imitated their gestures, which left him deformed for the rest of his
life, or made him a victim to St. Vitus' dance. Anyone who stepped upon
the linen the Rusalki had laid out to dry, lost all his or her strength, or
became a cripple, and those who desecrated the *Rusalnaya* (Rusalki
Week) by working, were punished by the loss of their cattle and poultry.
At times the Rusalki enticed into their haunts both youths and maidens,
and tickled them to death, or strangled or drowned them.

## Rusalki as field-spirits

In many parts of Russia (North, Wolga and Ural regions) the Rusalki
had much to do with the harvest, sometimes making it plenteous, and at
other times ruining it by rain and wind. The farmers in Belarus believed
that the Rusalki dwelled amid the standing corn. It was believed that on
Whitsunday Eve they went out to the corn-fields, and there, with joyous
singing and clapping of hands, they scampered through the rye or hung
on to its stalks, and swinged to and fro, so that the corn undulated as
if beneath a strong wind. In some parts of Russia there, immediately
after the end of the Whitsuntide festival, a ceremony of expelling the
Rusalki was performed. On the first Monday of *St. Peter's Fast* (begins
on the second Monday after Pentecost and takes 8 to 42 days) a figure
made of straw was draped in woman's clothes, so as to represent a Rusalki.
Afterwards a *Khorovod* was formed (an East Slavic pagan circle dance and
chorus singing combination), and the assembled company went out to the
fields with dance and song, she who held the straw Rusalka in her hand
bounding about in the middle of the choral circle. On arriving at the fields,
the singers formed two bodies; one attacked the figure, while the other
defended it. Eventually the Rusalka-puppet was torn to pieces, and the
straw of which it was made was thrown to the winds. Then the performers
returned home, saying they had expelled the Rusalka. In the district of
Tula the women and girls went out to the fields during the Green Week
and chased the Rusalka, who was supposed to be stealing the grain.
Having made a straw figure, they took it to the banks of a stream and flung
it into the water. In some districts the young people ran about the fields
on Whitsunday Eve, waving brooms, and crying, *"Pursue! pursue!"*. W.R.S.
Ralston's wrote in his *Songs of the Russian People* that there were people
who affirmed that they had seen the hunted Rusalki running out of the
corn-fields into the woods, and had heard their sobs and cries.

## Spirits of children and women

Besides the full-grown Rusalki there are little ones, having the appearance of seven-year-old girls. These were supposed to be the ghosts of still-born children, or children that had died before there was time to baptize them. The Rusalki were in the habit of stealing such children after their death, taking them from their graves, or even from the cottages in which they were laid out, and carrying them off to their subaqueous dwellings. Within a mix of pagan lore and Christian dogma, it was believed that every Whitsuntide, for seven successive years, the souls of these children flew about, asking to be christened. If any person who heard one of them lamenting would exclaim *"I baptize thee in the name of the Father, and of the Son, and of the Holy Ghost"*, the soul of that child was saved, and would go straight to heaven. A religious service, annually performed on the first Monday of the St. Peter's Fast, in behalf of an unbaptized child would be equally efficacious. But if the child-soul, during seven years, neither heard the baptismal formula pronounced, nor felt the effect of the divine service, it became a Rusalki. The same fate befell those babies whom their mothers had cursed before they were born, or in the interval between their birth and their baptism. Such small Rusalki, who were abound among the Belarussian Mavki, were akin to small sized *Fairies* of the British-Celtic tradition. They made the grass grow richer where they danced, they floated on the waters in egg-shells. Some sea-Rusalki born of dead children were troubled by doubts about the future. In the district of Astrakhan is was believed that the sea-Rusalki came to the surface to ask mariners: *"Is the end of the world near at hand?"*. Besides children under conditions mentioned above, women who killed themselves, and all those who were drowned, choked, or strangled, and those who did not obtain a Christian burial, were liable to become Rusalki. During the *Rusalka Week* the relatives of drowned or strangled persons went out to their graves, taking with them pancakes, spirits and red eggs. The eggs were broken, and the spirits poured over the graves, after which the remnants were left for the Rusalki, while these lines were being sung:

*"Queen Rusalka,*
*Maiden fair,*
*Do not destroy the soul,*
*Do not cause it to be choked,*
*And we will make obeisance to thee."*

## Tickling creatures

On the people who forgot to do this, the Rusalki would bestow their
vengeance. In the Saratof district the Rusalki had a bad reputation. There
they were described as hideous, humpbacked, hairy creatures, with sharp
claws, and an iron hook with which they try to seize passers-by. If anyone
ventured to bathe in a river on Whitsunday, without having uttered
a preliminary prayer, they instantly dragged that person down to the
bottom. Or, if someone went into the woods without taking a handful of
*poluin* (wormwood) he ran a serious risk, for the Rusalki could ask him,
*"What have you got in your hands? Is it poluin or petrushka* (Parsley)*?"*.
If that person replied "poluin", they cried, *"Hide under the hedge!"*, and
the person was safe. But if he or she said "petrushka", they exclaimed
affectionately, *"Ah! My dushka"*, and began tickling their victim until foam
came out of the latter's mouth. In either case they seemed to be greatly
under the influence of rhyme.

In the vicinity of the Dnjepr, peasants believed that the wild-fires, which
were sometimes seen at night flickering above graves, or around the
tumuli called *Kurgáns*, or in woods and swampy places, were lighted by
the Rusalki, who wish thereby to lure incautious travelers to their ruin;
but in many places these wandering *Will-o'-the-wisps* were regarded
as being the souls of unbaptized children, and so as small Rusalki
themselves. In many parts of Russia the Rusalki are represented in the
songs of the people as giving riddles to girls, and tickling and teasing
those who cannot answer them. Sometimes the Rusalki are asked similar
questions, which they answer at once, being very sharp-witted.

# S

## Samca

*Samca* is a character in Romanian legends, a very ugly and scary female demon. She most commonly takes the appearance of a naked woman with disheveled hair growing down to her heels, dried out breasts that touch the ground, small eyes that shine as brightly as the stars, iron hands and long nails sharp as knitting needles or hooked as sickles, and a tongue of fire. This demon, whose large, ugly and crooked mouth always spits fire, was said to appear at the end of each month, around full moon, and usually took children under the age of four, who got so frightened that they immediately became sick. The Samca could also appear to women while giving birth. Sometimes she even made herself visible and began to knead the woman's body in a painful manner, scaring her so much that she either died instantly or remained crippled for life. Apart from her appearance as some kind of *Hag*, Samca could take different animal-forms: a very large and fierce pig, a grinning dog showing awful teeth, a hairless cat with fiery, bulging eyes, a crow with bloody eyes and small as a black spider.

Samca has 19 names: *Vestitia, Navadaraia, Valnomia, Sina, Nicosda, Avezuha, Scorcoila, Tiha, Miha, Grompa, Slalo, Necauza, Hatavu, Hulila, Huva, Ghiana, Gluviana, Prava* and *Samca.* In order to defend themselves against Samca, people needed to write all 19 of her names on a wall of their house. Another way was to get a gullible person to write the 19 names on a piece of paper. This was kept in the pocket and if the Samca attacked, it was not the bearer of this paper talisman who was hit but the writer of the spell instead. There was one exception to this rule. If the writer of this spell was someone of age, Samca would only make this person grit their teeth while he or she was sleeping.

## Samodiva

In Bulgarian, and South and West Slavic folklore, the *Samodiva* (Bulgarian: самодива; pl.: *Samodivi*; or *Samovila* / самовила; pl.: *Samovili*; or simply *Vila* / вила; pl.: *Vili*), are a kind of *Woodland-* and *Water-Nymphs*, related to *Rusalkas.* In Romania, they are known as *Iele.*

Samodivi, just like the Greek *Nymphs*, live inside trees, in abandoned
shacks or dark caves, or near rivers, ponds and wells. Mountains linked to
the Samodivi include Vitosha, Belasitsa, Pirin, Rila, Rodopi, the Balkan
Mountains in Bulgaria and the Rudina Mountains. However, Mount
Pirin is their traditional favorite. Samodivi enter the human world during
the spring, staying until autumn. During winter, they live in a mythical
village called Zmajkovo. In Macedonian folklore they were also said to
inhabit trees, especially oaks and willows, and that they lived in a far off
village called Patelevo. It was believed that Samodivi were the souls of
beautiful women, living in inaccessible caves near water springs, in the
middle of nowhere, or in abandoned windmills, sometimes depicted
with wings turned upside-down. They left their abodes in early spring,
avoiding people, and returned in autumn. They hid in the shadows of old
trees and uninhabited houses, which they left at night. Commonly they
were depicted as ethereal maidens with long, loose hair – and in some
cases with wings – dressed in a shirt and gown with a green bell, or in a
free-flowing, feathered white gown, which gave them the power of flight.
Like most of such maidens throughout Europe, they were able to bring
rain or drought. After dusk they would gather together near places with
water – lakes, ponds, and springs – where they would strip naked, wash
their white robes, and dry them in the moonlight. Then they bathed, and
later, in a clearing nearby, they sang and danced the Hora. They loved
music, especially the sounds of the flute. The party lasted until sunrise.
Although lovely in appearance, there was an insidious and dangerous
Dionysian pull in the Samodivi and men who joined their party could die
of exhaustion at dawn when the Samodivi vanished, as these spirits could
completely drain their energy.

The words Samodiva and Samovila have Indo-European roots meaning
"divinity", "rave", "wild", or "rage". Samodivi also appeared as working
women at the harvesting, they supported young married couples with
little children. In most cases, however, they were unfriendly to humans –
they held back springs, set bait for shepherds whom they killed because
they destroyed their clearings, kidnapped pretty girls and brides, or
caused problems for them out of sheer envy and malice. If a man stole
the veil (Bulg. *sjanka*) from a Samodiva, she transformed herself into
an ordinary woman and became obedient to him, but not with too
much advantage. Such a woman did not become a good mother and
housekeeper, because she used every moment to return to herself the lost

freedom of the Samodiva, bypassing the performance of her duties. They acted on their own, they were capricious, wicked and obsessive towards their beloved, not leaving him alone, if even for a moment. They were interested only in him, and often due to this obsession they led him to his death. They sometimes rode deer, which were sacred to them, using snakes as a whip. If someone hunted a deer, they would immediately kill the hunter, or strike him with a deadly disease. People called this disease *samodiw*; if a sick person accidentally crossed a location that housed a Samodiva, he or she would die on the spot. They could change their faces into animal faces, usually that of a wolf. Popular belief held that people could protect themselves from the Samodivi with garlic, a dead woman's bone, snake skin, ash, olibanum, the act of saying goodbye, and fire or cigarette smoke. The only person who could withstand the darker features of the Samodivi was a *Junak*. The Samodivi would socialize with the Junak, if he was good to them. A Samodiva could form an alliance with him and even bear him children. Junak (Bulgarian: Юнак) is a term peculiar to the Southern Slavs, that originated in Bulgarian epic poetry, denoting a great hero and champion; a brave and very strong young man with special qualities.



## Sântoaderi

The *Sântoaderi* were a group of either seven or nine demons, looking like young men with long feet with hooves, wearing capes. They are found in Romanian folklore and it was believed that they would mysteriously appear in a village, where they would sing, beat their drums, and cause illnesses like rheumatism by wrapping people up in chains or stamping on their bodies. Mircea Eliade noted a similarity between the Sântoaderi and the *Zine*, or *Fairies*, who were also believed to travel through the night as a procession of dancers. There is a folk-belief that on the 24th day after Easter, the Zine and Santoaderi meet together to play, and should be offered bouquets of flowers.

## Sânzienele

In Romanian folklore, the *Sânzienele* are good *Fairies* of the *Iele*-class, but when their celebrations are not respected, they become evil Fairies. Sometimes Sânzienele are synonymous with *Drăgaicele*, manifesting – according to folk belief – on the day of Saint John the Baptist (24 June).

*Iana Sânziana* is regarded as a benevolent entity instead of a neutral one. According to Mircea Eliade in *Zalmoxis: The Vanishing God* (Chicago 1972), the Sânzienele come from a Roman cult, related to the goddess Diana – *Sanctae Dianae*:

> *"Pârvan supposes that the Dacian-Roman Diana (Diana sancta, potentissima) was the same deity as Artemis-Bendis of the Thracians (Herodotus, IV, 33). This equivalence, however probable, has not yet been proven, but there is no doubt that under the Roman name of Diana, syncretized or not, an aboriginal goddess was hidden. The cult of this goddess survived after the Romanization of Dacia. Diana Sancta din (of) Sarmizegetusa became Sânziana (San(cta) Diana), a central figure in Romanian folklore. Religious and linguistic continuity was ensured mainly because the transformation process took place in a popular, i.e. rural (country and wild) environment."*



## Sárkány

A *Sárkány* (*dragon*; pl.: *Sárkányok*) is a legendary monster found in Hungarian mythology. It usually appears as a scaly, winged, reptilian beast, but it could also be a mixture of other beings. Dragons were part of Hungarian culture prior to the 18th century. They were associated with natural weather phenomena and either made or appeased the violent forces of nature. They could create rainstorms and tornadoes. The rumble of the thunder was the roaring of Sárkányok, battling above the clouds, striking the clouds with their tails which crashed in the heat of the fight and, as a consequence, caused floods of rain pouring over the Hungarian fields. It is a description of Sárkányok which occultists (see Karl Spiesberger's *Naturgeister* and others) would describe as *Sturmgeister* or *Boreas* (Storm-Elementals) often regarded as a separate class of *Elementals*, related to the Elementals of the Air-Element *(Sylphs)*. According to folklore, the creatures usually live inside hollow trunks, dens, or in abandoned caves in the mountains.

In Hungarian folklore some unique birth-process was attached to the Sárkány. In some regions it was believed that they were born through a trans-formative process of another being. In the Csallóköz region, for example, it was believed that the Sárkány evolved either from an old hen or from a 7 or 13-year-old rooster, when the former either dives into the mud or, in the case of the latter, retreats into the hiding place of the house, from where only a *garaboncier* (Hungarian magician) can charm it out, already in the form of a dragon. In other regions, the belief was that Sárkányok can be born in a more normal way from other Sárkány. The female, after being pregnant for seven years, suckles her child for another seven years. According to the Hungarian ethnographic dictionary *(Magyar néprajzi lexikon)*, the Sárkány is known in two forms; in folklore and myth:



- *"The serpent with the loins is a terrifying snake with supernatural powers. It has the shape of a wing, resembles a horse in front and a snake behind, with scaly hard skin, long and rounded, long teeth, flaming hair, blows sparks and vomits flames. Its colors vary: yellow, white, black, red, blue, but it can also be red-tongued, red-bodied, red-black with scaly tail, black-yellow winged."*
- *"The dragon, like the horse of the garaboncier, is associated with storm, hail and treasure. It becomes a fish hidden in a swamp or a snake, hidden under a rocky cliff, that for seven years has not been seen by human eyes."*

However, Csulyak Gaspar Miskolczi (1627-1696) gives a different and less spectacular description. He wrote: *"they have no wings, but are only very old and grown snakes"*.

**Geography**
There are several locations in Hungary and Eastern Europe named after the Sárkány:
- *Sárkány*, village in Romania, Transylvania, Brasov county
- *Sárkány-tó* is a remnant of the ancient flood and the ancient Balaton ditch
- *Sárkány-barlang* small limestone cave under Wawel Hill in Krakow
- *Bősárkány* village in Győr-Moson-Sopron county, Csorna district
- *Bakonysárkány* municipality in Komárom-Esztergom county, Kisbér district
- *Szilsárkány*, municipality in Győr-Moson-Sopron county, Csorna district
- *Sárkányfalva*, municipality in Slovakia, in the district of Érsekújvár in Nitra
- *Šarkan*, a hamlet on the outskirts of Nagymegyer

*Sirin* (1905) by Ivan Yakovlevich Bilibin (1876-1942)

РАЙСКАЯ ПТИЦА СИРИНЪ
Книга Граг
нографъ
гл. Д, и чи
И. БИЛИБИНЪ. 1905.

## Sątopef'an

In Kashubian folklore and dialect the *Sątopef'an*, is an evil spirit in the form of a big-eared bat that throws money into a well, or through the chimney into a house, for people who have sold their souls to the demon.

## Seemaćić

The Bosnian/Serbian/Croatian *Seemaćić* is a local kind of male *water-spirit*, like a male Mermaid, who likes to eat pancakes and lives in the Adriatic Sea.



## Shahapet

The *Shahapet* (Սհահապետ), also called *Khshathrapti*, *Shavod*, *Shoithrapaiti*, *Shvaz* and *Shvod*, were usually friendly guardian spirits of Armenian, East-Slavic and Persian folklore or mythology, who typically appeared in the form of serpents. They inhabited houses, orchards, fields, forests and graveyards, among other places. The Shvaz-type was more agriculturally oriented, while the Shvod was a guardian of the home. A Shvod who is well-treated may reward the home's inhabitants with gold, but if mistreated might cause strife and then leave.

## Shatany

*Shatany* are odd-looking Belarusian mythological characters, described by Nikolai Nikiforovsky in his work *Нечистики. Свод простонародных в Витебской Белоруссии сказаний о нечистой силе* (Nechistiki. The Code of Common Folk Tales of Unclean Powers in Vitebsk Belarus). In the *Мифологическом словаре* (Dictionary of Mythology) the word "shatana" is given as a synonym of Satan. According to folklore, Shatany are neutral characters who do not bear evil, but are not famous for their good deeds either. They act as symbols of idleness, callousness and intrusiveness. In Belarusian mythology Shatany are known as creatures leading a completely pointless and useless way of life. They are of no use at all. Shatany can wander aimlessly along roads, fields and forests all day long, doing nothing useful. These creatures are very clingy and constantly distract others from their work. Shatany can also cling to a person and incline them to the same pointless staggering. Belarusian folklore says that evil mythological characters (such as the witch) like to tease Shatany.

Shatany are also cowardly creatures – they hide or run away from their abusers. It happens that Shatany die from pranks and attacks of evil spirits and creatures. But Shatany cannot communicate with anyone in a normal way, even with each other, and in case of trouble they don't rescue and help one another. When Shatany are tired of wandering around, they sometimes make shoes from cane. These shoes quickly wear out, and the canes break from the constant futile wobbling.

## Shtriga

Originally a *Shtriga* is a vampiric witch in Albanian mythology and folklore, that sucks the blood of infants at night while they sleep, and then turns into a flying insect (traditionally a moth, fly or bee). Only the Shtriga herself could cure those she had drained. The Shtriga is often depicted as a woman with a hateful stare (sometimes wearing a cape) and a horribly disfigured face. She usually lives in hidden places in the forest and has supernatural powers. The term Shtriga is also used with the meaning of "witch", when referring to a bad and ugly old woman who casts evil spells upon people. The male noun for Shtriga is *Shtrigu* or *Shtrigan*. The Albanian word *shtrigë*, definite: *Shtriga*, derives from the Latin *Strīga* (evil spirit, witch), related to Italian: *Strega*, Romanian: *Strigă* and Polish: *Strzyga*. According to legend, only the Shtriga herself could cure those she had drained (usually by spitting in their mouths). Those who were not cured, inevitably sickened and died.



The name can be used to express that a person is evil. According to northern Albanian folklore, a woman is not born a Shtriga; she becomes one, often because she is childless or made evil by envy. A strong belief in God could make people immune to a witch as He would protect them. Usually, Shtriga were described as old or middle-aged women with grey, pale green, or pale blue eyes (called white eyes or pale eyes) (Albanian: *sybardha*) and a crooked nose. Their stare would make people uncomfortable, and people were supposed to avoid looking them directly in the eyes because they have the *evil eye* (Albanian: *Syliga*).

### Protection

To ward off the Shtriga, people could take a pinch of salt between their fingers and touch their (closed) eyes, mouth, heart and the opposite part of the heart and the pit of the stomach and then throw the salt in direct

flames, saying: *"syt i dalçin syt i plaçin"* or *"plast syri keq"* – or one could
just whisper one of these sentences 3–6 times. In some regions of Albania,
people used *hudhër* (garlic) to send away the demon and her evil eye or
they placed a puppet in a small house especially built to trap this evil.
Newborns, children or beautiful girls have been said to catch the evil eye
more easily, so in some Albanian regions when meeting such a person,
especially a newborn, for the first time, people might say *masha'allah!* and
touch the child's nose to show their benevolence and so that the evil eye
would not catch the child. In Catholic legend, it is said that Shtriga can
be destroyed using holy water with a cross in it, while in Islamic myths it
is said that Shtriga can be sent away or killed by reciting verses from the
*Qur'an*, specifically *Ayatul Kursi 225 sura Al-Baqara*, and spitting water
on the creature. Edith Durham in *High Albania* (London, Phoenix Press,
2000), recorded several methods traditionally considered effective for
defending oneself from Shtriga. A cross made of pig bone could be placed
at the entrance of a church on Easter Sunday, rendering any Shtriga inside
unable to leave. They could then be captured and killed at the threshold
as they vainly attempted to pass. She further recorded the story that after
draining blood from a victim, the Shtriga would generally go off into the
woods and regurgitate it. If a silver coin were to be soaked in that blood
and wrapped in cloth, it would become an amulet offering permanent
protection from any Shtriga.

## Shubin

The *Shubin* is a spirit of the mines. The legend of Shubin is distributed
mainly in the mining towns of the Donbass region of Ukraine and the
popularity of legends about Shubin has led to his name being used in the
Donbass region for bars and even for a popular brand of beer: *Sarmat
Dobriy Shubin*. The spirit is usually good, but can be wicked. There is
no single point of view about the etymology of the word. Explanations
include:

- The nickname of a miner, whose soul, according to legend, walks in a
  fur coat at the bottom of the mine with a torch in his hand and burns
  the gas (firedamp).
- The name of the cruel mining master Shubin, who terrorized workers
  underground.
- The sound from methane *(Shu-Shu)*, which often accumulates in the
  mines.

## The good Shubin

According to one version, Shubin is the ghost of a dead miner. Another is that he was a good mining master who worked in the late 19th century in one of the mines in Donbass. He had a gift for predicting collapses and methane emissions. Therefore, before each shift, the master would go down in the mine and, if he felt something was wrong, he warned of the danger. Hence, Shubin is the name of what the coal miners also called *The Spirit*, that comes to their aid in a dangerous hour. In the Ukrainian mining towns, many people claim to have seen this spirit with their own eyes. Once, when a man was in the mine, the lights went down. He was in complete darkness, lost his orientation, and could not find the exit. He fell into despair but suddenly he saw lights far away. The spirit drew near, holding a flashing beacon. The man was afraid, but obediently followed until he was removed from the labyrinth of darkness. Some miners say that Shubin can be good or bad, depending on which person he meets.

## The evil Shubin

Thus not all legends about Shubin depict him as a good spirit. Anthracite miners of the area claim that this ghost is vindictive and often plagues them with accidents in the mines. There is a legend that once, long ago somewhere in Donbass, a man came in search of a better life. He visited a tavern to request help in finding a job. Drunken miners said they would give him a test. The newcomer would have to go down the mine, light a torch, and walk a few meters. If he was not afraid, he could become a miner. The man did not guess the true purpose of this test. In fact, the miners wanted to determine whether there was methane in the mine, which always gave them a lot of trouble. If the gas exploded, it would save the lives of other miners who were due to work the next day. The drunken miners cynically thought it was better for a beginner to take the risk. At a certain concentration, the gas (firedamp, or methane) burned, but did not explode. In such a case, a fur coat gave the miner some protection from skin burns. That's why the newcomer put on a fur coat. Then he did what he was ordered to do, but unfortunately there was an explosion. Ever since that accident, the newcomer's spirit has haunted the mines, taking vengeance for the wrong that was done to him. Sometimes he is voracious and causes terrible accidents that take the lives of dozens of miners. To cast the evil spirit from the east Ukrainian Lugansk Oblast mines, the metropolitan bishop Ioanniky of Sliven specially descended into a mineshaft in the Sverdlovsk region and said prayers there.

**Shubin in Russia**

Shubin is also known in Russia. There, in some areas you can even hear the phrase "ему пришел шубин" (he got a Shubin). This means that a man got into a very dangerous and desperate situation. The story goes that in the Urals in the 19th century lived a cruel master named Shubin, who slew people working underground, for which he was killed. Since then he is said to haunt underground drains and is usually displayed in the image of a stooped old man, (also) in a fur coat and with pitted felt boots, acting as a death omen. The Russian miners believed that those who saw Shubin were unlikely to remain alive.



**Similar spirits**

In the beliefs of some Ukrainian miners Shubin appears as a female spirit called *Bila Koroleva* (White Queen). Once, a miner from Sverdlovsk region went missing. After a long search he was finally found in the mine naked. He had gone mad and was taken to a mental hospital. Then some other miners also went mad. All of them talked about the "white queen", a beautiful woman who tried to cheat them, but the miners could not bear her towering beauty and completely lost their wits. People have long mocked these stories, and the White Queen seems to have disappeared. In Poland the Wieliczka salt mines are believed to be inhabited by the *Skarbnik* (Treasurer). In German speaking regions there are *Kobolds* in the mines as guardians of underground mines and precious stones, and there are spirits like the *Bergmönch*. Wales of course, has its *Knockers* and *Coblynau*.

# Sirin

*Sirin* (Russian Сирин) is the name of a legendary figure of Russian folklore. They are creatures resembling the Greek *Harpies*. Externally a Sirin resembles a huge owl, but they have the head and chest of a beautiful woman which wears a crown or has a halo. According to legend, these creatures once lived near the Garden of Eden or in the area around the Euphrates River. They show distant reference to the Greek tales of the *Sirens*. The Sirin sang songs for the saints about future joys – for mortals, however, the beings were dangerous; whoever listened to their songs forgot everything earthly, followed the Sirin and ran to their death. It was said that loud noises, such as cannon shots or bells ringing should scare them off. Sirins could draw men to the land of the dead. They were the magical birds of sorrow and grief. In contrast to the *Alkonost*, the birds of happiness and hope. The Sirin tended to be evil to humans, while the Alkonost were not and became symbolic of happiness. It was believed that only the truly happy could hear them. According to folk tales, at the morning of the *Apple Feast of the Saviour Day* (a celebration of transfiguration on August 19), Sirin flies into the apple orchard and cries sadly. In the afternoon, the Alkonost flies to this place, beginning to rejoice and laugh. Alkonost brushes dew from her wings, granting healing powers to all fruits hanging on the tree she is sitting on.

The legend of Sirin might have been brought to Russia by Persian merchants in the 8th-9th century. In the cities of Chersonesos and Kiev the Sirin is often found on pottery, golden pendants, even on the borders of Gospel books of the 10th-12th centuries. The Sirins often appear as illustrations in the *Book of Genesis* where they are depicted as birds sitting in paradise trees. The creature is seen as a metaphor for God's word going into the soul of a man. Sometimes she is seen as a metaphor of heretics tempting the weak. The Russian-American writer Vladimir Nabokov used the pseudonym "Sirin" with his Russian work.

## Skarbnik

*Skarbnik* (treasurer in Polish) – скарбник/*Skarbnik* in Ukrainian, кладенец/*Kladenetz* in Russian, дзедка/*Dzedka* in Belarusian), also *Karzełek* (a small one), is a Slavic class of spirits that live underground (especially in mines) and guard the natural resources of the earth and the treasures buried there. They were also the rulers of the underground world, where they took care of the souls of miners who died while working in the mine. The Skarbnik was a sympathetic figure, he warned miners of the danger of bumps, floods and fires, he could also befriend the miners and lead them to veins of ore. But just like the *Bergmönch* and other mine- or mountain-spirits, the Skarbnik could also be very strict, vindictive and harsh with people who were lazy, unreliable, stingy or malicious in the mine. To people who were evil or insulted him he was deadly, pushing them into dark chasms or having parts of tunnels crashing down upon them. According to miners' lore, hurling rocks, whistling, or covering one's head are actions that are offensive to Skarbnik, who will then warn the offender with handfuls of pelted soil in their direction before taking serious action. The Skarbnik usually

appeared in the form of an old, bearded miner with a stick in his hand.
He could also assume the shape of a goat, horse, dog, mouse, frog, spider
or fly, or he kept himself invisible for the eye, but the miner could sense
his presence or hear him knocking.

## Skrzak

The *Skrzak* or *Skrzek* is a little flying *Imp* in Polish and Wendish folklore.
It was believed that since the earthquakes that have released the gods
from the Void, many underground labyrinthine mazes have come to
exist. One of the many inhabitants of these tunnels are the Skrzaks.
Living primarily in dark, high ceilinged enclosures, these creatures attack
trespassers without mercy. If their target was able to avoid the razor
sharp fangs and claws, the maniacal laugh that these Imps emit would
instead drive a person mad. Their pursuit is relentless and their cackling
consistent. These small creatures tend to have human-like appearances,
even though their flesh is purplish-black, and they rarely walk but instead
fly with the large wings on their backs.

The information above was based on a work of Herbert Gottschalk:
*Lexicon Der Mythologie. Safari-Verlag,* Berlin, 1973. However, Barbara
Podgórska and Adam Podgórski in *Wielka księga demonów polskich.
Leksykon i antologia demonologii ludowej* (Kos, 2018) gives a very
different description of the creature. Skrzak is another name for a *Skrzek*.
According to the beliefs of the Wielkopolska-region, it is a caring demon,
taking care of farms. By others he is considered to be quite a negative
creature, because after the death of his master he takes on his soul as
his own. His abode is the fire place and he enters the house through the
chimney. So in the second description the Skrzak is a kind of household-
spirit with a dark agenda.

## Şobolan

In Romanian folklore *Şobolan* is a demon that looks like a giant rat.
Rural Romanian folklore tends to attribute human characteristics to the
Şobolan. Little is known about this entity.

# Spiriduş

In Romanian and Moldavian traditions, the *Spiriduş* (pl.: *Spiriduşii*) is a
devil incarnated – often depicted as a creature that looks like a chicken.
This creature lives in a household, bringing good luck to the owner as
a kind of *Spiritus familiaris*. The purpose of these familiars once they're
summoned, is to act as messengers or intermediaries, between the master
of the home in which the Spiriduş was born, and the Devil. The master
can use the Spiriduş to request from the Devil any mortal desire, in return
for his soul in the afterlife. Spiriduşii hatch from eggs: usually a left-over
egg that has to be kept under the armpit and stay there for forty days.
Once hatched, that chick is actually a Spiriduş, which will need to be
kept in a new, red pot filled with onion skins. It will then fulfill all of its
master's wishes, and upon his death can be sold for two bits. There are
however several local variations on this theme. In Moldova, the egg is
small, coming from a hen believed to have been trampled by the Devil.
So the Spiriduş that will come out, although it does good to the master, is
an envoy of the Evil One, and after the man's death, his soul will belong
to the Devil. According to Moldavian beliefs, the abandoned egg must
be kept for nine days in an uninhabited house without crosses or icons,
and after these nine days, a tiny black human baby will emerge, the Devil
himself, which will carry out all the master's commands. It will be kept
in a bottle, a jar or *"small pots of marble or white clay"*, being fed with
walnut kernels. According to popular belief, the Spiriduş may also appear
in the form of a penny, which has the power to attract money from rich
people. Such a Spiriduş could be purchased in Bucovina, from a witch
who fetched water from nine wells and then put a clean coin in this water.
In character, the Spiriduşii can roughly be compared to the protective
*Genius* in Roman mythology, the *dwarf, elf* and *Kobold* in the mythology
of the Nordic peoples, the *Lutin* (as a family demon) of the Walloons, the
*Brownie* in Scottish fairy tales, the *Leprechaun* in Irish mythology and the
*Domovoj* in Russian folklore.



# Spor

*Spor*, derived from *sporysz* (ergot) is a frumentaceous (resembling
wheat or grain) *field-spirit* in Slavic folklore, personifying fertility and
fruitfulness. It was believed that the spirit was responsible for a rich
exuberant harvest and growth of crops. In Belarus it appears in an
anthropomorphic form, depicted as a man with white, curly hair. In the

Lublin region, the spirit appeared in zoomorphic shape, as a hamster or a rat with a pouch, and also in the form of a snake, dog, cat, or frog. It is associated with the parasitic ergot fungus, which was locally known as *the mother of grain* (ergot) and believed to bring good crops.

## Srala Bartek

In Slavic beliefs *Srala Bartek* (also: *Sral, Srela, Srala, Strala, Srola, Srella, Kręciek*) is a *field demon* stuck in a whirlwind or appearing itself in the form of a small whirlwind, found throughout Poland, and especially popular in Zagłębie Dąbrowskie. Srala Bartek usually does have a human appearance though, and can be encountered as a small shaggy man, wearing a red outfit and a wide-brimmed hat, under which he hides three horns protruding from his head. According to prevailing beliefs, Srala Bartek usually appeared during haymaking and harvest time. He circled around the ground in a column of whirling air, teasing people and laughing loudly. He ruined sheaves, blew up the hay, and scattered the harvested grain in such a way that it could not be tied up again, or destroyed the thatch which covered roofs. He was also capable of more substantial mischief, like even kidnapping a peasant together with his horse and cart. In order to protect oneself from its harmful effects, the last handful of harvested hay had to be placed crosswise. When encountering Srala Bartek, another effective way was to spit or cross oneself three times and one could also hurt him or drive him away by throwing a new, well-sharpened knife at him. He would then disappear, moaning and cursing. Another way to annoy Srala Bartek was to spit in his direction while simultaneously slapping oneself on the buttocks.

## Stichija

The *Stichija* or *Stija* (pl.: *Stichiję, Stije*) is one Bulgarian name for two different creatures. It was either a female *water-demon* or *household-spirit*, which depended on the region. In general Stichije were described as creatures with feminine curves and very long hair. They lived in the depths of lakes and rivers; they lured bathers to themselves and drowned them. The Stichije wrapped their hair around their victims legs, or grabbed the unfortunates with their hair in some other creative way. In the area of Bitola however, the Stichija was called a house-demon, resembling a huge snake (just like the *Stopan*), which appeared in places

where there was some treasure hidden or where someone's possessions were stored. The Stichija did not move far from the places it guarded. It was believed that in every household there were Stichije; cottages without them were considered unlucky.

## Stopan

The *Stopan* (Bulgarian: *Stopan, Zmiya-stopanka, Zmiya-domakinka*; Macedonian: *Domashir, Domaħ(k)in*; Serbian: *Zmija chuvarkuħa, Kuharica, Chuvarkuħa, Zmija Čuvarkuća*) is a *household-spirit* of the South Slavs. A Stopan is the spirit of some distinguished ancestor. It usually lives in the house in the form of a snake and protects the family and the whole household from misfortune. The creature is associated with the cult of ancestor-worship; the fate of the household depends on it, or even the whole village as a single family – like the Genii of the Romans. In comparison with the similar East Slavic *Domovoy*, the South Slavic household-snake is less occupied in the typical household-function of the guardian of livestock. The folkorist O.V. Kutarev notes as a similarity in relation to the Stopan, about the East Slavic Domovoy and *Roda*, that to all of them meals were sacrificed. They were all considered as managers of destinies of the descendants, and in honoring these guardian spirits an image resembling the dead ancestor could be used. A Stopan that lacked the respect from the household members, became very annoyed. It made noises at night, and would sent bad dreams and illnesses. An offering, called *stopan gozba*, was then prepared for him. The sacrifice was always made by the oldest woman in the family, who killed a black hen and let the blood flow into a pit in the ashes of the fireplace of the house. Then the roasted hen and a cake were taken up to the attic and placed in the corners as food for the Stopan, while the woman poured wine into the fire saying: *"Raduj się, stopanie, wesel się, chato!"* (Be joyful, Stopan, be happy, friend!). If after two weeks the food was found untouched, it meant that the Stopan had accepted the sacrifice.

## Strigoi

In Romanian folklore the *Strigoi* (feminine: *Strigoaie*) are troubled vampiric spirits that have risen from the grave, attributed with the abilities to transform themselves into an animal, become invisible, and to refresh their vitality from the blood of their victims. Strigoi is a Romanian word that originates from a root related to the Latin terms *strix* or *striga* with the addition of the augmentative suffix "-oi". Otila Hedeşan notes that the same suffix appears in the related terms *Moroi* and *Bosorcoi* and considers this parallel derivation to indicate membership in the same "mythological micro-system". The root 'strix' has been related particularly to *owls* and is also related to the Romanian verb *striga*, which means "to scream". Cognates are found throughout the Romance languages, such as the Italian words *Strega*, or the Venetian word *Striga*, which mean "witch". The Italian *Stregone* even has the parallel cognate augmentative suffix and means "sorcerer." In French, *Stryge* denotes a bird-woman who sucks the blood of children. The Greek word *Strix*, Polish *Strzyga*, and the Albanian word *Shtriga* are also cognate. In the late Roman period the word became associated with witches, or a type of ill-omened nocturnal flying creature. A Strix (Late Latin *Striga*, Greek στρίγξ), referred to night-time entities that craved human flesh and blood, particularly that of infants'. Tudor Pamfile, in his book *Mitologie românească*, compiles all appellations of *Strigoi* in Romania *Strâgoi*, *Moroi* in western Transylvania, Wallachia and Oltenia, *Vidmă* in Bucovina, and also *Vârcolacul*, *Cel-rau*, or *Vampire*. The Strigoi-types described are:

- *Strigoaică*: a witch and the name of the Romanian feminine Vampire.
- *Strigoi viu*: a living Strigoi or sorcerer.
- *Strigoi mort*: a dead Strigoi, the most dangerous. The Strigoi which emerges from its grave to torment family members until they get sick and/or die.

One of the earliest mentions of a historical Strigoi was Jure Grando Alilović (1579-1656) from the region of Istria. This villager is believed to have been the first real person described as a Vampire, because he was referred to as a *Strigoi*, *Štrigon* or *Štrigun* in contemporary local records. Grando Alilović is supposed to have terrorized his village not only while he was alive, but also for sixteen years after his death. Eventually his dead body was decapitated by the local priest and villagers. The Carniolan scientist Johann Weikhard von Valvasor wrote about Jure Grando Alilović's life and afterlife in his extensive work *Die Ehre deß Hertzogthums Crain* when he visited Kringa during his travels. This was the first written document on Vampires. *Striga* are mentioned by the Moldavian statesman and soldier, Dimitrie Cantemir, in his work the *Descriptio Moldaviae* (1714-1716). He thought that the belief in Striga was mostly limited to the inhabitants of Moldavia and Transylvania.

However, he associated them with witches or warlocks rather than blood-drinking undead Vampires. An 1865 article on Transylvanian folklore by Wilhelm Schmidt describes the Strigoi as nocturnal creatures that preyed on infants. He reports a tradition in which, upon the birth of a child, one tosses a stone behind oneself and exclaims *"This into the mouth of the Strigoi!"*. The belief in Strigoi or Vampires has survived in Romania up to modern days.

## Strzyga

*Strzyga* (pl.: *Strzygi*, masculine: *Strzygoń*) is usually a female demon in Slavic mythology, that stems directly from the mythological Strix of Ancient Rome and Ancient Greece. The demon is somewhat similar to a *Vampire*, and is predominantly found in Polish and Silesian folklore. According to Aleksander Brückner, the name Strzyga is derived from *Strix*, Latin for owl and a bird-like creature that in Roman and Greek folk mythology fed on human flesh and blood. It is unclear how the word Strzyga was adapted by the Polish people, although it might have been through the Balkan peoples. The term Strzyga could also sometimes mean a *Vampire*, or *Upiór*. After the 18th century, there was a distinction between Strzyga and Upiór; the first was more connected to witchcraft, while the latter was more of a flying, vampiric creature. People who were born with two hearts and two souls, or two sets of teeth (the second one barely visible) were believed to be Strzygi, just like somnambulists or people without armpit hair. Furthermore, a newborn child with already developed teeth was also believed to be a Strzyga.

Persons identified as a Strzyga were chased away from human dwelling places. During epidemics, people were getting buried alive, and those who managed to get out of their graves, often weak, ill and with mutilated hands, were said to be Strzygi. It is said that Strzygi usually died at a young age, but according to belief, only one of their two souls would pass to the afterlife; the other soul was believed to cause the deceased Strzyga to come back to life and prey upon other living beings. These undead creatures were believed to fly at night in the form of an owl and attack night-time travelers and people who had wandered off into the woods at night, sucking their blood and eating their insides. Strzyga were also believed to be satisfied with animal blood, but only for a short period of time. According to other sources, Strzygi were believed not to harm people, but to herald someone's imminent death. In which they resemble the Irish *Banshees*.

**Methods of protection**
When a person suspected of being a Strzyga died, decapitating the corpse and burying the head separate from the rest of the body was believed to prevent the Strzyga from rising from the dead; burying the body face down with a sickle around its head was believed to work as well. Other methods of protection from the Strzyga (some of which were similarly used against Vampires) included:
• Burning the body.
• Hammering nails, stakes etc. into various parts of the Strzyga's body.
• Putting a flint into its mouth after exhumation.
• Pealing the church bells (the Strzyga then turns into tar).
• Slapping it across the face with one's left hand.
• Burying it again, outside of the village, and pinning it down with a big rock.
• Scattering poppy seeds in the shape of the cross in every corner of the house.
• Exhumation in the presence of a priest and burying the body again, after additional rituals (such as putting a piece of paper with the word "Jesus" written on it under the Strzyga's tongue).
• Putting small objects in the Strzyga's grave to make it count them.



## Stuhać

*Stuhać* or *Stukhach* (Serbian: Стухаћ *Stukhaħ*) is a demonic and horrifying creature, a kind of devil or malicious *Vila* in the folklore of Serbia and especially Herzegovina. Although phonetically the word is consonant with *Zduhach*, there is nothing in common between these mythical creatures. The Stuhać lives in high mountains and barren areas; what it looks like is not described. However, it is known that it wears braids made of human ligaments on its feet, so that it would not slip on mountain slopes. When those ligaments were worn out, he would pull some fresh ligaments from some poor victims legs, to make new ones. To defend oneself against the Stuhać, it is necessary – according to belief – to grab its feet and lift them up to the level of ones hands, thus scaring it.

## Şüräle

The *Şüräle* (Bashkir *Shurale*, Tatar *Shurale*, *Şüräle*, also known as *Urman iyase*, *Urman iyäse*, and *Yarımtıq* in Tatar of the Ural and Bashkir) is an anthropomorphic mythical male creature of Tatar and Bashkir folklore, a personification of the forest-spirit. The image of Şüräle is close to that of Satyrs and L(y)eshis. He has long fingers, a horn on its forehead, and a woolly body. He lures victims to a thicket and can tickle them to death. The Şüräle closely resembles other similar folkloric characters such as *Arçuri* of the Chuvash, *Pitsen* or *Picen* of the Siberian Tatars. He can shapeshift into many different forms. As a human, he looks like a peasant with glowing eyes, with his shoes on backwards. Usually the Şüräle is described as a short, hunchbacked creature with long, thin fingers, long legs, a beard and a small horn on his forehead. A person who befriends a Şüräle can learn from him the secrets of magic. Farmers and shepherds would make pacts with the Şüräle, to protect their crops and sheep. The Şüräle has also a dark side, including leading peasants astray, making them sick, or tickling them to death. They are also known to hide the axes of woodcutters and when a Şüräle crosses their path, people get lost in the woods. To find the way back, you had to turn your clothes inside out and wear your shoes on opposite feet. The creature lures horses away from the herd and rides them, whereby he can exhaust them to the point of death. A Şüräle can be caught by smearing tar on the horse's back. It is afraid of water, so it flees from it by jumping over a river or a brook. Inspired by the Tatar folklore, Ghabdulla Tuqay wrote a poem called *Şüräle* and Şüräle was Tuqay's pseudonym. The first Tatar ballet by Farit Yarullin was also named after Şüräle.

## Susulu

*Susulu*, also known as *Susuna*, *Susona*, *Suna* or *Sona*, is a unique entity and a legendary aquatic creature with the upper body of a human female and the tail of a fish. She is the daughter of the Sea King in Turkic folklore. "Su" means "water" in Turkish. *Susulus* (pl.) are a species of supernatural creatures that appear as unlucky omens, both foretelling disaster and provoking it, just like *Mermaids*. They are conventionally depicted as beautiful young women with pale faces and long green flowing hair, suggesting a connection with floating weeds and days spent underwater in faint sunlight. They are believed to be the ghosts of young women who died a violent or untimely death, perhaps by murder or suicide, but especially by drowning, and swim up rivers towards freshwater lakes. They can be seen after dark, gathering together in the moonlight and calling young men by their names, luring them into the water and drowning them.

## Szëmich

In Kashubian folk-beliefs the *Szëmich* was a benevolent spirit of the forests, and a guardian of pleasant silences and gentle hums.

## Szépasszony



The *Szépasszony* ("beautiful lady" in Hungarian) is often related to witches. She is a seductive demoness with long hair and a white dress. She appears and dances in storms and hail, and seduces young men. Sometimes a Szépasszony awaits people who somehow end up in a forbidden place, punishing them for their curiosity. Folk tradition also claims that they kidnap babies and sleep with the Devil. They are usually depicted as evil, although some ancient Hungarian myths interpret them as servants of *Arany Atya* (Golden Father), the chief god in the pre-Christian Hungarian religion. However, according to ethnographer Ferenc Bakó, Szépasszony was originally one of the goddesses of the ancient religion, a figure similar to Venus, the goddess of love. With the Christianization of the world, it was standard procedure that the gods of the old religions were turned into demons; a process that solely had a religious-political objective. This process occurred even before the Christian era; the conqueror demonized the gods of the subjugated peoples.

# T

## Tęsknica

*Tęsknica*, *Tęsknota* (longing) or *Osmętnica* is a Slavic demon, personifying a state of morbid reverie, languor or longing. According to folklore she fell from the sky along with the stars, from a black storm cloud. She was a pale specter, wearing a garland of dry fern on her head, wrapping herself in a gray cloth pulled out from under a dead man's couch, and putting on her feet clogs that she had fashioned herself from green reeds plucked from a lake, or from threads growing over the waters. She would walk slowly, with her head lowered, and would usually sit by cemeteries or statues at the crossroads. When she found sad, weeping, lonely girls, she would sit by them, embrace them in her skinny arms and kiss them on the lips, placing a heavy hand on their hearts. Longing mostly affected young women who had not yet had children. These women were in no pain and had no scars on their bodies, but when afflicted by longing they lost their vigor, did not drink or eat, suffered from insomnia, and became weak and numb. Usually such girls did not live long.

## Topielica

In Slavic mythology, the *Topielica* (pl.: *Topielice*; drowned or drowned women) is a malevolent demon or "drowner", inhabiting bodies of water, and a female variety of the better known *Utopiec*. Topielice were the souls of young girls who had drowned themselves out of desperation or bitterness, or were murdered by drowning. They appeared as young girls with long light colored hair. Calling for help, or singing, attracted young men, whom they tried to lure into the water to drown them. European folklore preserves a lot of varieties on this theme of the female water-demon who lures victims into the water with their charms or singing etc. under many different local names.

## Tündérek

In Hungarian folklore the *Tündérek* (sing.: *Tündér*) are translated as *Fairies*. However, here we have to take into account that the definition of the word "Fairy" is not consistent and uniform. The tiny cliché Fairy-

creatures of Anglo-Saxon folklore, depicted as hovering around flowers,
for example, are now popular in Hungary, but were in fact unknown in
traditional Hungarian folk culture. The etymology of the word tündér is
not clear - some academics recognize the Sumerian root *dingir*, meaning
"god(s)", "sky". The word *tenger* (sea) is derived from the same root,
and the figure of *Tündér Ilonain* in the Hungarian folk tales seems to
be derived from the Sumerian god *Dingir Ilama*. *Dingir* is a compound
of the Sumerian words "judgment" and "to bring". According to István
Kiszely the word is of Turkish origin. The first record we have is from the
15th century *Müncheni kódexből* (Codex of Munich), part of the oldest
known Hungarian translation of the Bible, called *Bible of Hussites* (or the
*Hussite Bible*). It was written at Tatros (today Târgu Trotuş, Romania) in
1466. Today it is located in Munich at Bavarian State Library:

> *"És ők [a tanítványok], hogy láták őt [Jézust] a tengeren járatta [járni],
> alajték [vélték, gondolták] őtet tündérletnek és üvöltének."*

(And they [the disciples], when they saw him [Jesus] walking on
the sea, thought him to be a Fairy/tündérletnek and shouting.)

In the Middle Ages, besides *kísértet* (ghost), the word *tündér* was used
in other, specifically negative connotations, as the Hungarian-Latin
dictionary of Albert Molnár Szenczi (1604) shows: *"szörny, csodalény;
varázsló; szemfényvesztő; az, aki kénye-kedve szerint különféle alakot
tud ölteni"* (monster, wondrous creature; sorcerer; conjurer; conjurer of
the eye; one who can assume various forms at will). These descriptions
suggest the use of the word as an adjective in the sense of "fleeting,
vanishing, elusive", which is mainly a characteristic of poetic language;
for example, as "changeable" in a sentence by the poet Berzsenyi Dániel
(1776-1836):

> *"Tündér szerencsénk változandó, / Hol mosolyog, hol utálva néz ránk."*

(Our Fairy-luck is changeable, / Sometimes smiling,
sometimes looking at us with hatred.)

In the Hungarian folk beliefs there are few – mainly legendary – data
about Tündérek. Most of the data are old and difficult to interpret. It is
certain that there is no clear-cut, unified image of Tündérek in Hungarian

folklore, both in the past and in the present. The greatest influence on Hungarian lore was undoubtedly the Fairy cult of the Balkan peoples. This is the origin of the expressions *Fehér asszony* (white woman), *Szép asszony* (beautiful woman) *Kis asszonyok* (little women). The influence of the Slavic peoples is also shown by the fact that the terms *tündérkedik* (fairy tales) and *Tündérország* (Fairyland), which referred to Transylvania, were used in the 16th and 17th centuries, primarily in a pejorative sense, i.e. they did not exactly denote positive things. Transylvania was believed to be the "Home of the Fairies" or Fairy-land.

The term Tündér was used mainly in the southern Great Plain, Transdanubia, Transylvania, Moldavia, Bukovina and in many places in the Highlands. In these areas, the creatures are young, long-haired, mostly white-clad, beautiful women, usually appearing in groups. Their favorite places of appearance are abandoned paths, crossroads, bridges, ditches and lakes. They like to sing, play music, bathe and sometimes hold big dances or dinners. They can fly and change shape (e.g. into swans or whirlwinds). Men are seduced, carried off or led astray; babies are exchanged, horses are stolen for their nightly amusements (in Bukovina, on certain days, poppies were used to spray the stables against them). Those who disturb their revels, get in the way of their processions or step on their dance halls are afflicted with diseases: according to popular belief, paralysis, muteness, madness, and sore feet are caused by the Tündérek . However, good Fairies can save a person in distress (e.g. they can rescue a drowning person in a lake). There are several legendary Hungarian Tündérek with names that usually relate them to some natural location, mountain or river:
* *Ramocsa*: the name of the ramocsa flower (*henye boroslán*) and the Ramocsa field.
* *Tarkő*: his kingdom is located in the north-eastern part of Szeklerland.
* *Olt*: Daughter of Tarkő, who was turned into a river by her mother.
* *Maros*: the younger sister of Olt, who also hurries to her father in the form of a river.
* *Dála*: Székelydálya is named after her.
* *Firtos*: the Fairy of Mount Firtos.
* *Tartod*: The Fairy of Mount Tartod and brother of Firtos.
* *Rapsóné*: wife of the Rabonban Fairy *Rapsó*, sister of Firtos and Tartod.
* *Torja*: Fairy of Torja (Transylvania).
* *Kecskekő*: Fairy of the mountain of Kecskekő (Transylvania).

# U

## Uboże

The *Uboże, Ubożę* (in plural often: *Uboża, Ubożęta, Bożęta*) is a figure
from old Polish beliefs, a caring household-spirit, ensuring prosperity,
often derived from the souls of deceased ancestors. His figure appears
in literature in the 15th and 16th centuries, but later disappears when its
role is taken over by its Russian equivalent; the *Domovik* or *Domovoy*.
According to a fragment of a 15th century sermon, the Uboża were left
with dinner leftovers, especially on Thursdays. Having eaten, the Uboża
were supposed to chase away evil forces. The etymology of the word
*uboże* comes from the stem *bog-*, meaning "grace, wealth". Deriving
the term from the word *ubogi* (poor) is erroneous, as it contradicts
the function of the *household-spirit* whose job it was to make sure the
household was prosperous.

## Ubyr

*Ubyr* (Bashkir: *Ubyr*, Tatar: *Ubyr*) goes back to the common Turkic *obcr*
or *obr*, a root which means "to suck in", "to draw in" or to "suck out". It is
a bloodthirsty ghoulish and vampiric being in the folklore and legends
of the Turkic peoples: the Kazan Tatars, the Tatar-Misharis, the West
Siberian Tatars (also *Uvyr, Myatskayi*) and Bashkirs (in some groups,
also *Myasekay*). According to both the Мифологический словарь/
Гл. ред. Мелетинский Е.М. – М.: Советская энциклопедия, 1990 (A
Mythological Dictionary/General Ed. by E.M. Meletinsky. – M.: Soviet
Encyclopedia, 1990) and Мифы народов мира/под ред. Токарева С.
А. – М., Советская энциклопедия, 1992 г. – т.2 (Myths of the Peoples
of the World / ed. Tokarev S.A. – M., Sovetskaya Encyclopedia, 1992 –
Vol.2), an Ubyr replaces a sorcerer's soul and controls him during life.
At night, the Ubyr sometimes leaves the body of the sorcerer, usually
through a hole that he has under his arm. Then Ubyr takes on the image
of a fiery ball, a fiery wheel, a dog, a cat, a pig, and sometimes a man.
According to the folk-beliefs, the Ubyr steals cows' calves, sucks cows' and
mares' milk, making them sick, drinks cattle's blood, and sends illnesses
to people. If one wounds an Ubyr at night, then in the morning the
wound will be found in the same place on the sorcerer's body. After his

death such a sorcerer lives on in his grave, coming out at night through a hole (according to the beliefs of the Tatar-Misharis, it wanders on the ground) and continues to cause harm. For example, by "swallowing clouds", he causes drought. In scientific literature the creature is described for the first time by the Tatar writer and ethnographer Kayum Nasyri in his book *Поверья и приметы казанских татар* (1880) (Beliefs and omens of the Kazan Tatars):

> *"The Ubyr, Upyr at the Ukrainians, at the Chuvash Vubar (actually a Vampire, a bloodthirsty animal found in South America), according to the Tatar notions, is such a fabulous creature, which, although sometimes acting separately and independently, always has an abode in one specific person, who is therefore called убырлыкши – "вампир-человек" (Ubyrlykshi – "Vampire-human")."*

### Ubyr-characters

In fairy tales there are also "Ubyr-characters" like the Bashkir *Ubyr ebay* or *Tatar ebi* (old woman Ubyr) or the Bashkir убыр ҡарсыҡ (*Ubyr kapsik*) who was feeding on the blood and the spinal cord of people and animals. The *Ubyrly karsik* was a *Baba Yaga*-variety; the witch who overhears where the children are making noise, and who is often called a "horned old woman". The Bashkir убыр ҡатын (*Ubyr katyn*) is a female Vampire; just like the Bashkir убыр ҡәйнә (*Ubyr kene*).

An Ubyr is said to have no back, only a front (compare the Swedish *Huldra* or *Skogsrå*). In the Bashkir language there are several names for a disease caused by a close encounter with an Ubyr. Urinary incontinence for example is believed to be a disease one gets under the influence of the creature. The shirt of a child who is sick from the effects of a Ubyr must be washed in the river before it can be worn again. Убыр ауыры (literally "the heaviness of Ubyr") is a painful pathological condition.

Apart from some overlap with Baba Yaga and the Skogsrå, the Ubyr also has a link to the *Will-o'-the-wisp* or *Ignis fatuus*. Wandering fires are called in Bashkir *Ubyr uty*, (literally: "Vampire fire"). When the people see a wandering light, they utter: *"Go away, disappear, cursed one!"* and while doing so, they quickly unbutton the buttons of their collar. A person who gets an illness caused by an Ubyr throws a pinch of ritual salt in a westerly direction and locks his or her door carefully before going to sleep.

# Upyr

The *Upyr*, *Upir* or *Upiór* (from pre-Slav. *Ǫpir*; standard-Slav. *Upyre*;
modern Polish *Upiór*, and also *Wąpierz*, *Wupi*; pl. in Ukrainian *Opiritsya*)
is a pan-Slavic vampiric creature, a dead man, rising from the grave at
night, who harms people and cattle, drinks their blood and causes damage
to the economy. The characteristic feature of the Upyr is his unusually red
face (general feature) and red eyes (typical for the Ukraine and Bulgaria).
The redness remains even after death from the blood it drank.

## Etymology

The word *upyr* or *upir* is known in the major Slavic languages: Czech and
Slovak: *upír*, and (perhaps East Slavic-influenced) *upiór*, Ukrainian: упир
(*upyr*), Russian: упырь (*upyr'*), Belarusian: упыр (*upyr*), from Old East
Slavic: упирь (*upir'*). The exact etymology is unclear. Among the proposed
proto-Slavic forms are ǫpyrъ and ǫpirъ. Another, less widespread theory,
is that the Slavic languages have borrowed the word from the Turkic term
*ubır* or *ubar*. Czech linguist Václav Machek proposes the Slovak verb
*vrepiť sa* (stick to, thrust into), or its hypothetical anagram *vperiť sa* (in
Czech, archaic verb *vpeřit* means "to thrust violently") as an etymological
background, and thus translates *Upír* or *Upyr* as *"someone who thrusts,
bites"*. An early use of the Old Russian word is in the anti-pagan treatise
"Word of Saint Grigoriy" (Russian Слово святого Григория), dated back
variously to the 11th-13th centuries, where pagan worship of *upyri* is
reported. Tolstoy was rather picky on not confusing the Upyr – whom he
describes as "pure Slavic" – with the *Vampire*:

> *"You, God knows why, call them vampires, but I can assure
> you that their real Russian name is: Upyr; and since they are
> of purely Slavic origin, although they occur throughout Europe
> and even in Asia, it is also unreasonable to stick to the name
> twisted by the Hungarian monks, who thought of turning
> everything in the Latin way and made a vampire of Upyr."*
> – A.K. Tolstoy, "Упырь" (The Upyr)

The term Upyr was introduced to the English-language culture as
"vampyre", mentioned in 1813 by Lord Byron in *The Giaour*, described
by John William Polidori *The Vampyre* in 1819, and popularized by Bram
Stoker's *Dracula*. In Slavic folk culture however, the Upyr has features that
are strongly present in *Strzyga*, and so Adam Mickiewicz has theorized

Upyr to be developed from the ancient Roman and Greek *Strix*. In the territory of present-day Ukraine (e.g. in the Chigirinsky Uyezd), the term *Martvyets* was used to describe the Upyr. The Upyr also roughly corresponds to the *Vordalak* in East Slavic tradition. The belief in the *Opiritsya*, usually translated as *Ghouls*, was most strongly spread in the territory of Southern Russia (the modern Ukraine). It was believed that they could cause famine, pestilence, cattle diseases and drought, causing the communities to accuse and lynch innocent people.

## The unclean soul

Upyrs are associated with ideas about the existence of two kinds of dead people: those whose soul after death finds peace in the "other world", and those who continue their posthumous existence at the border of the two worlds. Common Slavic belief indicates a stark distinction between soul and body. The soul is not considered to be perishable. The Slavs believed that upon death the soul would go out of the body and wander about its neighborhood and workplace for 40 days (compare the Tibetan belief of 40 days in Bardo prior to reincarnation) before moving on to an eternal afterlife. Thus pagan Slavs considered it necessary to leave a window or door open in the house for the soul to pass through at its leisure. During this time the soul was believed to have the capability of re-entering the corpse of the deceased. The passing soul could either bless or wreak havoc on its family and neighbors during its 40 days of passing. Thus, upon an individual's death, much stress was placed on proper burial rites to ensure the soul's purity and peace as it separated from the body. The death of an unbaptized child, a violent or an untimely death, or the death of a grievous sinner (such as a sorcerer or murderer) were all grounds for a soul to become unclean after death. A soul could also be made unclean if its body were not given a proper burial. Alternatively, a body not given a proper burial could be susceptible to possession by other unclean souls and spirits. Slavs feared unclean souls because of their potential for taking vengeance. From these deep beliefs pertaining to death and the soul derives the Slavic concept of Upyr, a manifestation of an unclean spirit possessing a decomposing body. This undead creature needs the blood of the living to sustain its body's existence and is considered to be vengeful and jealous towards the living.

Upyrs left their graves at night, carrying their heads in their arms, or, if the head was not detached, with glowing "wolf-like" eyes. Some of them caused menace during the daytime, climbing up bell towers and killing everyone who heard their shriek. They drank human blood, and used their superhuman strength to tear their victims to shreds. They could also kill with their breath or their shrieks. They harassed people at night, making them suffocate, or sleepwalk. There were claims of husbands (and wives) becoming Upyrs and visiting their widowed spouse after death. They would do the same chores they did during their lifetime, and sometimes harassed the family. Thanks to their humanoid appearance they easily penetrated houses. Before the cock crows for the third time they had to return to their graves. It was believed that one could kill an Upyr by piercing its corpse with an aspen stake. If this did not help, the corpse was usually burnt. Folklore however differs about the classic *"ghoulish corpse from the grave-Upyr"* and the Upyr as some kind of vampiric spirit that can possess ordinary living people and cause the same kind of havoc. Ivan Franko, in his ethnographic note *Сожжение упырей в Нагуевичах* (Burning of Upyrs in Nagujevici), describes how in the 1830s in Franko's homeland, in the village of Nagujevici, live people were dragged through the fire, suspecting Upyrs in them.

## Upyr detection

It was considered that people who were Werewolves or sorcerers during their lifetime or those who were excommunicated and anathematized (heretic, apostate, some criminals, for example maniacs) became Upyrs after they died. An Upyr could also be a person who was cursed before death, a person who died suddenly, or someone whose corpse was desecrated. Other origins included a dead person over whom an animal had jumped, suicide victims, witches, unbaptized children and those who were killed by another Upyr. It was also believed that those who were physically different in a community were potential Upyr candidates: redheads, the left-handed, those with a limp, unibrow, a double set of teeth or with a gray mark on their back and religiously "different" (e.g. Lutherans in Catholic communities). Suspicious traits among the living also included walking by moonlight, having a big head, or no armpit or pubic hair. Many of these ideas are reproduced in the legends and ethnographic records of *Strzygas*, therefore Upyrs are often described as having two hearts and two souls just like the Strzyga or the *Dwojedushnik*. Women who died during or after childbirth were particularly vulnerable to the transformation. It was feared that they would return to the orphaned child as Upyrs to feed it at night. That is why in Silesia, for example, those who died in childbirth were buried by the edge of the cemetery, near the wall. Lack of rigor mortis, a flushed face or blood beneath the nails were signs that a deceased person could become an Upyr or *Wąpierz*. The signs of its misdeeds among family or neighbors could be fatigue, pallor, sweating or recurring nightmares. An Upyr could haunt its family if the family burned a photograph or portrait of the deceased. A dead person buried in an old shirt could also become an Upyr. A way to recognize an Upyr was to have an innocent child ride a horse to a cemetery and have them indicate the grave of the Upyr. An Upyr could be seen in the mirror in the evening, so in the Sieradz region people would not look into mirrors after dusk.

**Remedies against the Upyr**



It was said that the dead should be taken out of the house through a special exit or hole, because if they were taken out via the main door they could become Upyrs. Dead people suspected to be or become an Upyr had garlic heads, bricks, or pieces of iron placed in their mouths before burial. Branches of wild rose, hawthorn, or blackthorn were put into their coffins. The coffins were sprinkled with poppy-seeds, so the Upyrs would have a chore (picking up all the seeds) to occupy them. In Pomerania the method for keeping the Upyrs busy was to give them little knots, or nets, or other small things to untangle in the grave. If a person that had died was thought to be an Upyr, or if someone's grave was believed to be an Upyr's grave, a "Vampire burial" was performed. The head could be cut off and put between the legs of the corpse, the corpse could be burned, nailed to the coffin, or repositioned to lie face-down. If an Upyr harassed a human at night, the remedy was to stop the Upyr from returning to its grave – at dawn it would disappear or change into black tar. Another protective measure was to drink the Upyr's blood or eat some soil off its grave.

**Local Upyr folklore variations**

- Near Warsaw, a body found on the road was treated as a potential Upyr and branches were thrown over it. In spring those stacks of branches were burned, so that the soul of the dead underneath would be purged of its sins.
- Near Kraków, a way to free an Upyr's soul was recorded in 1847: one was supposed to stake the Upyr's head with a nail, and then put paper with writings by a teacher/professor underneath its tongue. Then a priest would be asked to cut the Upyr's head and reposition it face-to-the-pillow in the coffin.

- Near Słupia, a young man who committed suicide due to unrequited love was thought to be an Upyr. After burying him in a secluded hole, the Upyr was supposed to appear and attack people and cattle. It disappeared when the rooster called at dawn.
- In the village of Liszki a strange story was told about a woman who found an Upyr in one of three coffins at night. She cut its liver out to make a meal for her husband. The Upyr later harassed the family until they all fell ill and died.
- In Lubelskie, the dead were buried face-down with their hands tied with blessed herbs to prevent them from becoming an Upyr.
- According to Bulgarian beliefs, an Upyr has no bones but just cartilage, at least as long as it is young.
- In the Transylvanian region, it was believed that Upyrs do not like garlic and onions, so garlic was hung in the house and the door was greased with it.
- In Pokuttia, a Ruthenian woman who was said to be "loved by an Upyr", was taken out of her house after her death via a hole made in the wall, and then buried at a crossroads, in accordance with her wishes.
- In Volhynia, after taking out the baked bread, the housewife would cover the stove so as not to die with her mouth open and become an Upyr, devouring everyone.
- A story from Ukrainian farmers from Chigirinsky Uyezd was recorded, about an Upyr who protected a Cossack against a hangman.
- A story from 1701, recorded by travelers to Mykonos, described a fight of several days between some inhabitants and an Upyr. The dead inhabitant was said to enter houses, knocking over candles, disturbing people so that whole families moved their beds to the square outside, to spend the nights there. The dead man's heart was removed and then burned. When this (and prayers, fasts, and masses) did not help, the exhumed body was burned again.
- Around Gradiška, Serbia, until the end of the 19th century, a story circulated about a dead father haunting his son after his death, asking for food. After one visit, six more family members fell ill and died. After the commission found the father's unusual appearance during the exhumation, he was declared an Upyr. The executioner pierced his heart, and the body of the deceased was burned.

# Ursitoare

In the Oltenia region of Wallachia, Romania, the three *Ursitoare* are
supposed to appear three nights after a child's birth to determine the
course of its life. They are similar to the Greek *Fates* or *Moirai*. This
traditional belief was part of Romanian tradition for hundreds of years.
Similar trios of female spirits that come at night to the newborn's cradle
and weave its fate, exist in South Slavic folklore, among the Serbians,
Macedonians, Croatians, Bulgarians and Montenegrans.

# Ustreł



The *Ustreł* (also: *Usov*, Bulgarian: усов) is a demon of southeastern
Bulgarian folklore from the regions Burgas and Malko Tyrnovo, close
to the *Vampire*. The Ustreł is also considered a folk representation of
disease. The demon arose from the spirit of a child who was conceived
on a Saturday, but who died after birth without being baptized. After
nine days of death, the dead child would turn into a Ustreł, who would
dig a hole in the grave and get out. It was active only at night, looking for
blood; it spent its days in the grave. He started sucking the blood of cattle,
sheep, oxen, and when he gained strength he would also attack people.
According to folk-belief the Ustreł did not attack on Saturdays, because at
that day he would lose his strength. The creature feared the wolf, which,
unlike humans, could see it, and it also avoided fire. An Ustreł was always
tormented by thirst, so it had to drink blood. The animal it attacked
would then die the same night. On the victim one could locate where
an Ustrel had bitten by a bruised and swollen spot. When the Ustreł was
satiated and had gained strength, it did not return to its grave, but sat
among the horns of livestock or the udders of cows. He could change
his weight and be very light, but also very heavy. The Ustreł changed its
appearance depending on its period of existence. He went through three
stages of development:

1. During the first months it resembled a bagpipes' bellows, smooth and
   bulky, without legs, wings, tail or neck. Its face was similar to a pig's
   snout, but shorter. Its eyes were human-like but with very red corners
   and eyelids with which it kept blinking. Instead of a nose it had two
   holes. Its limbs were very short and it had long, black, curved claws. It
   had no bones. During this period of existence, it could only be killed
   with a hawthorn spike.
2. When it gained strength and began to appear between the horns of

animals, it resembled an owl without feathers, legs or beak, but with membranous wings. When it was captured, it cried like a baby. During this period of existence it could be killed with a hawthorn stake or a silver coin.

3. In its last stage of development, after about six months, it could turn into a human or an animal. When it took on the appearance of a human, it differed only in that it had no cartilage dividing its nose and instead had a single hole.

A *Sybotnik* (i.e. a man born on a Saturday) could also kill an Ustreł. The demon could also be banished by fire obtained by rubbing dry crackling lime. Therefore, when an illness appeared, animals or people were led through such a fire and the sick were led out of the village.



## Utopiec or Topnik

*Utopiec* (pl.: *Utopce*; locally known as *Topic, Topnik, Topek, Utopnik, Utoplec, Utopek* or *Wasserman*) is a vicious *water-demon* of the "drowner-class" in Slavic beliefs. Utopce were born from the souls of drowned or aborted fetuses. Similar to *Wodniki*, they inhabited all kinds of water reservoirs (including wells and roadside ditches in some legends) and drowned bathers, passersby and animals crossing the river. In some places they were also responsible for flooding rivers and flooding fields and meadows. Utopce took the form of tall, very thin people with slimy green skin, a large head and dark hair. They could also appear as a child or a child-sized man in soaked, muddy clothes. It is believed it sometimes wears a red cap, which it can also use to lure its victims to the water by hanging it on a tree branch or bush. Whoever wandered by and plucked it off, would be grabbed by the demon and pulled to a watery death. It could also take on a more terrifying look: a hairy human torso supporting a red head. During the new moon the Utopce would come ashore. They would often lure people to them by playing puzzles with them. A person who tried to cheat in solving the riddles was immediately drowned. The Utopiec was feared throughout Slavic lands in areas where there were many bodies of water (e.g. Warmia and Masuria, river basins), especially during autumn and spring, when it posed a real threat to human life. In some folk tales, however, Utopce seek contact with people, make friends with them, and sometimes warn them of various dangers (this is especially true of Silesian Utopce).

# V

## Vadleány

The *Vadleány* is a female creature of the Central European, especially
Hungarian, folklore. She is an elusive forest-spirit – her name means
"wild girl" – who seduces wanderers and shepherds, saps their strength
and makes the forest rustle. She is usually naked and her long hair reaches
to the ground. She can sometimes be lured and caught with a boot (as she
tries to put both her feet into one boot). The term Vadleány is also in use
as a pseudonym for teenage girls from Russia or Scandinavia.

## Vâlvă

In Romanian folklore a *Vâlvă* (pl.: *Vâlve*) is either used for a person with
special powers, or a female spirit. In case of the human version Vâlve are
said to be children who are conceived on holidays. In rural areas it is said
that these children are born with a red *tichiuță* or fleshy donut-shaped
growth on their head. This has to be removed by surgery. If these deformed
children survive they become *Solomonari*, people with some special kind of
magical ability.

As nature-spirits the Vâlve are believed to walk over the hilltops at night,
and are roughly subdivided into *Vâlve Albe* (White Vâlve), who are
considered beneficial, and *Vâlve Negre* (Black Vâlve), who are considered
evil. In certain contexts, they are believed to have assumed a human form
(especially when they came to protect villages from a storm). They are
shapeshifters, however, and may appear under various guises, such as
shadows or black cats. The Vâlve include several types, including:

- *Vâlva Apei* (of the water), considered as a sort of guardian of the water
  sources and fountains;
- *Vâlva Bucatelor* (roughly, "of the morsels"), protector of the poor
  people, and of crops;
- *Vâlva Băilor* (of the mines), defender and protector of mines and
  tunnels, whose departure means that the deposit is coming to an end;
- *Vâlva Banilor* (of the money), protector of money;
- *Vâlva Comorilor* (of the treasures), protector of treasures, who can also
  signal the spot where these are buried;

- *Vâlva Pădurii* (of the forest), protector of woodlands, similar to *Muma Padurii*;
- *Vâlva Ciumei* (of the plague), controlling bubonic plague and other diseases;
- *Vâlva Zilelor* (of the days), protector of the days (there is one for each day of the week);
- *Vâlva Cetăţilor* (of the citadels), defender of ancient ruins.

**Vâlve of the mines**
The best known among oral tradition are, still, the *Vâlve of the mines*. Legends about them flourish around traditional metal exploitation areas in Romania, such as Roşia Montană, a place extremely rich not only in gold, but also in folklore and myth. There, the people still say that you cannot find any gold in the mines without the help of a Vâlvă Albe. But if one gets too greedy, or spends the money foolishly, or if someone steals the gold or money from the family it was originally intended for, the white Vâlvă will become a Vâlve Negre and will avenge the injustice and disrespect to her. Miners say that anyone can hear her knocking through the galleries just in the next corridor, even if there is no knowledge of that place in the rock or if you know for sure no one can be there at that time. She is producing that strange knocking sound in her search for gold which she will show the miners, to help them not get lost, or warn them in case of danger.



# Vampire

In the last three centuries, *Vampires* became worldwide the most used term for a blood or energy sucking creature, that mostly attacks after sunset. Although popular movies suggest otherwise, "Vampire" is a blanket-term for a large variety of often totally different creatures. The Vampire-phenomenon is known on all continents. In Europe the highest number of vampiric beings is located in Eastern Europe and the Balkan. Many creatures that are not known for preying on blood attack humans or animals to steal their energy or life force. This habit is well known of creatures of the *Alp*-type, while the *Incubi* and *Succubi* are a class of their own as these prey exclusively on sexual energy, which they absorb directly from the victims orgasms that they induce by direct second chakra stimulation. Several British water-spirits also exhibit Vampire-like behavior. The vast majority of vampiric beings operates nocturnally.

## Origin of the word Vampire

There is disagreement about the etymological origin of the word "Vampire", which is commonly used in Europe. The only certainty is that the Hungarian term *Vampire* in turn derived from Polish, dominated international literature by 1732 at the latest. Originating in the Slavic language area, the word spread to Western Europe, where it was modified in the individual countries; in Italy, Spain and Portugal, for example, the creature is called *Vampiro*, in Denmark and Sweden *Vampyr*. The Baltic languages also know the word, which is associated with the Bulgarian *Vapir*, which comes from a Macedonian dialect and means something like "winged creature". Others trace the word "Vampire" to the Serbo-Croatian or Lithuanian languages. In southern Russia, Bohemia, Montenegro, and parts of Serbia, the Vampire creature is called *Wukodalak, Vurkulaka,* or *Vrykolaka,* which means "wolf-haired" derived from Greek. The Serbs know the terms *Vampir, Lampir, Lapir, Upir* and *Upirina*. In Albanian, the Vampire creatures are called *Vampir* or *Dhampir*. The latter consists of the parts of speech *dham* (tooth) and *pir* (drink), the term Dhampir is however also used for the child of a human and Vampire, which usually acts as a Vampire-hunter and killer. In Ukraine the figure is called *Upyr*, in Belarus, Bohemia and Slovakia *Upir*, and in Poland the terms *Upior, Upierzyc,* and *Wapierz* are common. The suffix *pir* stands for a "winged or feathered being". The first designation as Upir is found for a prince named *Upir Lichyi* mentioned in 1047 AD in the vicinity of Novgorod, in northwestern Great Russia. In western Russia, there are also places called Upiry and Upirov, whose inhabitants boast that they are descended from Vampires. South-Russia has its *Upuir*, the Croatian name for a Vampire is *Pijawica* and the Turks have their Ubir.

## Animated corpses

Vampire stories or stories of animated corpses were numerous in Russian and Slavonic folklore, all of them based on the same belief – that in certain cases the dead, in a material or dense etheric shape, leave their graves in order to destroy and prey upon the living. This belief is not seen as peculiar among the Slavs, but W.R.S. Ralston mentions it as *"one of the characteristic features of their spiritual creed"*. Animated corpses also play a part in the traditions of other countries. Among the Scandinavians and especially in Iceland, they were the cause of many fears, though they were not supposed to be impelled by a thirst for blood so much as by other carnal appetites, or by a kind of local malignity. In Germany tales of horror similar to the Icelandic are not unknown, but the majority of them are to be found in districts which were once wholly Latvian or Slavonic, such as East Prussia, Pomerania, or Lusatia. The ordinary Modern-Greek word for Vampire, βουρκόλακας, is undoubtedly of Slavonic origin, being identical with the Slavonic name of the *Werewolf*, which is called in Bohemian *Vlkodlak*, in Bulgarian and Slovak, *Vrkolak*, etc., the Vampire and the *Werewolf* having many points in common. The Belarussians hold that if a Vampire's hands have grown numb from remaining crossed in the grave, he makes use of his teeth, which are like steel. When he has first gnawed his way through all obstacles, he then attacks the babies he finds in a house, and after that the older inmates. If fine salt be scattered on the floor of a room, the Vampire's footsteps may be traced to his grave, in which he will be found resting with rosy cheek and gory mouth. The Turkish *Ubirs* were usually reported as bloated in appearance, and ruddy, dark in color; these characteristics were often attributed to the recent drinking of blood.

The causes of vampiric generation were many and varied in original folklore. In Turkic and Slavic traditions, any corpse that was jumped over by an animal, particularly a dog or a cat, was feared to become one of the undead. Ubirs are reanimated corpses that kill living creatures to absorb life essence from their victims. The Kashoubes (Polish Slavs of the Danzic region) say that when a *Vieszcy*, as they call the Vampire, wakes from his sleep within the grave, he begins to gnaw his hands and feet; and as he gnaws, one after another, first his relations, then his other neighbors, sicken and die. When he has finished his own store of flesh, he rises at midnight and destroys cattle, or climbs a belfry and sounds the bell. All who hear the ill-omened tones will soon die. But generally he sucks the blood of sleepers. Those on whom he has operated will be found dead the next morning, with a very small wound on the left side of the breast, exactly over the heart. The Lusatian Wends hold that when a corpse chews its shroud or sucks its own breast, all its kin will soon follow it to the grave. The Wallachians say that a *Murony* – a sort of cross between a *Werewolf* and a Vampire, connected by name with *Mahr* or *Nightmare* – can take the form of a dog, a cat, or a toad, and also of any kind of blood-sucking insect. When he is exhumed, he is found to have long nails of recent growth on his hands and feet, and blood is streaming from his eyes, ears, nose and mouth.

## Soul-body relation

Common Slavonic belief indicates a stark distinction between soul and body. The soul is not considered to be perishable. The Slavs believed that upon death the soul would go out of the body, and wander about its neighborhood and workplace for 40 days (compare the Tibetan belief of 40 days in Bardo prior to reincarnation) before moving on to an eternal afterlife. Thus pagan Slavs considered it necessary to leave a window or door open in the house for the soul to pass through at its leisure. During this time the soul was believed to have the capability of re-entering the corpse of the deceased. Much like the spirits mentioned earlier, the passing soul could either bless or wreak havoc on its family and neighbors during its 40 days of passing. Upon an individual's death, much stress was placed on proper burial rites to ensure the soul's purity and peace as it separated from the body. The death of an unbaptized child, a violent or an untimely death, or the death of a grievous sinner (such as a sorcerer or murderer) were all grounds for a soul to become unclean after death. A soul could also be made unclean if its body were not given a proper burial. Alternatively, a body not given a proper burial could be susceptible to possession by other unclean souls and spirits. Slavs feared unclean souls because of their potential for taking vengeance. From these deep beliefs pertaining to death and the soul, derives the invention of the Slavic concept of Upyr/Vampire. A Vampire is the manifestation of an unclean spirit possessing a decomposing body. This undead creature needs the blood or life energy of the living to sustain its body's existence and is considered to be vengeful and jealous towards the living. Although this concept of Vampire exists in slightly different forms throughout Slavic countries and some of their non-Slavic neighbors, it is possible to trace the development of Vampire belief to Slavic spiritualism preceding Christianity in Slavic regions. These applications are similar to the Turkish culture.

## How to end Vampire attacks

Methods of destroying suspected Vampires varied, with staking as the most commonly cited method, particularly in South Slavic cultures. Ash was the preferred wood in Russia and the Baltic states, or hawthorn in Serbia, with a record of oak in Silesia. Aspen was also used for stakes, as it was believed that Christ's cross was made from aspen (aspen branches on the graves of purported Vampires were also believed to prevent their risings at night). Potential Vampires were most often staked through the heart, the mouth was targeted in Russia and northern Germany, and the stomach in north-eastern Serbia. But a Bohemian Vampire, when staked in this manner in the year 1337 – says the German folklorist Wilhelm Mannhardt – merely exclaimed that the stick would be very useful for keeping off dogs; and a Strigon (or Istrian Vampire) who was transfixed with a sharp thorn cudgel near Laibach, in 1672, pulled it out of his body and flung it back contemptuously. Piercing the skin of the chest was a way of "deflating" the bloated Vampire. This is similar to a practice of "anti-Vampire burial": burying sharp objects, such as sickles, with the corpse, so that they may penetrate the skin if the body bloats sufficiently while transforming into a Revenant.



Decapitation with a grave-digger's shovel was the preferred method in German and western Slavic areas, with the head buried between the feet, behind the buttocks or away from the body. This act was seen as a way of hastening the departure of the soul, which in some cultures, was said to linger in the corpse. The Wends say that if a Vampire is hit over the back of the head with a shovel, he will squeal like a pig. The Vampire's head, body, or clothes could also be spiked and pinned to the ground to prevent their rising. Romani people drove steel or iron needles into a corpse's heart at the time of burial and placed bits of steel in the mouth, over the eyes, ears and between the fingers. They also placed hawthorn in the corpse's sock or drove a hawthorn stake through the legs. In a 16th century burial near Venice, a brick forced into the mouth of a female corpse has been interpreted as a Vampire-slaying ritual, by the archaeologists who discovered it in 2006. In Bulgaria, over a 100 skeletons with metal objects, such as plough bits, embedded in the torso have been discovered. Further measures included pouring boiling water over the grave, or complete incineration of the body. In the Balkans, a Vampire could also be killed by being shot or drowned, by repeating the funeral service, by sprinkling holy water on the body, or by exorcism. In Romania, garlic could be placed in the mouth, and as recently as the 19th century, the precaution of shooting a bullet through the coffin was taken. For resistant cases, the body was dismembered and the pieces burned, mixed with water, and administered to family members as a cure. In Saxon regions of Germany, a lemon was placed in the mouth of suspected Vampires.

## Vântoase

Vântoase (sing.: *Vântoasa*) are creatures present in Romanian folklore, as a sort of female spirits *(Iele)*. Popular beliefs describe them as capable of causing dust storms and strong winds, similar to *Harpies*. They live in the forests, in the air, in the lakes and use the winds to travel. They are sometimes said to cause winds when they dance the chorus. The Vântoase are also believed to be capable of attacking children, and the only protection against them is the mysterious "grass of the winds". The name Vântoase comes from the Romanian word for wind: *vânt*.



## Vârcolac

In Romania the *Vârcolac* is a being with both a mythological and folklorist connotation. In Romanian mythology it is a demon that eats the Sun and the Moon, thus generating the Moon phases and eclipses. The Russian dictionary translates vârcolac as "lunar eclipse", a "specter formed by a corpse" and a "demon". The general assumption is that a Vârcolac arises from a corpse that has been lying in its grave for seven years and comes out in the form of a small black child, who is going to suck the blood of the living. It can visit the same victims with intervals for several weeks, while they slowly get more and more exhausted and waste away. After the ninth visit, the victim usually dies within a few days. A small red patch would then be visible on the victims arm. The Vârcolac was believed to be able to enter a room even through the smallest hole, like a keyhole, just like a *Nightmare* or *Incubus*. Therefore the creature was extremely feared. In folklore the Vârcolaci can also arise from other sources, such as: unborn children, those born with abnormalities, people who have killed a brother or sister, the seventh or ninth child of the same couple, or even an action contrary to a tradition can generate a Vârcolac. The Vârcolac-man will transform during an eclipse, and most of the time, it is his soul that will ascend into the sky and eat the Sun or Moon. If the soul's connection to the body is severed during the transformation, the soul is lost forever. The etymology of the word "vârcolac" seems to come from Bulgarian or Serbian, from *vylx* + *dlaka* meaning "wolf-haired". In Norse mythology *Sköll* is a demon who eats the Sun and the Moon. When the term Vârcolac is used to denote the classic *Werewolf*, instead of a sheer mythological being, the term is a synonym for the *Vyrkolaki*.

## Vedmak and Vedma

In Slavic folklore, a *Vedmak* (Belarusian: вядзьмак, вядзьмар; Bulgarian: вещер; Croatian: vještac; Macedonian: вештер; Russian: ведьмак; Czech: *Vědmák*; Ukrainian: відьмак; Polish: *Wiedźmak*; Serbian: вештац) is a warlock or male witch, the female equivalent (witch) being *Vedma*, but unlike the latter, the Vedmak could also possess positive qualities, like healing people or animals. On the other hand, they are thought to be people connected to the Devil, and capable of bringing harm by sending illnesses, killing cattle, spoiling a harvest, etc. A Vedmak can turn into any animal or any object. Vedmak stems from Proto-Slavic *vědět* (to know) and Old East Slavic вѣдь (knowledge; witchcraft, comparable to the use of the term "cunning" in English folklore). The words Vedmak or Vedma were also used as an insult.

## Vetevana

In Estonian folklore the *Vetevana* is a male water creature in the beliefs of various peoples. The term is however vague and can include both *deities* (e.g. *Ahti*) and *male Mermaids*. In general the Vetevana can be compared to the English *Merman*, the German *Wassermann*, the Finnish *Vetehinen,* or the Russian *Vodjanoi*. He was regarded as mostly hostile to humans.

## Vila

A *Vila* (pl.: *Vile* or *Vily* – Russian: *вила*; Ukrainian: *віла*; Serbo-Croatian: *Vila*; Polish: *Wiła*; Slovene: *Vila*; Bulgarian: *Vila, Diva, Juda, Samovila, Samodiva, Samojuda*; Old East Slavic: *Vila*; Slovak: *Víla*; Czech: *Víla, Samodiva, Divoženka*) is a Slavic *Fairy*, similar to a *Nymph*, female, beautiful and with long blonde hair. It is the South Slavic and Russian equivalent of the *Mamuna* and *Rusalka*. Vile are described as group beings and are predominantly associated with the water element, but also appear in forests, fields and mountains. The related *Rusalkas*, whose worship is closely linked to the cult of the dead, in contrast to the *Vila*, usually have a disastrous effect on the men who encounter them. In western Slavic Poland it is known in a degraded form as a *Bogeyman* or *demon* bringing madness to people. Procopius of Caesarea already reports about their worship in the context of the pre-Christian cult in the 6th century. However, he does not give the Slavic name, but refers to them as "Nymphs". (Some researchers believe that the belief in Vile is a result of Balkan Slavs borrowing the

Greek belief in Nymphs.) Medieval Russian treatises associate them with the goddess *Mokosh*. Their worship was still an explicit part of church prohibitions in the 11th and 12th centuries. Modern ethnographic documents attest to the belief in the *Wilen* above all in the South and East Slavic regions; in Bulgaria a Samovila festival was celebrated at Pentecost.

In folklore *Vile* are believed to have originated from the souls of girls who died young. They inhabited forests *(Samoviel)*, mountains *(Zagorkinie)*, rivers and lakes *(Brodarice)* and clouds *(Oblakinie)*. They were able to ride on clouds and move them with their eyes. They usually appeared in groups and could take the form of beautiful winged girls with light and almost transparent bodies, naked or thinly clad, but also horses, swans, falcons, or wolves. Sometimes – just like field daemons – they turned into whirlwinds as well. According to some, Vile could also turn themselves into snakes. They are usually well-disposed towards humans. Sometimes they helped young men get married, warned of hailstorms, helped farmers in need or predicted the future, and even marriages between a Vile and a human occur in the stories. However, they take revenge for insults and can also confuse people and lead them off the path, or worse when really angry, they could destroy fields by causing hailstorms, gales or droughts. It also happened that the Vile danced to death the men they met, blinded them or drove them mad, bringing on them desires impossible to satisfy. In Slovakian folklore, Vile are *Revenants*; brides who died before the wedding and find no rest in the grave. Dancing with them is considered to be life-threatening for a young man.

In old Polish, the word *Wiła* meant "a crazy person", which is evident in *Rozmowie Mistrza Polikarpa ze Śmiercią* (The Conversation of Master Polikarpa with Death), a late medieval dialog in verse, written probably by Mikołaj Rej in the early 15th century. According to Aleksander Bruckner, it may have resulted from the belief that people who saw these creatures, fell into madness: in some languages the word "Wiła" came to mean a demon – in others, its victim. Perhaps this is the origin of today's word *szaławiła* (light-hearted).

## Vitryanik

In Slavic folklore the *Vitryanik* is a demonic character, an evil spirit of wind and mountains. Among the southern Slavs the *Vitryanic* is a

mountain spirit, which blows a strong wind. Whoever tries to catch him, he kills with the power of the wind. In the beliefs of the Slavic peoples, the Vitryanik causes drought, brings snowstorms, casts on people and cattle deterioration and illness, even leprosy. Often after its attacks on cattle, the milk of a cow is mixed with blood or the cow stops giving milk at all. In some regions he is regarded as being the same creature as the *Bosorkun*, who is especially harmful to people at night and on Ivan Kupala (June 23/ July 7), on the day of Luke (December 13/26) and on the days of Saint George, the patron saint of cattle (April 23/May 6).

## Vodyanitsa



The *Vodyanitsa* (Russian: водяница; pl.: *Vodyanitsy*) is a beautiful green-haired *Water-Maiden* of Russian folklore, often described as the wife of a *Vodyanoy*. This water-spirit sometimes appears in the form of a gold-finned fish or a white swan. Vodyanitsy prefer forest lakes, mill ponds, wells, and (less often) the sea as their habitat. They are considered harmless spirits, although they sometimes tear nets and damage millstones. Marine Vodyanitsy are more aggressive than tose who live in freshwater and are dangerous to ships. According to some beliefs, the main difference between the Vodyanitsy and other water-spirits is that she is a baptized drowned girl. The term is often used as a synonym for *Rusalka*.

## Vodyany or Wodnik

In Slavic folk-beliefs the *Vodyany* or *Wodnik* (also: *Vodník, Vodenjak, Vodyanoj, Wodjanoj, Wodylnik, Wodnikami, Łobasta; Hastrman* in German) is a male demon of inland water reservoirs and also their ruler. It is a water-sprite, affectionately called *Dyedushka* (Grandfather). He generally inhabits the depths of rivers, lakes, or pools (and wells in Kashubian folklore), but sometimes he dwells in swamps, and he is especially fond of taking up his quarters in a mill-stream, close to the wheel. Every mill is supposed to have a Vodyany attached to it, or several of them, if it has more wheels than one. Consequently millers were generally obliged to be well-versed in the black art, for if they do not understand how to treat the water-spirits, all will go ill with them. The Vodyany is often interchangeable with drowning in folklore. In this context, a child that got drowned without being baptized and then grew up in water for seven years, or a child without baptism drowned by its mother, became an Vodyany. There were also beliefs referring Vodyany to generally demonic figures associated with the underworld, the devilish world – here a Vodyany was created from silt accumulated at the bottom of a reservoir, or from clay. During the winter the Vodyany sleeps, but with the early spring he awakens, wrathful and hungry, and manifests his anger by various spiteful actions. In order to propitiate him the peasants in some places buy a horse, which they feed well for three days; then they tie its legs together, smear its head with honey, adorn its manes with red ribbons, attach two millstones to its neck, and at midnight fling it into an ice-hole, or, when the thaw has set in, into the middle of a river. Three days long the Vodyany has awaited his present, manifesting his impatience by groans and water upheaval. After he has received his due, he becomes quiet. Fishermen propitiate him at the same season of the year by pouring oil on the water, begging him, while doing so, to be good to them; and millers once a year sacrifice a black pig to him. A goose also, is generally presented to him in the middle of September, as a reward for his having watched over the farmer's ducks and geese during the summer months.

## Appearance

The Vodyany is usually represented as a naked old man of about 2 feet tall with fishy, green eyes, a wrinkled face and long, disheveled hair with seaweed in it, and with amniotic membranes between his fingers. He is usually dressed in red and in such a way that it was sometimes difficult to distinguish him from an ordinary (albeit little) human person. Vodyany could also appear in the form of a child, a woman, a maiden, or a deceased neighbor. Wherever he stood, a puddle of water was left behind. Wodnik also took the form of aquatic animals, often appearing as a pike, or at the head of a school of fish as the largest of them. He could also turn into a horse, emerging from the water. Sometimes he is represented, like the western *Merman*, with a fish's tail. The Vodyany is much given to drinking, and delights in carouses and card-playing. He is a patron of bee-keeping, and it is customary to enclose the first swarm of the year in a bag, and to throw it, weighted with a stone, into the nearest river, as an offering to him. The person that does this, will flourish as a bee-master, especially if he/she takes a honeycomb from a hive on St. Zosima's day (celebrated by the Orthodox Church on April 4), and flings it into a millstream at midnight.

## Behavior

When a Vodyany appears in a village it is easy to recognize him, for water
is always dripping from his left pant leg and the spot on which he sits
instantly becomes wet. In his own realm he not only rules over all the
fishes that swim, but he greatly influences a lot of fishers and mariners.
Sometimes he brings them good luck; sometimes he lures them to
destruction. Sometimes he gets caught in nets, but he immediately tears
them asunder, and all the fish that had been enclosed in them swim out
after him. A fisherman once found a dead body floating about in the water,
so he took it into his boat. But to his horror the corpse suddenly came
to life, uttered a wild laugh, and jumped overboard. That was one of the
Vodyany's pranks. A sportsman once waded into a river after a wounded
duck. The Vodyany got hold of him by the neck, and would have pulled
him under if he had not cut himself loose with his axe. When he got home
his neck was covered with blue marks left by the Vodyany's fingers.

Sometimes the Vodyany will jump on a horse and ride it to death; so,
to keep him away while horses are fording a river, the peasants signed a
cross on the water with a knife or a scythe. One should not bathe, say the
peasants, without a cross round one's neck, or after sunset. It is especially
dangerous to bathe during the week of the *Feast of the Prophet Ilya,*
formerly *Perun the Thunderer* (Orthodox Church, August 2), for then
the Vodyany is on the lookout for victims. During the day he generally
lies at the bottom of deep pools, but at night he sits on the shore combing
his hair, or he sports in the water, diving with a splash and coming up
far away. Sometimes, also, he fights with the wood-sprites, the noise of
their combats being heard from afar. In Bohemia, fishermen are afraid of
assisting a drowning man, thinking the Vodyany will be offended and will
drive away the fish from their nets, and they say he often sits on the shore
with a club in his hand, from which hang ribbons of various hues: with
these he allures children, and those whom he gets hold of he drowns. The
souls of his victims the Vodyany keeps, making them his servants, but
their bodies he allows to float to shore.

W.R.S. Ralston, who collected most of the above information in his *Songs
of the Russian People,* writes that the Vodyany have their subaqueous
dwellings well-stocked with all sorts of cattle, which they drive out into
the fields to graze by night. They have wives and children too, under the
waves, the women sometimes being women who have been drowned, or

on whom a parent's curse was placed within the power of the Evil One.
Many a girl that has drowned herself has been turned into a *Rusalka* or
some such being, and then has married a Vodyany. On the occasion of
such a marriage, or indeed of any subaqueous wedding, the Vodyany
indulge in such revels and mad pranks that the waters are wildly agitated,
and often carry away bridges or mill-dams; at least, that is how the
peasants explain such accidents as arise when the snows melt and the
streams wax violent. When a water-sprite's wife is about to bear a child
he assumes the appearance of an ordinary mortal, and fetches a midwife
from some neighboring village to attend to her. Once a water-baby was
caught by some fishermen in their nets. It splashed about joyously as long
as it was in the water, but wailed sorely when it was taken into a cottage.
Its capturers returned it to its father on his promising to drive plenty of
fish into their nets in the future – a promise which he conscientiously
fulfilled.



## Volkolak

The *Volkolak*, *Volkodlak* or *Volkulak* (Russian: Волколáк; Belarusian:
ваўкалáк, *Vaukalak*; Polish: *Wilkołak*; Ukrainian: вовкулáка, *Vovkulak*)
is in Slavic folklore a human *Werewolf*-variation, often someone who
for a certain time can change (or was changed) into a wolf. Instead of a
half man – half beast creature, the Volkolak was often described as an
ordinary wolf, sometimes showing oddities in appearance and behavior,
indicating its human origin. A Volkolak retains his human mind, but
cannot speak. According to folk beliefs, transformation into wolves is the
most common type of "were-transformations" among the Slavs. It has
been known since antiquity. It is present to some extent with all Slavic
peoples, but especially among the Belarusians, Poles and Ukrainians.
The motif of a person turning into a wolf was present in the folk beliefs
of all Slavs, but it was best preserved with Ukrainians, Belarusians and
eastern Poles. In the Russian regions the word *Volkolak* is recorded only
in the southern areas, and in the rest of the territory people who turn
into wolves, were simply called Óборотень *Oberotem* (*Werewolf*), but the
beliefs about them are very similar to beliefs about Volkolaks. In Slovaks,
and especially in Czech, beliefs about Werewolves are few; in Lusatia
they are also reduced and are found mainly in Lower Lusatia. In South
Slavic beliefs Werewolves and *Ghouls* resemble each other, and except in
Slovene, these images are almost merged.

Variations on the word "Volkolak" are extremely common and widespread within the Slavic languages or languages influenced by them:

- Russian: *Volkolak(a)* (Mosalsky district, Kaluga province), *Volkodlak* (Smolensk; probably a word from a book, influenced by South Slavic languages), *Volkulak* (Voronezh, Kursk, Orlov), *Vukula* (Smolensk, Voronezh)
- Belarusian: *Vaukalak(a)*, *Vaukolak(a)*, *Vaukulak*, *Vaukulak*
- Belarusian Ukrainian and West-Poland dialects: *Vocukolak*, *Vovkulach*, *Vocukulach*, лужицкие *Wjelkoraz*
- Ukrainian: *Vovkulak(a)*, *Vovkolak*, *Volkulak*; southwestern dialects: *Vovkun* and *Vovkunitsa*, *Vovkolab*
- Ukrainian Hutsul dialects: *Vovkunka*
- Ukrainian Transcarpathian dialects: *Vovkunak*, *Vovchur(ies)* Ukrainian Lemkovsky dialects: *Vovkurad*, *Vovkorab*
- Old Polish: Wilkołek (predominantly), *Wylkolek*, *Vylkolek*, *Wilcolec*, *Wylkolecz*, *Wilkołak*, *Wylkolak* (earliest form – first mentioned in 1455 in Latin-Polish dictionary)
- Polish: *Wilkołak*, *Wilkołek*, *Wilkołap*
- Slovak: *Vlkolák*, *Vlkodlak*, *Vilkolak*, *Vrkolak*
- Czech: *Vlkodlak* (glutton), probably a book-word influenced by South Slavic languages, in popular speech found only in Polish dialects as *Vyl'kodlak*)
- Old Slavonic: *Vl'kodlak*, *Vurkolak*, *Voykolak*, *Voykolak*
- Bulgarian: *Vvrkolàk*, *Vvlkolàk*, *Vvrkolakt*, *Vlkodlak*, *Vvrkodlak*, *Vvrkodlak*, *Vvrkodlak*, *Frkodlak*, *Frkolak* (from the Greek βουλκολάκας, which is borrowed from Slavic languages), *Vrkokolak*, *Vrakulak*, *Urkulak*, *F'kulak*, *Vrakalàk*, *Vrakalok*, *Vrkolak*
- Macedonian: *Vrkolak*, *Volkolak*
- Old Serbian: *Vlkodlaci* (pl.) (first mentioned in the Serbian (Ilovica) Kormčja)
- Serbo-Croatian: *Vukódlak*, *Vlokódlak*, *Ukodlak*, *Kodlak*; Croatian: *Vùkodlak*, *Kudlak*;
- Croatian: *Čakovsky*: *Vukozlàk*, *Kozlàk*, *Kodlàk*
- Timoska Krajina (East Serbia, Timok valey region): *Vrkolak*
- Slovene: *Volkodlák*, *Vukodlák*, *Okodlák*, *Kódlak*, *Verkodlák*, *Kodlakon*, *Volcodlac* (word mentioned in 1592)
- Proto-Slavic: *vl̥ko-dlakъ* (presumably) from dialect *vl̥ko-t/dlak(-ъ)*
- Romanian: *Vârcolác*
- Greek: βρυκόλακες – *Vrikolakes*

- Dalmatian: *Valtudluk, Vukolak*
- Trans-Romanian: *Vacodlac*
- Albanian: *Vurkollák, Vurvollák*
- Turkish: *Vurkolak*
- Lithuanian: *Vilkólakis, Vilkakis*

The neologism *Vurdalak*, was introduced into the Russian language by
A.S. Pushkin (the poem *Vurdalak* from the cycle *Songs of Western Slavs*,
1835) and A.K. Tolstoy (the Gothic story *The Vurdalak Family*, 1839)
and was used mainly in relation to Ghouls and Vampires, which is a
combination and distortion of several Balkan forms.



**Wolf-man or Bear-man**

Etymologically the first part of the name Volkolak comes from the
word wolf (Proto-Slavic *vḷkъ*) and changed accordingly in the specific
languages. The second part, according to the classical hypothesis,
corresponds to the Church-Slavic *dlaka*, Serbo-Chorvian *dl̀ka*, Slovenian
*dláka*, meaning: "hair", "pelt", "wool", "horse or cow hair", hence the
Russian *kudla*. According to another version, now accepted by the
majority of researchers, the second element probably derives from
the Balto-Slavonic *dlak(i)as* (bear), Prussian *tlokis / clockis (klokis)*,
Lithuanian *lokỹs*, Latvian *lâcis*, Latvian *lōcś*; which is related to the Greek
ἄρκτος, Hittite *ḫartagga* (bear-man), etc. In this context, the Proto-
Slavonic reconstruction of the second part, as *dlaka* (bear), is proposed.
In this connection it is noted that the term *dlak* (wolf) may be of the
same origin as the Lithuanian *vilktakis* and is identical in meaning to the
Visigothic *Ber-ulfus*. The combination of the abilities to turn into a wolf
and a bear is described in the old Russian book *Charovnik* and in the
beliefs of Transcarpathia. "Volkodlak" could also mean *"a man with the
features of a bear or wolf"*.

**Folk-beliefs**

It was believed that sorcerers, in order to turn into wolves, read a spell
and jumped, stepped over, tumbled or climbed over an object endowed
with magical power, or threw it over themselves, etc. A sorcerer usually
had to perform the same actions in the reverse order if he wanted to
reverse the transformation. Sorcerers transformed themselves into
wolves at their will in order to harm people. There were beliefs about
people whose propensity to periodic werewolfism was a kind of curse

they carried from their moment of birth, as a result of the behavior of their parents, or as punishment for their own sins in a former lifetime. Various zoomorphic features, such as hair resembling wolf fur, were considered to be a distinctive feature of such wolfhounds in human form. Transformation often occurred at night or at certain times of year. It was often believed that such wolves did not have control over their behavior when in wolf form, when they attacked livestock and people, even loved ones. Sometimes cannibalism was attributed to them. According to some folk beliefs a sorcerer or witch could also turn another person into a wolf, usually for revenge, by throwing an enchanted wolf skin on him/her, tying a belt around the victim, enchanting the door through which their victim had to pass, and more. A very popular story was the transformation of all the guests of an entire wedding into wolves. The period of transformation ranged from a few days to several years. Unwilling Volkolak or Werewolves suffer from fear and despair, miss human life and do not mix with wolves. It was often believed that they did not eat raw meat, subsisting on wild foods and food stolen from humans. Many ways were mentioned by which they could supposedly be helped back to their original form.

**Origins**

Speaking about the antiquity of the ideas about the transformation of people into wolves in the Slavic lands, we can mention the tribe of *Nevrovs*, who lived in the 6th to 5th centuries BC somewhere on the territory of modern Ukraine and/or Belarus. According to Herodotus (c. 484-430 BC) in his *History* members of this tribe became wolves for a few days a year, probably in winter: *"These people are apparently witches. The Scythians and the Hellenes living among them at least claim that every Nevrov annually turns into a wolf for a few days and then takes human form again"*. Possibly, a ritual "transformation" is meant. The comparison of the "werewolfing" of the Nevrovs with the Slavic festive dressing-up is for some researchers one of the arguments for the hypothetical Slavic nature of the Nevrovs. The earliest evidence of ideas about the transformation into wolves are, apparently, mentioned in the Italian and Byzantine chronicles of supernatural abilities of the Bulgarian *Bayan Magesnik* (c. 910-970) *"It is said, that Boyan so mastered magic, that once he inadvertently turned into a wolf or a beast like him"*. In *The Tale of Igor's Campaign* (1185) the Polotsk (Belarus) prince Vseslav Brjachislavich (c. 1101) transforms into a wolf at night and reaches Tmutarakan' in this form during the night (however, it is possibly only meant as a metaphor):

The changing into a wolf, together with other animals, is also mentioned
in the poem about the singer Boyan and the Prince Igor Sviatoslavich. The
Serbian Ilovica and Russian Kormchikas of 1262 and 1282, respectively,
mention wolf-dogs (the first mention of the word) chasing clouds and
eating the moon and sun. In *Russian bylinae*, Volkh Vseslavievich (Volga
Svyatoslavich) turns into a wolf : "*To other wisdom he, Volh, learned to be
a grey wolf*", "*Volga felt like a lot of wisdom... prowling about the pure fields
as a grey wolf*".

In the 15th to 18th centuries, beliefs in Werewolves in Polish lands
were repeatedly mentioned in local and foreign historical chronicles
and demonological works. Polish authors in their works, within the
framework of the prevailing ideas in Europe, denied the possibility
of a real transformation, indicating its imaginary nature, created by a
diabolical deception. One of the earliest recorded cases is the report of
the capture in the woods of a Masurian peasant with abundant vegetation
on his body, numerous scars, allegedly from canine fangs, and suspicious
behavior. He was accused of attacking his neighbors' cattle in wolf form,
which he gradually acquired on the day of John the Baptist and during
Christmas. He was locked in the cellar of the castle of the Prussian
duke Albrecht (1490-1568), but the expected transformation into a
wolf never happened, and he was later apparently burned alive. In the
seventeenth and eighteenth centuries, becoming a wolf was one of the
charges in Polish witch-trials. Most mythological tales and beliefs about
wolves, as well as other characters in Slavic folklore, were recorded in the
nineteenth and twentieth centuries. In the twentieth century, traditional
representations of werewolfing faded away, which is probably due not
only to the general decline in traditional beliefs, but also to the decline in
wolf numbers, although in some regions stories of wolf transformations
still retain some popularity. In modern urban demonological
representations, original Slavic views of the Volkolak are replaced by the
image of Werewolves (lycanthropes) from western popular culture.

**The Slavic wolf-cult theory**
The wolf is one of the central, most mythologized, dangerous and revered
wild animals in Slavic folk tradition. The Slavs probably once had their
traditional wolf-cults. Among the main characteristics of the wolf
image; living in the wild, predation, connection with blood, chtonicity,
connection with darkness, connection with the dead, its way of mating,
male and erotic symbolism, connection with unclean forces (the wolf can
be identified with unclean forces, suffer from them, or, on the contrary, be
dangerous because of them) and some demonic properties. Furthermore
the rampant presence of wolves in winter, which coincides with a period
of activation of evil forces, the intermediary function of the wolf between
people and God and people and evil, the definition of the wolf as an
"alien", the connection with crossing boundaries and critical moments,
the closeness of the image to images of a bear on the one hand, and a dog
on the other. The use of its body parts and the word "wolf" as a magical
means *"for the acquisition of frightening properties, aggressiveness, vitality
and health"*, played a role as well.

Apart from the theory supported by researchers like Claude Lecouteux,
who explain the *Werewolf* by the projected etheric doubles in wolf shape
of shamans and witches capable of such an art, it is widely believed that
the *Werewolf*-phenomena in general links to totemism, in which rites
of disguise in the skins of totemic animals were performed. The Slavs
had a widespread custom of dressing up in wolf masks and costumes
on New Year's holidays, on Shrovetide and on some other occasions,
which may be regarded as an imitation of "werewolfing". During the
destruction of pagan beliefs and the strengthening of Christianity,
the attitude toward wolves changed from neutral to negative. Also
werewolfing, once seen as a sign of *"an individual's accession to a divine
or sacred animal"*, became viewed negatively and considered a *"sign or
symbol of unclean power or its attributes"*. Relying on the fact that – with
the exception of transformations of entire weddings – accounts of wolf-
shapeshifting of women among the Slavs are very rare, we could conclude
that representations of Volkolaks are a folklorization of the archaic
rites of male adolescent initiation. The ancient Slavs were supposedly
accompanied by ritual rebirth into wolves, and the subsequent "wolf"
unions of young warriors who isolated themselves from society, lived in
the forest (and also engaged in robbery). Echoes of these phenomena are
seen, for example, in Polish and Ukrainian rites of initiation into male

communities in the 19th century and in Ukrainian representations of the Zaporozhe Cossacks and noble robbers of the early 19th century. It has also been suggested that representations of werewolfing might be traced back to the Indo-European worship of the wolf god – the god of warriors, the world of the dead and fertility. Representations of the transformation of the people on a wedding into wolves, are also associated by some researchers with totemism, as wedding groups once signified clan groups. There are, however, also skeptical opinions concerning these theories, denying the connection of ancient customs and beliefs with later representations, which may well have arisen independently.

## Vubar or Vupăr

*Vubar* (Chuvash *Vupăr*, in the upper dialect also *Vopăr, Lopăr, Lapăr, Vapăr*; Mari: *Vuver*; Udmurt: *Ubyr*; Komi-ziryan: *Üpyr*; Karachai: *Obur*) is an *Alp*-type evil spirit in Chuvash folklore. The Vubar appears at night and, taking the form of domestic animals, a fire snake or a man, pounces on sleeping people, causing suffocation and nightmares – (вăпăр пуснă *Văpăr pusnă* (Vubar crushed), вупăр çыпăçнă *Vupăr çupăçnă* (Vubar struck). Like the classical *Incubus/Succubus* the Vubar presses men in the form of a woman and women in the form of a man. Often it gets attached to one particular person which it visits frequently. According to local myths, old sorceresses turn into Vubars. By attacking sleeping people, they thereby improve their health. The sleeping person who is under attack cannot move or say anything. Vubars can also strangle people or spoil their health, thus causing them to suffer from a severe disease called вупăрлă хаяр *Vuparla haiar* (Vubar's evil). The Vubar does attack animals as well as people and can even cling to a calf lying by its mother's side. People and animals affected by a Vubar are helped by a Yomzia (medicine man) with incantations.

**Protection against a Vubar**
- When a Vubar is crushing a person, and someone close to him or her notices the attack, he or she should stand up and shout: *"God, what has happened to this man?"* This makes the Vubar frightened and it will disappear.
- It was recommended that they tell their pets about the Vubar's visit so that it would not come again. If a Vubar could be frightened off during the attack, it turned into some black object, for example into a scrap

of felt. Then it was recommended to immediately destroy this foreign objects or to burn it. The next morning the person who visited the house in the guise of a Vubar could then be spotted with a burnt face or with a broken leg, or some other kind of wound.

- To get rid of Vubar, the Northern Chuvash, before going to bed, tied a neck cross on the forehead, or put it in their mouths..
- They also considered it useful to smell the sweat between your toes before going to bed.
- It is impossible to catch a Vubar with one's bare hands. There was a custom after waking up to throw a handful of ashes into the street after Vubar, saying, *Вупăр урăх ан кил, вутлă кĕл canamăn!* (*"Vubar, don't come again, I'm throwing fire ashes!"*)
- In ancient days people believed that Vubars actually caused eclipses. When a Vubar was devouring the Sun, thus causing an eclipse, the Chuvash elders wrestled with Vubar (shouting and frightening him, throwing burning logs, onions and metal objects in the direction of the moon or the sun). While trying to ward off a Vubar from the moon or the sun, it is also possible to pour ashes on a window sill or to use a slingshot made from a rowan tree, and the Vubar will at once leave the body alone.

## Vupkăn

The *Vupkăn* (bringer of misery, damager – also *Opgan* or *Vupgan*; Chuvash: Вупкăн) is an evil spirit in Chuvash mythology. The Chuvash consider the Opgan to be the cause of many terrible diseases, including epidemic diseases and mental illnesses. The demon is shaped like a dog, but makes itself invisible and approaches people like a swift wind, causing a disturbance in their minds. Three black sheep were sacrificed to appease him. The first is given to the *Vupkăn aşşĕvupgan* (Father Vupkan), the second to the *Vupkan amăşĕ* (Mother Vupgan) and the last sheep to the *Vupkăn turro* (Vupgan god). A Vupgan is a very destructive being. Only through cunning is it possible to get rid of it.

# W



## Wëkrëkùs

In Kashubian folklore the *Wëkrëkùsa* is an inferior spirit who cares for loners, outsiders, misfits, etc. At the same time he was the spirit of failure and also favored those who ridicule others.

## Wiedźma

In Polish beliefs the *Wiedźma* (knower, pl.: *Wiedźmy*) was originally not a human, but a semi-demonic being (an intermediate form between demon and human) that is usually translated rather erroneously as "witch". In pre-Christian Slavic societies a witch was a woman with knowledge related to herbalism, medicine and nature. A witch with magical abilities or traits was addressed with the rather strange term *Ciotą* (Faggot). Probably until the mid-ninth century the term Wiedźma was in the eastern Slavic areas originally not a pejorative. As a result of the expansion of Christianity and the stigmatization of folk and pagan rituals, the custom of accumulating and preserving knowledge by individuals in select families fell into oblivion. Wiedźmy were accused of witchcraft, so nowadays a Wiedźma is often equated with a *Czarownicą* (sorceress). There are still women practicing witchcraft in eastern Poland. Some of them coming from the Orthodox tradition are called *Szeptunkami* (whisperers). *Ragana* (knower) was the Baltic term for a witch, a term originally only used for a *Fairy* or a sorceress. In Prussia, Ragana was the goddess of death and transfiguration, and also a witch. Her sacred animal was the toad.

## Wieszczy

A *Wieszczy* (pl.: *Wieszcze;* "soothsayer", "fore-teller"; also *Vjesci*) is a vampiric figure from Slavic demonology, a form of posthumous existence of the human soul, similar to the images of a *Upior*, however, in many areas it has its own separate identity, distinguished by specific features. Distinctions between the Wieszczy and an ordinary *Upior* were mainly present in the beliefs of the Kashubians, the Kociewieks and the people of Kuyavia. However, characteristic beliefs attributed to the Wieszczy also appeared in other regions of the country, where this character was regarded either as an autonomous demonic being, or as a specific variety of Upior. Data on the physical characteristics of this figure are lacking. The most frequently mentioned trait in ethnographic studies, which made it possible to determine at birth whether a person would become a Wieszczy after death, was to be born with the so-called *czapce* (caul, or helmet). When a child had two teeth at birth is was considered to be an Upior. The people of the Skarszew area called such a person born with a caul or cap a soothsayer, and they reported the custom that, when the caul was dried and hidden, and the child had reached seven years of age, the dried caul should be grated into powder and given to the child to drink, and then everything would be all right. If this did not happen, the body of such a person would not undergo the process of rigor mortis (stiffening) after death, but would remain as limber as when he or she was alive. The inhabitants of Krotoszyn and Ostrzeszów believed that a Wieszczy occurs when one of two close friends, close relatives or peers dies.

The Wieszczy did not lose its vitality while being buried, which made it dangerous to living people, and its exceptional harmfulness manifested itself in a very characteristic way. When the person becoming a Wieszczy was buried, he or she began to chew on the clothes he/she was buried in (like the German *Nachzehrer*). Then, the first thing that happened was that all the close relatives became ill and died one by one. When no close relatives were left, it attacked the less close relatives, and when all the relatives were dead, it rose from its grave, climbed the highest building in the village (usually a church steeple or a bell tower) and shouted loudly or rang the church bells. This was supposed to cause illness and death, even to strangers living in the area where the shouting or the sound of the bells could be heard. He also rang the church bells before various natural disasters took place. This is most likely the origin of the name of the demon – Wieszczy (soothsayer) *"the one who foretold or predicted some event"*, in this case: death.

## Wietrzyca

In the tradition of the Polish Highlanders the *Wietrzyca* or *Wietrznica* is an evil atmospheric spirit, which appears during a strong wind or hurricane. According to the legends, it snatches various objects, and can rob people of their speech and break their bones. To fight the spirit, one had to use a consecrated knife, which was thrown into the air. When the knife hit the Wietrzyca, it fell to the ground covered in blood and the wind would immediately stop.

## Wurdulac

In Russian, the word *Wurdulac* (Russian: вурдалак) first appeared in the early 19th century, and it became common due to Alexander Pushkin's 1836 poem of the same name, which was part of the *Songs of the Western Slavs*-cycle. It is the corrupted form of the West Slavic word "Volkodlak" (Russian: волкодлак), which literally means "wolf's-coat" or "wolf's-hide" (i.e., it designates someone "wearing" a wolf's skin; a *Werewolf*). The meaning of the term Wurdulac, however, also spelled *Wurdalak* or *Verdilak*, took on a more autonomous position as a special kind of "Russian *Vampire*" that must consume the blood of its loved ones and convert its entire family. This notion is apparently based on Alexey K. Tolstoy's novella *The Family of the Vourdalak*, which tells the story of one such Slavic (actually, Serbian) family. In Russia the common name for Vampire (or Wurdulac) is *Upyr* (Russian: упырь). Nowadays the three terms are regarded as synonymous, but in 19th century they were seen as separate, though similar entities.

## Wurlawy

Freely translated from Sorbian in German, *Wurlawy* means something like "Wild Women of the Spreewald" (Spree-forest). In the Wendish legend, the Wurlawy were peculiar old, gray forest women, who are described as not very friendly, but on the other hand took care that everyone came home on time in the evening after work. In the old days, when girls went to the spinning room in winter, they were allowed to spin until ten o'clock in the evening. Then everyone hurried home. Those who spun longer were visited by the Wurlawy. This fear of meeting a Wurlawa at a late hour may have served local parents of young girls.

# Y

## Yovnik

*Yovnik* (Osetnik, Belarusian: *Yovnik, Asetnik*) is a character from
Belarusian mythology. Like the *Ovinnik*, the Yovnik lives in the ovine – a
shed in the farmyard, where the sheaves were dried before threshing. In
the village, houses were built with a bathhouse, and the ovine was often
combined with it. Unlike the infamous Ovinnik, the Yovnik is considered
a good character. Yovnik's main concern is maintaining the fire in the
drying oven of the barn, so that sheaves and grain dry out properly
after harvest and, as a consequence, grain is well threshed and stored
for winter. In Belarusian folklore Yovnik is a symbol of industriousness,
order and rationality, practicality and housekeeping. The Yovnik is an
incredible hard worker and humble being. The Yovnik is described as
a mysterious and secretive creature, constantly hiding from people in a
corner, near the stove, black with soot and smoke, with eyes that burn like
embers.

It is difficult to see the Jovnik. Occasionally he comes to the window of
the barn to cough up dust and soot; even more rarely he steps over the
threshold of the barn to inspect the stacks of sheaves or to watch the
threshing and at those working in the ovine. When people enter the
ovine, the Yovnik quickly hides and keeps a close eye on the unexpected
visitors. If a visitor visits the ovine with bad intentions, the Yovnik can act
very harshly. Having waited for the moment when the person is asleep,
the Yovnik can disturb his sleep, make smoke and even suffocate the
visitor with the smoke or, in extreme cases burn him, together with the
goods that are stored there. Also, if bad owners have angered the Yovnik,
he may burn down their whole place. The Yovnik is not afraid of fire,
because he himself does not burn in ordinary fire. However, he can be
burned by lightning and be killed by an unexpected thunderclap. Chaff
dust easily catches fire when the lightning strikes, and in such a situation
the Yovnik burns up without leaving a speck of dust behind. If this has
happened to one Yovnik, another Yovnik will not go to the ovine or barn
built in the same place as the old one: the ovine will be left without a
Yovnik forever.

# Z

## Zagorkinia

The *Zagorkinia* is a female Slavic Serbo-Croatian demon, a type of *Vila*. Her dwelling place was in inaccessible mountainous places. She shunned people, against whom she usually had an unfriendly attitude. However, she provided help to those who got lost or had an accident in the mountains.



## Zână

Zână (pl. *Zâne*; *Zînă* and *Zîne*; *Ḑână* and *Ḑâne* in old spellings) is the Romanian equivalent of the Greek *Charites* (a kind of *fairy*-godmother). The word Zână comes from the Roman goddess *Diana*. Zâne were regarded as beautiful creatures and the opposite of monsters like *Muma Pădurii*. These characters make positive appearances in folklore and reside mostly in the woods. They can also be seen as the Romanian equivalent of Fairies, or of the Germanic *Elfen*. They vary in size and appearance, and can transform to blend into their surroundings for protection and cover. They can appear openly in the woods and coax travelers to follow them in order to help them find their way. They may also hide in the woods and quietly guide those in need through the forest by means of signs and "breadcrumbs". They give life to fetuses in the womb and bestow upon them great gifts such as the art of dancing, beauty, kindness, and good luck. In folk tales, it is told that one should not upset them because they also have the power to do bad things or put a curse on the wrongdoer. They also act like guardian angels, especially for children going into the forest, or for other good people.

## Zaraza

*Zaraza* (also: *Czarny mór, Morawica, Mór, Morowce powietrzne, Powietrze, Czarna śmierć, Pomór, Pomorek* or *Przymorek*) is a Slavic plague-demon who is the personification of the most dangerous, epidemic infectious diseases. She is a female, gloomy specter, lean, with disheveled hair, dressed in white or black. Sometimes Zaraza goes around the villages in the guise of a pale, thin woman, covered with a sheet.

In the nineteenth century in the Sandomierz region, when a man fell
ill with typhus, a fusillade was fired into the four corners of the ceiling,
under which the sick man lay, to drive the plague from the room. In 1888,
a cholera epidemic broke out in Machow, Poland. According to one of the
residents, a couple of men who were standing guard saw the specter of
this disease as a black, tall lady with disheveled hair walking through the
village.

## Zburător

*Zburător* or *Sburător* is a supernatural being in Romanian folklore,
described as a *"roving spirit who makes love to maidens by night"*. The
Zburător is also compared to an *Incubus*, but is described as a more
malevolent demon. Once every seven years, at night, it attacks a woman,
slipping into her home through an open window. While she is asleep,
it kisses her so gently that she may not even wake up. The next day,
the woman awakes feeling drained of energy, her body throbbing with
pain, and she is easily agitated. The Zburător is also referred to in some
regions as a *Zmeu* (a dragon-like creature), although it has more human
aspects than the Zmeu. Dimitrie Cantemir, writing about the myth in
*Descriptio Moldaviae* (1714-1716) stated that "Zburător" meant "flyer"
(Latin: *volatilis*), and according to the beliefs of the Moldavians it was
*"a ghost, a young, handsome man who visits women in the middle of the
night, especially recently married ones and does indecent things with them,
although he cannot be seen by other people, not even by the ones who
waylay him"*.

## Zduhać

A *Zduhać* (здухаћ) or *Vetrovnjak* (ветровњак) in Serbian tradition,
and a *Dragon Man* in Bulgarian, Macedonian and southern Serbian
traditions, were men believed to have an inborn supernatural ability
to protect their estate, village, or region against destructive weather
conditions, such as storms, hail, or torrential rains. It was believed that
*Zduhaći* (pl.) – like the Italian *Benedanti* (Good walkers) and *Maledanti*
(Bad walkers) and the Serbian *Kresnik* and *Kudlak* – could leave their
bodies in their sleep, to intercept and fight with demonic beings imagined
as bringers of bad weather. Having defeated the demons and chasing
away the stormy clouds they brought, the protectors would return to

their bodies and wake up tired. Although Zduhaći could be women and children, most were adult men. In many regions it was believed that the Zduhaći were born with a caul – white or red, depending on the regional belief. The mother would dry the caul and sew it into a piece of garment always worn by the child, such as a little pouch attached under the child's armpit. In the clan of Kuči, eastern Montenegro, the mother would preserve the caul hiding it from all eyes, and hand it to her son in his puberty. The caul was supposed to protect him when he flew as a Zduhać. If the caul was destroyed, the child's supernatural powers would be lost. A birthmark of a Zduhać in Herzegovina could be a tuft of hair growing on his shoulder or upper arm. In the Montenegrin coastal area, the caul played no role in the birth of a Zduhaći, who were rather born on certain Fridays at a set hour. It was also believed in Herzegovina that male children conceived on the eve of major holidays would become Zduhaći. The appearance of Zduhaći did not differ much from that of ordinary people, but they had some traits that set them apart. They were deep sleepers, very hard to wake up, often drowsy, pensive, thoughtful, and solemn. Their faces were often puffy, eyes shadowy. They were wise and shrewd, successful in whatever they were doing and resourceful in dealing with problems; their households were prosperous. In Semberija, Zduhaći were said to be good scapulimantic diviners (soothsayers using shoulder bones), and to be able to communicate with domestic animals. The clan of Paštrovići from the Montenegrin coastal region claimed that the Zduhaći could hear anything that happened anywhere in the world; if someone stepped on a Zduhać's foot, they could hear that too. The clan of Kuči held that the Zduhaći were outstanding long jumpers.

The Zduhaći of a gang would leave their bodies in sleep and gather at an agreed place, before flying into a battle. They used various weapons, such as spindles, beech buds, sharp splinters, leaves, stalks of straw, fluff, flakes, sand, long twigs, dogwood stones, pine cones, eggshells, and other light objects. As believed in Herzegovina, Zduhaći uprooted gigantic firs and oaks and fought with them. However, the most powerful Zduhać weapon was a *luč* (resinous stick of wood that burned at both ends to give light or used as kindling) or a charred wood splinter. A Zduhać who was hit with this weapon would surely die. People therefore avoided igniting the sticks at both ends, and took care not to leave splinters half-burned. In addition to the weapons, each Zduhać carried a milk bucket and a pick measure; an alternative to the latter could be a shovel or broom from a threshing floor. If a group of Zduhaći succeeded to seize the pick measures of the enemy group, they used them to transfer the crop yield from their enemies territory to their own. Confiscating the milk buckets meant that the milk proceeds would be transferred. According to the clan of Kuči, Zduhaći used their pick measures, milk buckets, and other containers to take away the total yield of the enemy territory. Zduhaći battles were furious. They were accompanied by powerful storms and whirlwinds that uprooted trees and kicked up dust. In Montenegro, it was considered dangerous to throw stones into the wind, because that might knock out an eye of a Zduhać, who would then kill the culprit. A fighting Zduhać was supposed to retain his pick measure and milk bucket, while trying to seize these objects from an enemy Zduhać; he should hit and not be hit. The victorious group of Zduhaći would loot the yield of all agricultural produce from the territory of their defeated foes. The harvest in the coming season would thus be excellent for the victors and poor for the defeated Zduhaći. After the battle, the soul of the Zduhać would return into his body, and he would wake up weak and exhausted. If he was wounded, he would be sick for some time afterwards, or die if his wound was mortal. There are records of seriously ill men who claimed that they were wounded in Zduhać battles. In the Montenegrin Littoral the view was held that the health of a mortally wounded Zduhać could still recuperate, if he avenged his injury before the eighth day of his injury had passed.

## Zlydni

*Zlydni* in the mythology of Ukrainians and Belarusians are demonic beings, spirits hostile to man, causing them misfortune and adversity. They are invisible and live in the house or sit on the shoulders of humans. Sometimes Zlydni are considered to be identical with such related beings as the *Dolya, Nedolya, Gore-Zloschastie, Likho, Beda* (Ukraine) and others. Belarusians depicted Zlydni as a snake or an invisible woman who had no tongue, eyes or ears. In other places, Zlydni were represented in the form of skinny shabby animals living in the house behind or under the stove (the most common dwelling place for most house-spirits). In general Zlydni resemble hunchbacked cats or dogs. Often these strange creatures wear tall boots and earflaps. They are constantly engaged in all sorts of sabotage. As soon as they leave their place behind or under the stove, they try to disturb the peace and make as mess of everything.

Belarusians believed that Zlydni preferred to settle in the homes of those who want to get rich quickly. It is said that in the house where Zlydni settle, the owners are often hampered by health problems or diseases, while the plants or crops in their garden do not grow or also suffer from some sort of plague.

It was believed that it is very difficult, but not impossible, to get rid of beings like Zlydni or Nedolya. To get rid of them, they had to be put in a sack and thrown into the swamp. They could also be tied up and left on the road, lured under a rock, buried, etc. They would then cling to and bother whoever set them free. In fairy tales this is usually a jealous neighbor or a landlord. In Russian folklore Zlydni are usually referred to as *Nedoli* (bad Dolya), *Nedolya, Gore, Beda* or *Gore-Zlopchastia*. In Polish folk tales, a similar character that lives behind the stove, could appear in the guise of a pigeon, saying: *"I am your misfortune"*. This creature is disposed of in the same way as the Zlydni. In folk witchcraft, there is another ritual with a similar purpose, called "transfiguration", in which problems are solved by talking to an object, which is then left at a crossroads. This parallels the ancient Jewish scapegoat-ritual in which two goats were taken, one to sacrifice to Yahweh and one to lay on all the sins and misfortunes of the community, which was then sent into the desert and – in this way – fused with the demonized figure of Azazel. In modern Ukrainian the word *zlydni* is used to mean "poverty".

## Żmij

The *Żmij* is the equivalent of the classical European *dragon* in Slavic mythology. Its name there is *Żmij* in Polish and Old Polish, *Smei* or *Zmej* (Змей) in Russian and Bulgarian, *Zmij* in Old Church Slavonic and Ukrainian, and *Zmaj* (Змај) in Bosnian, Serbian, Croatian and Slovenian. The word *Smok* (Смок) is also used in contemporary Polish and Belarusian, which in Bulgarian designates vipers, and in Romania a similar creature is known called *Zmeu*. Slavic dragons originally represented elemental forces of nature, with male dragons personifying the male elements of Fire and Air, and female dragons representing Earth and Water. Most of the above names are the masculine forms of the Slavic term for "snake" (Russian: змея; Bulgarian: змия; Serbian and Croatian: *zmija*; Polish: *żmija*), and so the old Slavic mythology sees the male dragon *(Żmij)* who dwells in the sky and breathes fire is seen as a counterpart of the female dragon *(Żmija)* who dwells under the earth and controls the water. The image common today of the dragon living in caves, yet breathing fire, is an obvious attempt to bridge the (apparent) contradiction of the two symbols.

Russia and Ukraine know the dragon as *Smei/Smij Gorynych* (Змей Горыныч). It is three-headed and green, walks on his two hind legs, has rather small front legs and can spit fire. In Macedonia, Croatia, Bulgaria, Bosnia, Serbia and Montenegro the dragon (*Zmaj*, *Zmej* or *Lamja*) is multi-headed (with three, seven or nine heads) and spits fire. In Serbia, Bulgaria, and Bosnia, it is called *Aždaja* (Аждаја) or *Ala* (Ала). The Romanian word for dragon, *Zmeu*, was in all likelihood adopted from Bulgarian.



## Zwodziasz

*Zwodziasz*, also known as *Zwodzijos*, is a demon in Slavic folklore. It was said to lead people astray and lure them into the wilderness, causing them to lose their way and often indirectly becoming the cause of their sudden death. In tales of people from Kalisz and its surroundings, Zwodziasz is portrayed as a nightjar or goatsucker, a small nocturnal bird of the swallow-family.

## LITERATURE AND DIGITAL SOURCES

- Abercromby, John – *The Pre- and Proto-historic Finns, both Eastern and Western with the Magic Songs of the West Finns – in two volumes*, published by David Nutt in the Strand, London, 1898
- Árnason, J.; Powell, G. E. J. and Magnússon, E. trans. – *Icelandic Legends* – Richard Bentley, London, 1864
- Arrowsmith, N. – *Field Guide to the Little People: A Curious Journey Into the Hidden Realm of Elves, Faeries, Hobgoblins & Other Not-so-mythical Creatures* – Llewellyn Worldwide., 1970/2009
- Barb, A.A. – *Antaura. The Mermaid and the Devil's Grandmother: A Lecture* – Journal of the Warburg and Courtauld Institutes, 1966
- Bardon, Franz – *Die Praxis der Magische Evokation* – Rüggeberg Verlag Wuppertal, 2003
- Bartsch, Karl – *Sagen, Märchen und Gebräuche aus Meklenburg*, vol. 1 – Vienna, Wilhelm Braumüller, 1879
- Beaumont, William Comyns – *Britain The Key To World History* – London, 1948
- Benwell, G. and Waugh, A. – *Sea Enchantress: The Tale of the Mermaid and her Kin* – Hutchinson, London, 1961
- Blau, Lajos (Ludwich) – *Das Altjüdische Zauberwesen* – 1897-98 Budapest / Graz, 1974
- Blécourt, W. de, – *"I Would Have Eaten You Too": Werewolf Legends in the Flemish, Dutch, and German Area* – 2007
- Bonnefoy, Yves, – *Asian Mythologies* – University of Chicago Press, 1993
- Bottiglioni, Gino – *Leggende e tradizioni di Sardegna (testi dialettali in grafia fonetica)* – 1922
- Briggs, Katharine – *An Encyclopedia of Fairies – Hobgoblins, Brownies, Bogies and Other Supernatural Creatures* – Pantheon Books, USA, 1976
- Calmet, Dom Augustine – *The Phantom World: The History and Philosophy of Spirits, Apparitions &c. Two Volumes in One* – Philadelphia: A Hart, Late Carey & Hart, 1850
- Campbell, J.G. – *Superstitions of the Highlands and Islands of Scotland* – James MacLehose and Sons, Glascow, 1900
- Conway, Moncure Daniel -*Demonology and Devil-Lore 1 & 2* – revised publication of the 1897 editions by VAMzzz Publishing, Amsterdam, 2015
- Conybeare, Frederick Cornwallis – *Testament of Solomon* – Jewish Quaterly Review of October 1889 – revised edition VAMzzz Publishing, Amsterdam, 2015
- Corstorphine, Kevin & Kremmel, Laura R – *Horror in the Medieval North: The

*Troll, The Palgrave Handbook to Horror Literature* – ed., 2018

- Courtney, M.A. – *Cornish Feasts and Folklore* – Beare and Son, Penzance, 1890
- Craigie, W.A. – *The Oldest Icelandic Folklore*, 1893
- Davidsson, O. *The Folk-lore of Icelandic Fishes*, 1900
- Dennison, W. Traill – *Orkney Folklore, Sea Myths* – Edinburgh University Press, 1891
- Dörler, Adolf Ferdinand (collected and edited by) – *Sagen aus Innsbruck's Umgebung, mit besonderer Berücksichtigung des Zillerthales* – Innsbruck, 1895
- Edmondston, Thomas – *An Etymological Glossary of the Shetland & Orkney Dialect* – Adam and Charles Black, 1866
- *Encyclopedia Brittanica online*
- Folkard, Richard – *Plant Lore Legends & Lyrics* – 1884, revised edition by VAMzzz Publishing, Amsterdam, 2021
- Frazer, Sir James George – *The Golden Bough: A Study in Magic and Religion* – edition 1906-15
- Genesin, Monica & Rizzo, Luana (Hrsg.) – *Magie, Tarantismus und Vampirismus; Eine interdisciplinäre Annäherung* – Verlag Dr. Kovač, Hamburg, 2013
- Gibbings W. W. – *Folk-lore and Legends* – *Germany,* London, 1892
- Gieysztor, Aleksander – *Mitologia Słowian* – Warszawa: Wydawnictwo Uniwersytetu Warszawskiego, 2006
- Gill, W. Walter – *A Second Manx Scrapbook* – Arrowsmith, London Bristol, 1932
- Grimm, Jacob – *Deutsche Mythologie* – Göttingen: Dieterich, 1835
- Hageland, A. van – *La Mer Magique* – Marabout, Paris, 1973
- Hall, Manly Palmer – *The Secret Teachings of All Ages: An Encyclopedic Outline of Masonic, Hermetic, Qabbalistic and Rosicrucian Symbolical Philosophy* – 1928
- Hanaur, J.E. – *Folk-Lore of the Holy Land – Moslim, Christian and Jewish* – Edited by Marmaduke Pickthall, London Duckworth & Co, 1907
- Henderson, William – *Notes on the folk-lore of the northern counties of England and the borders* – Longmans, Green, 1866
- Hlidberg, J. B. and Aegisson, S.; McQueen, F. J. M. and Kjartansson, R., trans. – *Meeting with Monsters* – JPV utgafa, Reykjavik, 2011 .
- Huizinga-Onnekes, E.J. – *Groninger Volksverhalen* – bewerkt door K. ter Laan, J.B.Wolters' Uitgevers Maatschappij N.V. Groningen – Den Haag, 1930
- *Jewish Encyclopedia online*
- Johnston, Sarah Iles – *Restless Dead: Encounters Between the Living and the Dead in Ancient Greece* – University of California Press, Berkeley-Los Angeles-London, 2013

- Karakurt, Deniz – *Türk Söylence Sözlüğü* (*Turkish Mythological Dictionary*) (OTRS: CC BY-SA 3.0), 2011
- Kivilson, Valerie A. & Worobec, Christine D. – *Witchcraft in Russia and Ukraine, 1000–1900: A Sourcebook* – Cornell University Press, Northern Illinois University Press, 2020
- Kreuter, Peter Mario – *Der Vampirglaube in Südosteuropa. Studien zur Genese, Bedeutung und Funktion. Rumänien und der Balkanraum* – Weidler, Berlin, 2001, (Dissertation Universität Bonn, 2001)
- Lachower, Fischel & Tishby, Isaiah; translations by David Goldstein – *Wisdom of the Zohar – An Anthology of Texts* – London, 1994
- Landt, George – *A description of the Faroe Islands, containing an account of their situation, climate, and productions, together with the manners and customs of the inhabitants, their trade etc.* – 1810
- Lawson, John Cuthbert, M.A. – *Modern Greek Folklore and Ancient Greek Religion – A Study in Survivals* – Cambridge: at the University Press, London: Fetter Lane, E.C., 1910
- Lecouteux, Claude:
  - *Witches, Werewolves and Fairies: Shapeshifters and Astral Doubles in the Middle Ages*, Inner Traditions (Rochester, Vermont) transl. Clare Frock, 2003
  - *The Return of the Dead: Ghosts, Ancestors and the Transparent Veil of the Pagan Mind*, Inner Traditions (Rochester, Vermont) transl. Jon E. Graham, 2009
  - *The Secret History of Vampires: Their Multiple Forms and Hidden Purposes*, Inner Traditions (Rochester, Vermont) transl. Jon E. Graham, 2010
  - *Phantom Armies of the Night: The Wild Hunt and Ghostly Processions of the Undead*, Inner Traditions (Rochester, Vermont) transl., Jon E. Graham, 2011
  - *The Tradition of Household Spirits. Ancestral Lore and Practice*, Inner Traditions (Rochester, Vermont) transl. Jon E. Graham, 2013
  - *Demons and Spirits of the Land: Ancestral Lore and Practices*, Inner Traditions (Rochester, Vermont) transl. Jon E. Graham, 2015
  - *The Hidden Historie of Elves and Dwarfs – Avatars of Invisible Realms*, Inner Traditions (Rochester, Vermont) transl. Jon E. Graham, 2018
- Libera, Roberto – *Storie di streghe, fantasmi e lupi mannari nei Castelli Romani, Genzano di Roma* – Consorzio SBCR editore, 2010
- Lindley, Charles, Viscount Halifax – *Lord Halifax Ghost Book* – first edition Glasgow, 1936
- Lomas, Adriano Garcia – *Mitología y supersticiones de Cantabria* – 1964
- Luzel, François-Marie – *Contes populaires de Basse-Bretagne* – 1881
- Mackenzie, Donald Alexander
  - *Wonder Tales from Scottish Myth and Legend* – Blackie and Son Limited,

London, Glasgow, Bombay, 1917

- *Scottish Folk-Lore and Folk Life. Studies in Race, Culture and Tradition* – 1935
- *Elves and Heroes* – 1909
- *Teutonic Myth and Legend* – 2nd Ed. 1934
• Mannhardt, Wilhelm:
- *Roggenwolf und Roggenhund – Beitrag zur Germanischen Sittenkunde* – Verlag von Constantin Ziemssen, Danzig, 1865
- *Die Korndämonen, – Beitrag zur Germanischen Sittenkunde* – Harrwitz und Gossmann, Berlin 1868
- *Wald- und Feldkulte. Band 1: Der Baumkultus der Germanen und ihrer Nachbarstämme: mythologische Untersuchungen* – Gebrüder Borntraeger, Berlin, 1875
- *Wald- und Feldkulte. Band 2: Antike Wald- und Feldkulte aus nordeuropäischer Überlieferung erläutert* – Gebrüder Borntraeger, Berlin, 1877
- *Mythologische Forschungen* – Karl J. Trüber, Strassburg – London 1884
• Marliave, Olivier de – *Trésor de la mythologie pyrénéenne* – Toulouse, Esper, 1987
• Marliave, Olivier de et Pertuzé, Jean-Claude – *Panthéon Pyrénéen* – Toulouse, Loubatières, 1990.
• Masani, R.P., M.A – *Folklore of Wells, being a study of Water Worship in East and West* – Bombay, D.B. Takapokevale Sons & Co, 1918
• Mathers, S.L. MacGregor / Knor von Rosenroth – *Kabbala Denudata / The Kabbalah Unveiled* – Samuel Weiser Inc. York Beach, Maine, 1989
• McAnally, David Russell – *Irish Wonders: The Ghosts, Giants, Pookas, Demons, Leprechawns, Banshees, Fairies, Witches, Widows, Old Maids, and other marvels of the Emerald Isle* – The Riverside Press Cambridge, 1888
• McIntosh, A – *Faerie Faith in Scotland* (2005) in *The Encyclopaedia of Religion and Nature* – edited by Bron Taylor, 2006
• McPherson, Rev. J. M. – *Primitive Beliefs in the North-East of Scotland* – London, New York and Toronto – Longmans, Green and Co., Ltd., 1929
• Meyer, Elard Hugo – *Mythologie der Germanen*, Straszburg, Verlag von Karl J. Trübner, 1930
• Nadmorski, Dr – *Kaszuby i Kociewie. Język, zwyczaje, przesądy, podania, zagadki i pieśni ludowe w północnej części Prus Zachodnich* – Poznań, 1892
• Paracelsus – *Four treatises of Theophrastus von Hohenheim, called Paracelsus* (1493-1541) – English translation of the German, Baltimore: Johns Hopkins Press, 1941
• Petiteau, Frantz-E. – *Contes, légendes et récits de la vallée d'Aure* – éditions Alan Sutton, 2007

237

- Plancy, Collin de, – *Dictionnaire Infernal* – 1818
- Podgórscy Barbara and Adam – *Wielka Księga Demonów Polskich. Leksykon i antologia demonologii ludowej* – Katowice: KOS, 2005
- Rajki, Andras – *Mongolian Ethymological Dictionary* 2006-2009 – via *academia.edu*
- Ralston, W. R. S., M.A.
  - *Russian Fairy Tales – A choice collection of Muscovite folk-lore* – New York: Hurst & Co., 1872
  - *The songs of the Russian people, as illustrative of Slavonic mythology and Russian social life* – London, Ellis, 1872
- Ritter, Johann Nepomuk von Alpenburg – *Deutsche Alpensagen* – Vienna, 1861
- Rose, C. – *Giants, Monsters, and Dragons* – W. W. Norton and Co., New York, 2000
- Rosenthal, Bernice Glatzer (editor) – *The Occult in Russian and Soviet Culture* – Cornell University, 1997
- Rhys, John – *Celtic Folklore Welsh and Manx* – Library of Alexandria, 2020
- Ryan, W.F. – *The Bathhouse at Midnight – An Historical Survey of Magic and Divination in Russia*, Pennsylvania State University Press, 1999
- Sacaze, Julien – *Le dieu Tantugou, légende du pays de Luchon* – (in Revue de Comminges, Tome III, 1887, p. 116-118), texte « patois » et traduction littérale
- Saxby, Jessie Margaret Edmondston – *Shetland Traditional Lore* – Edinburgh, Grant and Murray, 1932
- Sébillot, Paul – *Le Folk-Lore de France, Tome Premier: Le Ciel et la Terre* – 1904
- Sikes, Wirt – *British Goblins: Welsh Folk-Lore, Fairy Mythology, Legends and Traditions* – London, 1880
- Simpson, J. – *Icelandic Folktales and Legends* – University of California Press, Berkeley and Los Angeles, 1972
- Sinastrari of Ameno – transl. Liseux, Isidore 1876 – *Incubi and Succubi or Demoniality – A Historical Study of Sexual contacts with Demons* – Revised edition by VAMzzz Publishing, Amsterdam, 2017
- Sluijter, P.C.M. – *IJslands Volksgeloof* – H. D. Tjeenk Willink & Zoon N.V., Haarlem, 1936
- Spada, Dario – *Gnomi, Fate e Folletti e altri esseri fatati in Italia* – SugarCo, Milano, 2007
- Spiesberger, Karl – *Naturgeister wie Seher sie schauwen – wie Magier sie rufen* – Richard Schikowski Verlag, Berlin 1978
- Stefánsson, V. – *Icelandic Beast and Bird Lore* -1906
- Summers, Montague – *The Vampire in Lore and Legend* – Toronto 2001 (previously published as: *The Vampire in Europe*, London, 1929)

- Ter Laan, K. – *Groninger Overleveringen* – Erven B. van der Kamp, Groningen, 1930
- Thompson, Francis – *The Supernatural Highland* – Robert Hale, London, 1976
- Thorpe, Benjamin – *Northern mythology : comprising the principal popular traditions and superstitions of Scandinavia, North Germany, and the Netherlands* – 1852
- Veen, Abe J. van der – *Witte wieven, weerwolven en waternekkers – Een beschrijving van alle geesten, elfen en andere wondere wezens uit Nederland* – 2017
- Vries, A. de, – *Flanders: a cultural history* – Oxford University Press, Oxford, 2007
- Wippel I. – *Schabbock, Trud und Wilde Jagd* – Verlag für Sammler, Graz 1986
- Wikimedia Commons Licence folklore data via *Armenian, Austrian, Basque, Belarusian, Catalan, Dutch, Estonian, Danish, German, Finnish, Icelandic, Italian, French, Latvian, Lithuanian, Norwegian, Polish, Portuguese, Russian, Spanish, Swedish, Swiss, Turkish, and Ukrainian* Wikipedia-files
- Wlislocki, Dr Heinrich von – *Volksglaube und religiöser Brauch der Zigeuner* – Aschendorffsche Buchhandlung, Münster, 1891


239

240

*Spirit Beings in European Folklore 1*
*Ireland, England, Wales, Cornwall,*
*Scotland, Isle of Man, Orkney's, Hebrides,*
*Faeroe, Iceland, Norway, Sweden and*
*Denmark*
by Benjamin Adamah, 250 pages,
Paperback, ISBN 9789492355553
www.vamzzz.com

*Compendium 1* of the *Spirit Beings in European Folklore*-series covers
the northwestern part of the continent where Celtic and Anglo-Saxon
cultures meet the Nordic. This book catalogs the mysterious creatures of
Ireland, the Isle of Man, England, Wales, Cornwall, Scotland, Hebrides,
Orkneys, Faroe Islands, Iceland, Norway, Sweden and Denmark. For
centuries, the peoples of these regions have influenced each other in
many ways, including their mythologies and folklore. The latter is
perhaps most evident in the various species of *Brook-horses* or *Water-
horses*. These semi-aquatic ghostly creatures come in all kinds of varieties
and are typical of the English or Gaelic speaking parts of Europe and
Scandinavia. Many other ghostly entities occur only in specific areas or
countries. Some even became cultural icons, such as the Irish *Leprechaun,*
the *Knockers* from Wales, the Scandinavian *Trolls* and *Huldras* or
the Icelandic *Huldufólk*. England has its *Brownies*, several kinds of
*Fairies* and locally famous *ghost dogs*. Iceland and Scandinavia seem to
"specialize" in spirit beings who appear fully materialized, such as the
different species of *Illveli* (Evil Whales) and *Draugr*, the returning dead.

*Compendium 1* discusses 292 spirit beings in detail, including their
alternative names, with additional references to related or subordinate
beings and a unique selection of illustrations.

CONTENTS:

**Spirit Beings in European Folklore 2**
*Germany, Austria, Alpine regions,
Switzerland, Netherlands, Flanders,
Luxembourg, Lithuania, Latvia, Estonia,
Finland, Jewish influences*
by Benjamin Adamah, 256 pages,
Paperback, ISBN 9789492355560
www.vamzzz.com

*Compendium 2* of the *Spirit Beings in European Folklore*-series covers the German-speaking parts of Central Europe, the Low Countries, the Baltic region and Finland. Via the Ashkenazi Jews, spirit beings from the Middle East entered Central European culture, which are also included. This originally densely forested part of the continent is particularly rich in nature-spirits and has a wide variety of beings that dwell in forests and mountainous areas (*Berggeister*) or act as atmospheric forces. Also dominant are the many field-spirits and variations of *Alp*-like creatures (*Mare, Nightmare*). There is an overlap with the Nordic and Eastern European *Revenant* and *Vampire*-types, and we find several water- and sea-spirits. Among the German-speaking and Baltic peoples, invoking field-spirits was an integrated part of agriculture, with rites continuing into the early 20th century. The Alpine regions have spirits who watch over cattle. In general, forest-spirits are prominent. Germany has its *Moosweiblein* and *Wilder Mann* (*Woodwose*), the Baltic region has its *Mātes*, and Finland its *Metsän Väki*. Then there are ghostly animals, and earth- and house-spirits such as the many kinds of *Kobolds*, the Dutch *Kabouter*, and the *Kaukas* of Prussia and Latvia.

*Compendium 2* discusses 228 spirit beings in detail, including their alternative names, with additional references to related or subordinate beings and a unique selection of illustrations.

# CONTENTS:



243

*Compendium 4* of the *Spirit Beings in European Folklore*-series covers an area that starts with Wallonia and continues via France and the Pyrenees, through the Iberian Peninsula, to Italy and Greece. This results in a very diverse and colourful collection of spirit beings, due to the many included Basque nature-spirits or *Ireluak*, the Spanish *Duendes*, the Celtic spirits of Brittany, the prankster Italian *Folletti* and the creatures from Greece. Some creatures from Breton folklore are particularly gruesome, such as the hollow-eyed *Ankou*, the *Werewolf*-like *Bugul-nôz*, or the ghostly and *Will-o'-the-wisp*-like *Yan-gant-y-tan*, who roams the night roads with his five lit candles. Most Italian ghosts are less gloomy, while the Iberian Peninsula is home to everything ranging from the 'Beauty' to the 'Beast'. Compendium 4 contains – amongst other things – many kinds of dwarf-spirits or *Goblins* (*Lutins, Nutons, Folletti, Farfadettes, Korrigans, Minairons*) various seductive and feminine spring creatures, *Wild Man*-varieties (*Basajaunak, Jentilak*) and an extensive section on the *Incubus-Succubus*. It is fascinating to discover how many types of European spirit beings (from *Kobold* to many female spring-spirits), described in the other Compendiums, can be traced back to creatures from Ancient Greece.

*Compendium 4* discusses 270 spirit beings in detail, includes their alternative names, additional references to subordinate beings and a unique selection of illustrations.

CONTENTS: